A Functional Curriculum for Teaching Students with Disabilities

A Functional Curriculum for Teaching Students with Disabilities

THIRD EDITION

Volume I
Self-Care, Motor Skills,
Household Management, and Living Skills

by
Michael Bender
Peter J. Valletutti
and
Carol Ann Baglin

pro·ed

8700 Shoal Creek Boulevard
Austin, Texas 78757-6897

pro·ed

This book is designed in Serif Gothic and Bookman Light.

Production Manager: Alan Grimes
Production Coordinator: Karen Swain
Managing Editor: Tracy Sergo
Art Director: Thomas Barkley
Reprints Buyer: Alicia Woods
Editor: Sue Motzer
Editorial Assistant: Claudette Landry
Editorial Assistant: Martin Wilson

Printed in the United States of America

1 2 3 4 5 6 7 8 9 10   00 99 98 97 96

To my wife, Madelyn,
for her inspiring love for all children
and her tireless efforts to protect them
—M.B.

To my brothers, Drs. Angelo
and Joseph Valletutti,
for their faith and encouragement
—P.J.V.

To my dear friend, Dr. Mary Brady,
a dedicated professional
and my first collaborator
on a curriculum for students
with special needs
in Los Angeles County
—C.A.B.

Contents

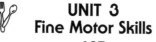

Preface

A Functional Curriculum for Teaching Students with Disabilities, the third edition of *Teaching the Moderately and Severely Handicapped*, is a major revision of the first and second editions. The major alterations made in the present edition have been impelled by several recent phenomena: (a) the changing perceptions of the nature of special education (e.g., inclusion, emphasis on a holistic approach, and the movement toward the development of independent living skills); (b) the identification of new and underserved populations (e.g., infants and toddlers, youth with attention-deficit/hyperactivity disorder); (c) modifications in service delivery (e.g., interagency cooperation and increased parental involvement); (d) recent federal legislation regarding education (e.g., P.L. 99-457, P.L. 101-476, and P.L. 102-119) and the civil and legal rights of persons with disabilities (e.g., Americans with Disabilities Act); and (e) reductions in targeted federal dollars.

The central problem, however, continues to be the nonproductive and, at times, destructive magical thinking engaged in by educators who believe that structural changes alone will automatically result in improvements in education. Unfortunately, many special students continue to receive an education that is not "special" whether they are placed in segregated or inclusive settings. Structural change that does not address the individual and special needs of students with disabilities or attend to the quality of instruction is merely cosmetic, not substantive. We consider this functionally oriented curriculum—if it is implemented by special education teachers, parents, and other trained personnel—to be a critical way of making the education of students with special needs an education that is truly special, regardless of the setting.

The first edition of this text, introduced in the 1970s, coincided with the movement for the educational rights of individuals with disabilities, as mandated by the landmark federal legislation P.L. 94-142. This was also the time when parent and advocacy groups, along with many other professionals, consolidated their efforts based on a collective mission not only to provide special education and related services to all children and youth with handicapping conditions but also to integrate them, whenever appropriate and feasible, in the public schools and the mainstream of society.

Instructional areas and emphases addressed by the first two editions, such as functional academics, interpersonal and social skills, and leisure education, represented a significant departure from the curriculum traditionally being taught in many special education programs. Of equal importance was the attempt to comprehensively and clearly identify appropriate instructional objectives, strategies, and resources that would promote independence, be age appropriate, be suitable for teaching in a natural environment, and be of lifelong functional value.

Much change has occurred since then. Evolving ideological currents have had a significant impact on guiding and determining the content of this new edition of the curriculum series. Several recent developments—the need for interagency cooperation, reduction in targeted federal dollars, emphasis on a holistic approach, the need for a competent core of human service professionals, and the movement toward independent living—have all resulted in major changes in this profession. For example, special education terminology has been modified. The word *handicapped* is no longer used to describe a person who is challenged by a disability. The rejection of the word *handicapped* has come about because the problems experienced by persons with disabilities are viewed as not being within the person him- or herself but rather as arising from social attitudes and perceptions and by society's failure to provide needed programs, services, and resources that will compensate for or minimize the effects of the individual's disability.

This change in terminology has been incorporated in the recent amendments to P.L. 94-142 (the Education for All Handicapped Children Act). These amendments—P.L. 101-476, the Individuals with Disabilities Education Act (IDEA)—reflect the changing concept of disabilities and the role of society in meeting the needs of individuals who have special needs. Of particular importance is the addition of the requirements for transition services, which focus on the successful movement of students from school to community, thus emphasizing the functional skills of independent living and community participation.

Moreover, the preferred descriptor, *disability,* should not be used as a label, as in "He or she is a 'learning disabled' or 'mentally retarded' child." Rather, as a way of accentuating the personhood of the individual, expressions should be used such as "the individual with learning disabilities." In this way, the disability is seen as merely one aspect or part of a total individual, thus minimizing the placement of undue emphasis on the disability by others and by the person him- or herself, while at the same time emphasizing the person in all his or her myriad dimensions.

The concept of the least restrictive environment (LRE) shapes the placement provisions of P.L. 94-142 and its subsequent amendments (P.L. 99-457) as well as P.L. 101-476 and its various state legislative counterparts. LRE led to the implementation of a continuum of educational placements and services—from placement in a regular or mainstreamed class as the least restrictive of possible environments to the most restrictive environment in a nonpublic residential setting. Central to individual placement decisions, however, was the fundamental premise that placement within this continuum should be shaped by the concept central to special education, namely, that the primary determinants are the individualized needs of the students, based on the idiosyncratic nature of their disability.

Although mainstreaming was, at its inception, identified as the least restrictive or the most normalized school environment, it has not always been successfully realized in practice. Too often, needed support services have not been provided to mainstreamed students and their teachers, and inordinate emphasis has been placed on location of service rather than on effective and efficient instructional practices. Teachers assigned to mainstreamed classes, more often than not, were ill-prepared pedagogically and psychologically to teach their students with special educational needs on either an individual or a group basis. Invariably, the curriculum was not modified to reflect the needs of those integrated special students who required instruction in practical knowledge and skills taught from a functional perspective and with a functional purpose. Functional curricular modifications, if they had been assiduously pursued, might have benefited the students without disabilities as well. Typically, the curriculum of the mainstreamed class is test driven and tradition bound, resulting in too much time wasted on the teaching of atomized and irrelevant knowledge.

Recently, however, the concept of mainstreaming has been redefined as part of the inclusion movement or the Regular Education Initiative (REI). The REI maintains that a dual system of regular and special education is unnecessary, inappropriate, and ineffective, and that students with disabilities, regardless of the severity of their disability, can and should be educated in the mainstreamed (regular) setting. This service delivery approach rejects the continuum-of-services concept and views all other alternate placements, except the regular or mainstreamed class, as too restrictive. The collaborative teaching movement emanates from the REI and attempts to respond to some of the problems that resulted from more restrictive placements and misguided mainstreaming. The collaborative approach requires regular and special teachers to work as a team as they plan instruction for and teach all the students (both those with disabilities and those who are not so challenged) in their assigned classes. As the collaborative approach is increasingly being employed, it will be necessary for all teachers, regular and special, to modify the existing regular class curriculum so that it addresses the adaptive behavior needs of all students, whether they have disabilities or not.

This curriculum, although meant primarily for teachers functioning within a special setting, has the additional goal of assisting collaborative teams of teachers as they analyze and modify existing curricula, subsequently design individualized curricula (Individualized Education Programs [IEPs] and Individualized Family Service Plans [IFSPs]), and cooperate with other human service professionals and related human service agencies to meet the life needs of regular as well as special students.

Curricular areas have also changed. For example, vocational education, often associated with skill development and traditional "shop" programs, is now often defined in terms of work readiness, supported employment, and career education. Curricula in the area of leisure education have also gained prominence—a justified development given that free time continues to increase for most people in our culture. The problem of meaningful utilization of leisure time, especially for older people with disabilities, is particularly acute because many are chronically unemployed or underemployed, and therefore not only have expanded free time but also lack the financial resources required for the productive use of that time.

Safety, as a curricular entity, has also gained increasing recognition, especially as more and more programs emphasize community-based education, which entails greater and more numerous threats to safety than the traditional, classroom-based approach. Safety elements should pervade all curricular areas, and therefore have been included in the lesson plans and learning activities of this edition.

Unserved, underserved, and increasing populations of children with disabilities continue to enter educational programs at a rapid rate. Some of this change is a result of recent legislative mandates, such as P.L. 99-457 (Education of the Handicapped Act Amendments). Part H, reauthorized as P.L. 102-119, IDEA Amendments of 1991, mandates the provision of comprehensive early intervention and family services for infants and toddlers and their families (birth through age 2). School programs are also now serving children and youth with disabilities who were not often identified in the 1970s and whose numbers have drastically increased in the 1990s. Examples include children with fetal alcohol syndrome (FAS) and those who have been damaged prenatally (or perinatally) through maternal substance abuse, the AIDS virus, syphilis, or gonorrhea.

Technology continues to play an increasingly important role in educational practice. The instructional use of the personal computer and other instructional technology (including interactive television) is increasing at a rapidly accelerating rate. The use of technology has proven to be of considerable assistance in planning (development of IEPs), in managing teaching (recording of formal and informal assessment data), and in communicating with parents (progress reports and report cards). The personal computer, with its capacity for miniaturization, adaptations, and peripherals, is also moving rapidly to address the habilitative needs of individuals with disabilities. In the near future, as a result of research with neuromuscular feedback and computers, we can expect some individuals who cannot walk—to walk. Other technological advances will make it possible for those who cannot see—to see in some fashion, and those who cannot hear—to hear in some way from implant devices and as yet unknown technologies. The use of assistive technology will also expand as continuing efforts are made to assist students in meeting the demands of an increasingly complex and demanding postindustrial society.

The role of parents (or parent surrogates) is essential to the implementation of this curriculum. Parental participation in decisions regarding placement, IEPs, and needed related services is essential to a holistic approach to educating exceptional children. The parental role in providing pertinent information to teachers should not be minimized, because parents can provide information that is essential for assisting in identifying goals and objectives, establishing educational and programming priorities, and determining areas of interest. Parents have a unique advantage in instructing their children in activities that are best introduced and practiced in the home setting and also in the community. Parents can also serve as effective carryover agents who provide practice sessions and reinforce newly acquired skills as the child performs them within his or her reality contexts.

Because of these various trends and factors, it seems appropriate to now produce a new edition of the curriculum. Teams of teachers, students, parents, clinicians, and other related service staff have been surveyed to find out what needed to be addressed in these three new volumes. Our overriding goal continues to be the presentation of new information and material that will assist teachers, other professionals, and parents in facilitating the functional performance of children and youth with disabilities in the full variety of life situations and contexts. As in past incarnations, the present curriculum assumes that the reader possesses a basic understanding of teaching methods and a fundamental level of expertise in analyzing educational tasks so that they may be used as a framework for evaluating the child's current level of performance and as a means of focusing on specific behaviors requiring remedial or instructional attention. Emphasis continues to be placed on teaching students in reality situations in the home, community, and workplace. Whenever home-based or community-based education is not feasible, teachers must provide realistic classroom simulations that offer students with disabilities opportunities to practice life skills in functional contexts and settings. The past successes of the curriculum have supported our view that reality contexts can be effectively simulated in a classroom setting only if the entire behavior is demonstrated with all its applicable dimensions (psychomotor, affective, and cognitive) expressed as a total, integrated act.

Long-range goals and specific teaching objectives have been identified, in this edition, as "general goals" and "specific objectives" to indicate their relationship to the development and subsequent revisions of the Individualized Education Program (IEP) and the Individualized Family Service Plan (IFSP). Although we have provided readers with suggested activities viewed from an age and grade-level perspective, readers applying the curriculum must appreciate the essential relationship between informal and formal assessment data and the decisions they make as to the relevant goals and objectives to be addressed. Although specific objectives have generally been placed in their developmental sequence, known sequences have been considered only if they make functional sense. Developmental milestones and traditional educational tasks have been deemphasized and eliminated from this curriculum if the identified behavior does not contribute to functional success for the intended population (e.g., drawing a geometric shape or matching wooden blocks of different colors). Furthermore, developmental profiles are less important as children get older, whereas they are central for infants and toddlers.

The curriculum is intended as a guide not only for individuals with disabilities but also for individuals who may be experiencing learning problems but who have not been classified as having a disability. In fact, many high-level goals and suggested activities are included to encourage program implementors not to have restricted or limiting views. There are many nondisabled students and adults, students and adults with mild disabilities, and students and adults with no formally defined disability who are functioning at a lower-than-expected level who would also benefit from the activities in the curriculum. These high-level goals and suggested activities are also meant to guide mainstreamed and collaborating teachers in their modification of regular curricula, which should do much to make inclusion more successful for both the students who have disabilities and those who do not.

As with past editions, this new edition has been designed as a guide to preservice and inservice teachers and other professionals who work directly as service providers to children and adults with disabilities. Parents, surrogates and foster parents, and other family members, as well as service coordinators (case managers), house parents in group homes/apartments or other alternate living arrangements, and counselors in activity centers and workshops should find this curriculum valuable as they interact with and instruct the individuals with whom they work and/or live.

The original curriculum also has had wide acceptance and use as a text for preservice teacher candidates and inservice teachers taking courses in curriculum development and teaching methods in special education at the undergraduate and graduate levels. The current edition has been updated to reflect the present needs of students taking these courses, especially as they interact in diverse practica experiences with previously unserved and underserved populations of individuals with disabilities.

The lists of Selected Materials/Resources attached to each unit is relatively brief because many of the essential materials needed in teaching a functional curriculum are the ordinary materials of life that are invariably found in the home, school, community, and workplace, and because well-designed and well-presented teacher-made materials are usually more appropriate, better focused, and more motivating to students.

The Suggested Readings appended to each unit list not only recent publications but some older, classic materials as well. These classics have been included because they retain their immediacy and appropriateness and thus should not be automatically eliminated from lists of relevant professional literature out of a passion for newness.

This new edition of the curriculum continues to provide information and suggestions that have proven to be of value in the past. The suggested activities provided in this new edition, a direct response to user recommendations and reviews, have been separated into two major categories: Teacher Interventions and Family Interventions. Further, four distinct age/grade levels for each of these interventions have been developed to reflect content deemed appropriate for the following levels: infant and toddler/preschool, primary, intermediate, and secondary. The suggested activities for the infant and toddler/preschool level are meant to meet the functional needs of infants and toddlers (birth through 2 years) and preschool children (3 through 5 years). Additionally, attention needs to be directed to the several alternative settings for teaching children, especially where infants and toddlers are concerned, because they are frequently educated in their own homes and in day-care settings.

Finally, this curriculum does not address all the dimensions of a functional curriculum because to do so is neither practical nor possible. It does not provide all the possible instructional activities that are applicable or would be interesting and motivating to students and adults with disabilities. It does, however, provide a structure and format from which a creative professional can extrapolate additional instructional goals and objectives, design learning activities, and suggest possible responses to the multitude of challenging questions that will arise from the actual implementation of the curriculum.

Acknowledgments

The development of this volume required collaboration with many education and health care professionals as well as the input of numerous parents. We would like to specifically acknowledge the contributions of Susan Harryman, RPT, and Priscilla Roberts, LPTA; Lana Warren, OTR/L; Marilee Allen, MD; Yvonne Caruso, RN; Margaret Morris, CCC-SLP; Dwight Baglin, school psychologist; and the following parents, who regularly commit their energies to the education and support of the many children who will benefit from these curricula: Madelyn Bender, Kathy Cooper, Mona Freedman, Michelle Grant, Joyce Bergstein, and Robert Stephens.

As always, the support of office professionals is invaluable. Of particular importance in this project was Carolyn Savage, administrative assistant and mother.

Sheréa Makle, publications specialist, selected and inserted the graphics, as well as refining many formatting inconsistencies.

General Goals

 ## UNIT 1. SELF-CARE SKILLS

I. The student will be functionally independent in toileting, provided there are no physical or developmental reasons for not being trained.

II. The student will be functionally independent in drinking and eating skills in a manner that allows for optimal performance in diverse situations.

III. The student will be functionally independent in dressing and undressing skills in a manner that allows for optimal performance in diverse situations.

IV. The student will be functionally independent in personal cleanliness and grooming in a manner that allows for optimal performance in diverse situations.

 ## UNIT 2. GROSS MOTOR SKILLS

I. The student will acquire those basic gross motor skills that will facilitate the later development of ambulations.

II. The student who requires assistive devices as an aid to ambulation will be able to use such assistive devices as canes, crutches, walkers, and wheelchairs to a degree that will allow him or her to function optimally.

III. The student will be able to move or walk, with or without assistive devices, to a degree that will allow him or her to function optimally in diverse settings.

IV. The student will acquire those gross motor skills that are an integral part of recreation and leisure activities.

 ## UNIT 3. FINE MOTOR SKILLS

I. The student will acquire those initial manipulative skills that will facilitate the development of more advanced fine motor skills and the functional use of the upper extremities.

II. The student will undress and dress using those fine motor skills that will allow him or her to function as optimally as possible.

III. The student will engage in leisure-time activities involving the use of the upper extremities and will do so using those fine motor skills that will allow him or her to function optimally.

IV. The student will acquire those fine motor skills that will enable him or her to use his or her upper extremities optimally in vocational/work activities.

V. The student will acquire those fine motor skills that will allow him or her to use his or her upper extremities optimally in operating simple appliances, objects, conveniences, and home accessories.

UNIT 4. HOUSEHOLD MANAGEMENT AND LIVING SKILLS

I. The student will be functionally independent in planning meals and in purchasing, storing, and preparing food in a manner that allows him or her to perform optimally.

II. The student will be functionally independent in purchasing and maintaining his or her clothes in a manner that allows him or her to perform optimally.

III. The student will be functionally independent in caring for his or her living quarters, appliances, and furnishings in a manner that allows him or her to perform optimally.

IV. The student will operate simple appliances, objects, conveniences, and home accessories.

Introduction and Curriculum Overview

A primary purpose of special education is to help students with disabilities lead successful and personally fulfilling lives now and in the future. A functional curriculum is designed to prepare students to function as independently as possible in an integrated society (Wheeler, 1987). A broad range of skills, therefore, must be included in the design of a functional curriculum for students with disabilities. It is axiomatic that the more severe the disability, the greater the educational need and challenge, and, thus, the more comprehensive the curriculum.

In addition, the skills needed by individuals with disabilities continue to expand as society becomes more complex. Moreover, with the renewed and increasing emphasis on inclusion and mainstreaming, it is imperative that curricula taught in these settings address the needs of students with disabilities who, given the nature of the traditional curriculum, are less likely to be expected to develop functional skills in these mainstreamed settings. Traditional ways of developing content for students with disabilities, such as through the watering down of the regular curriculum, do not work. If new entrants to the regular education mainstream are to be successfully integrated into the school and community, their programs must be modified in functional, real-life ways. In essence, *life is the curriculum.*

According to Gast and Schuster (1993), "A functional curriculum is a primary *external support* for children with severe disabilities" (p. 471). Gast and Schuster have identified a number of principles that should be observed in the development and implementation of a functional curriculum. These authors believe that the designer/instructor should:

> focus on teaching skills that are chronologically age-appropriate and immediately useful to the learner. Use ecological inventories and compile a community catalog of current and future environments that are important to the students. Define goals based on the prior step. Prioritize goals based on their potential for enhancing independence. Task analyze the skills needed to perform successfully. Conduct a discrepancy analysis to determine what the student can and cannot do. Use principles of applied behavior analysis. Provide instruction in integrated and community settings. (p. 471)

The need for acquiring functional skills has become the cornerstone for most programs involved in teaching special populations. Fortunately, for some mainstreamed students with disabilities, the principles and contents of this approach are increasingly being incorporated into regular educational programs.

DEFINING THE FUNCTIONAL APPROACH

The functional approach to educating students with or without disabilities is based on a philosophy of education that determines the format and content of a curriculum and that requires an instructional methodology emphasizing the application of knowledge and skills in reality contexts (Bender & Valletutti, 1985; Valletutti & Bender, 1985). Some authorities view this approach as being different from the developmental approach in that its emphasis is on teaching age-appropriate skills that are immediately applicable to diverse life settings (Gast & Schuster, 1993). Patton, Beirne-Smith, and Payne (1990), on the other hand, have posited: "The functional curriculum is a hybrid of the developmental and the behavioral curricula. It attempts to incorporate the best features of the two. Insofar as it emphasizes teaching interrelated classes of behavior and generalization within task classes, it is developmental, but it is behavioral in its emphasis on teaching skills that the infant or child needs now or will need" (p. 298). According to Kirk and Gallagher (1989), "Over the years, from research, common sense, and experience, a philosophy of teaching students with multiple and severe handicaps has evolved. Today our objective is to teach functional age-appropriate skills within the integrated school and nonschool settings, and to base our teaching on the systematic evaluation of students' progress" (p. 467).

Educators using the functional approach identify life skills, specified as instructional goals and objectives, and then seek to facilitate a student's acquisition of these skills. It is adult referenced in that it is a top-down approach, identifying behaviors essential to successful adjustment as a functioning adult rather than having a bottom-up design with its child-oriented focus (Polloway, Patton, Payne, & Payne, 1989). It fosters the development of skills that increase autonomy, as in self-care activities, and encourages constructive codependency, as in cooperative enterprises and mutual problem solving in the home, school, community, and workplace. It endeavors to make the individuals to whom it is applied as successful as possible in meeting their own needs and in satisfying the requirements of living in a community. It also strives to make the individual's life as fulfilling and pleasurable as possible (Cegelka & Greene, 1993).

The functional approach determines the nature of the instructional process. It requires that specified skills be taught in reality contexts. That is, skills are to be taught directly through typical home, school, or community activities, or, if a natural setting is not feasible, indirectly through classroom simulations (Brown, Nietupski, & Hamre-Nietupski, 1976; Polloway et al., 1989).

Conducting an ecological inventory has been suggested as a strategy for generating a functional curriculum that is community referenced. The steps involved in this process include identifying curricular domains (e.g., vocational and leisure), describing present and future environments, prioritizing the activities pertinent to these environments, specifying the skills needed to perform these activities, conducting a discrepancy analysis to determine required skills missing from the student's behavioral repertoire, determining needed adaptations, and, finally, developing a meaningful IEP (Brown et al., 1979).

A functional curriculum identifies *what* is to be taught, whereas the functional approach to instruction determines *how* a skill is to be taught. Whereas a functional curriculum is, in most cases, absolutely essential to instructional programs employed in special classes or special schools, it can also be particularly valuable to teachers of mainstreamed or inclusive classes. These teachers must make functional adaptations to existing curricula if life skills are to be addressed, despite the restrictions imposed by rigid adherence to the subjects traditionally found in school curricula. Teachers, therefore, must analyze the academically driven goals and objectives of traditional curricula and identify their potential practical applications.

DEVELOPING A FUNCTIONAL CURRICULUM

An analysis of the social roles that people play as children, adolescents, and adults can serve as the foundation for designing a functional curriculum (Bender & Valletutti, 1982; Valletutti & Bender, 1982). Social competency is thus primary in a functional curriculum. "Social competency dimensions are critical to the child's acceptability in the classroom, peer relationships, the efficiency and success of academic efforts, current life adjustment, and future social and vocational success" (Reschly, 1993, p. 232). Closely allied to the concept of a life skills curriculum is the concept of social competence, often referred to as "adaptive behavior." *Adaptive behavior* refers to the individual's effectiveness in meeting the demands and standards of his or her environment based on age and the cultural group to which the individual belongs (Grossman, 1983). According to Drew, Logan, and Hardman (1992), "Adaptive skills are necessary to decrease an individual's dependence on others and increase opportunities for school and community participation" (p. 257). Drew et al. specified that "adaptive skill content areas for school-age retarded children include motor, self-care, social, communication, and functional academic skills" (p. 258).

Curricular models based on the concept of career education emphasize effective participation by the individual in all of life's "occupations." Career education, thus, requires an educational program that starts early in the school career and continues into adulthood (Clark, 1979).

Brolin's (1986) Life-Centered Career Education (LCCE) model identifies 22 major competencies needed for effective functioning in school, family, and community. These skills are divided into three domains: daily living, personal/social, and occupational. Cronin and Patton (1993) have produced a life skills instructional guide for students with special needs. This guide provides information that addresses the importance of life skills instruction and insight as to how to identify major life demands and specific life skills. Professional sources such as these yield a wealth of information on ways of integrating real-life content into the curriculum.

Developers of reality-based curricula, whether identified as functional, life skills, adaptive behavior, or career education, must examine the situations faced by members of society and specify the behaviors expected of them as they function at different stages in their lives. The long-range orientation of education, however, requires that competencies needed by adults be given programming priority.

Functionally oriented curricula must have an adult-outcomes emphasis. This is especially true for those students with disabilities and their nondisabled peers for whom a higher education is neither desired nor appropriate. Adult-outcomes curricula have abandoned their vocational myopia and now deal more comprehensively and realistically with the many elements needed for successful personal and social adjustment in adulthood (Cronin & Gerber, 1982). Students categorized as having diverse learning and behavioral disabilities, as well as students who are at risk for school failure who have not been so classified, are more likely to be stimulated by learning activities that emphasize their present and future problems, needs, and concerns. Regardless of age or grade, students should be prepared for the challenges of life after they graduate or leave school.

If the social-role perspective is accepted, then teachers, parents, counselors, and other trainers must decide which competencies should be included in a curriculum with such a nontraditional approach. This task is not an esoteric or an insurmountable one, however. Through an examination of their own lives and the lives of other adults, educators can easily identify what life skills should be included in a functional curriculum. Moreover, listening and attending to the writings of the students themselves, especially during the adolescent years, will also prove a superb source of functional instructional goals and objectives (Polloway et al., 1989).

The process of selecting the goals and objectives and establishing the functional priorities of a life skills curriculum requires the designer to eliminate those traditional academic tasks that have little or no value. The determinant of inclusion is whether the skill in question is needed or may be needed by the individual now or at some time in the person's future. Patton, Beirne-Smith, and Payne (1990) have suggested that the selection should be governed by an objective's adaptive potential and its direct and frequent application to the individual's environment, the likelihood of its successful acquisition, its potential for improving the quality and level of services available to the individual, and its impact on the reduction of dangerous or harmful behaviors.

Once the functional curriculum has been developed, the student's IEP or IFSP must be formulated based on this general curriculum, with attention devoted to the establishment of instructional priorities. Priorities are determined, in part, on the basis of answers to the following questions:

- Will the acquisition of a skill with less-than-obvious functional relevance lead to the later development of a key functional skill? For example, will it be important to teach an individual to hop and skip because these movements will be incorporated in games, sports, and other leisure activities, such as dancing?

- Is the skill of practical or current value to the individual as he or she functions on a daily basis?

- Will the skill be needed by the individual in the future? A skill that is immediately needed must be assigned greater priority than a skill needed in the future. Age appropriateness is always to be honored whether it applies to the choice of suitable instructional materials or to establishing instructional priorities.

- Has the individual demonstrated an actual need for the development of a particular skill? Teachers, support personnel, and other instructors need to observe the individual to identify the areas in which he or she is experiencing difficulty and utilize these observations in setting programming priorities.

- Has the individual expressed the desire to acquire a specific skill? Students will often ask for needed assistance in acquiring a skill that has psychological importance. These self-identified needs should never be ignored and often will determine educational priorities.

- Do the parents believe that the acquisition of a particular skill will increase their child's adaptive behavior or performance in the home?

- Will the individual's acquisition of a specific skill improve his or her performance in school- and home-related tasks?

- Does the skill have survival value? Clearly, teaching a person how to cross a street safely has greater priority than teaching a youngster to chant or sing a nursery rhyme.

- Will the development of a particular skill facilitate the acquisition of skills pertinent to the goals of other human service professionals who are providing related services? (Valletutti & Dummett, 1992).

On the basis of the responses to these questions, and with essential input from parents and relevant human service professionals, teachers and trainers must develop the student's IFSP or IEP with its stated instructional priorities.

FUNCTIONALITY AS AN INSTRUCTIONAL PROCESS

In order to teach in a functional way, instructors must ask the questions, "Under what circumstances is this skill applied?" and "Why and when is this skill needed?" The answer to either question determines the functional scenario that structures the instructional plan and process. For example, if the short-term instructional objective is, "The student draws water from the sink," the response to the questions "Under what circumstances . . .?" or "Why and when is this skill needed?" may be, "when washing vegetables in preparing a meal," "when filling ice cube trays," or "when getting water to fill the fish tank." The responses to either of these two questions provide the creative vision out of which the lesson should emerge. The lesson might then involve making a meal for guests in which a salad is prepared and ice cubes are made for the meal's accompanying beverage.

Once the circumstances under which a skill is typically practiced have been identified, teachers, parents, and other instructors, if possible, should provide instructional activities in the skill's usual setting or, at a minimum, in its simulated setting. Whenever the realistic setting for a skill's application is the home, teachers must make the student's parents part of the instructional team by helping them to be effective teachers of their children, assisting them in carrying out functional "homework" assignments, such as doing simple household cleaning and home repairs. Teachers, of course, have primary responsibility for skills that are best developed in the school setting, such as teaching cognitive or academic skills in their functional applications. The community setting is the shared responsibility of both parents and teachers.

Whenever it is not possible to practice a skill in its reality context, learning experiences should be provided in classroom simulations. Instructional materials and equipment in a functional and functioning classroom also must be reality based. Furniture, decorations, appliances, and materials typically found in the home must then be found in the classroom as well. To simulate the community, the school might set up a mock traffic pattern in the gymnasium to practice safely crossing streets, establish a supermarket to practice shopping skills, and assign classroom duties as work tasks that mirror jobs available in the community.

THE SCOPE OF THE FUNCTIONAL CURRICULUM

A functional curriculum, if it is to meet the needs of students with disabilities, should be formulated in terms of the social roles people are required to play. Suggested instructional activities should be designed to assist students to fill these roles as successfully and productively as possible even when the curriculum is organized around traditional subject areas, and even when it is arranged around skill areas such as vocational, leisure, motor, communication, and interpersonal skills. Included among these roles are the individual as a

- socially competent person who works cooperatively with others for mutually agreed upon goals.
- capable student who learns from others, and, as a helper, assists others to learn.
- contributing member of a family unit.
- successful member of his or her own personal community (e.g., as a neighbor and friend).
- responsible and responsive citizen of the general community.
- skilled consumer of goods and services and participant in financial transactions.
- productive worker.
- skillful participant in diverse leisure-time activities.
- competent traveler who moves about the community while meeting all other social roles.

DEVELOPING INSTRUCTIONAL PLANS

Instructional plans serve as the blueprint for coordinating and teaching functional skills. In this curriculum, activities are presented in terms of Teacher Interventions and Parent Interventions. Subsumed under these interventions are four age and grade-level designations appropriate to teaching different age groups of children and youth with disabilities: infant and toddler/preschool, primary, intermediate, and secondary.

With its annual goals and their short-term objectives, the curriculum serves as the framework for systematically observing and assessing the student's performance in terms of both process and product. Evaluation occurs as the learner functions on a daily basis in natural settings and as he or she responds to structured and simulated activities. These observations, supplemented by more formally acquired data, aid in selecting what goals and objectives are to be placed, for example, in the student's IEP. Once these decisions are made, lesson planning can commence as follows:

- Lesson planning begins, based on instructional insights acquired from assessment data, with the selection of a priority *annual goal* and its associated *specific objective* from the student's IEP.

- Following this selection, a pertinent *lesson objective* is then constructed. The lesson objective, like the short-term instructional objective, is student oriented and has the dual purpose of structuring the instructional sequence and suggesting the assessment strategy and its performance criterion level. Toward these ends, a lesson objective has three key elements:

  - Clarification of the stimulus situation or conditions: "When given . . ." or "After being shown . . ."

  - Specification of a desired response: "The student will . . ."

  - Establishment of a performance level: "He will do so in four out of five trials" or "She will do so without assistance."

- Next, *materials and equipment* are listed even though a complete list is not really known until the total plan is developed. This segment is placed in the beginning of the plan, however, for ease in reading when the instructor skims the plan immediately prior to its implementation.

- The *motivating activity* is stated. Identifying an appropriate motivating activity may be a challenging task because it is not always easy to identify age-appropriate motivating activities that will capture the attention and encourage the involvement of the different age groups of students with disabilities who are functioning at depressed levels.

- *Instructional procedures* are then enumerated. These are instructor oriented and are sequenced in logical steps arising out of the motivating activity and leading to assessment. The instructional procedure itself is divided into four steps: initiation, guided practice, independent practice, and closure. Evidence that teaching is taking place must be carefully articulated in each of these steps. Demonstrations, assistance, and problem-solving challenges are ways of ensuring that instruction is occurring.

- The *assessment strategy* to be employed is then specified. This procedure should reflect the desired response and performance criteria indicated in the lesson objective. It is instructor oriented and should specify the method to be used in recording observational data.

- At this point, a proposed *follow-up activity or objective* is written to ensure that the sequence of instruction is honored. The hoped-for follow-up activity or objective is composed in positive terms because it can be pursued only if the student successfully meets the plan's lesson objective. If the learner fails to meet the lesson objective, a remedial lesson plan must be written on an ad hoc basis (because it is not possible to predict the reason for failure, especially given that the lesson was designed and taught with the likelihood of instructional success).

- A concluding section, *observations and their instructional insights,* is appended. This section is included in the instructional plan as one means of recording student data and for identifying one's insights as to programming implications for later reference and for use in completing checklists, writing progress reports, and designing and modifying the student's IEP.

Then, introductory information should be provided at the beginning of the instructional plan, such as the following:

- topic area

- name of the designer of the plan

- required time for implementation

- student(s) for whom the plan is intended

- relevant background information on the involved student(s)

Finally, an instructional (lesson) plan should be written in a simple and direct way and be relatively free from jargon so that parents, teacher aides, volunteers, and other appropriate instructors can readily understand it and implement it.

References

Bender, M., & Valletutti, P. J. (1982). *Teaching functional academics to adolescents and adults with learning problems.* Baltimore: University Park Press.

Bender, M., & Valletutti, P. J. (1985). *Teaching the moderately and severely handicapped: Curriculum objectives, strategies, and activities. Vol. 1: Self-care, motor skills and household management.* Austin, TX: PRO-ED.

Brolin, D. E. (1986). *Life-Centered Career Education: A competency-based approach* (rev. ed.). Reston, VA: Council for Exceptional Children.

Brown, L. F., Branston-McLean, M. B., Baumgart, D., Vincent, L., Falvey, M., & Schroder, J. (1979). Using the characteristics of current and subsequent least restrictive environments in the development of curricular content for severely handicapped students. *Journal of the Association for the Severely Handicapped, 4,* 407–424.

Brown, L. F., Nietupski, J., & Hamre-Nietupski, S. (1976). The criterion of ultimate functioning and public school services for severely handicapped students. In M. A. Thomas (Ed.), *Hey don't forget about me: Education's investment in the severely, profoundly, and multiply handicapped* (pp. 2–15). Reston, VA: Council for Exceptional Children.

Cegelka, P. T., & Greene, G. (1993). Transition to adulthood. In A. E. Blackhurst & W. H. Berdine (Eds.), *An introduction to special education* (3rd ed., pp. 137–175). New York: HarperCollins.

Clark, G. M. (1979). *Career education for the handicapped child in the elementary classroom.* Denver: Love.

Cronin, M. E., & Gerber, P. J. (1982). Preparing the learning disabled adolescent for adulthood. *Topics in Learning & Learning Disabilities, 2,* 55–68.

Cronin, M. E., & Patton, J. R. (1993). *Life skills instruction for all students with special needs: A practical guide for integrating real-life content into the curriculum.* Austin, TX: PRO-ED.

Drew, C. J., Logan, D. R., & Hardman, M. L. (1992). *Mental retardation: A life cycle approach* (5th ed.). New York: Merrill/Macmillan.

Gast, D. L., & Schuster, J. W. (1993). Students with severe developmental disabilities. In A. E. Blackhurst & W. H. Berdine (Eds.), *An introduction to special education* (3rd ed., pp. 455–491). New York: HarperCollins.

Grossman, H. J. (1983). *Classification in mental retardation.* Washington, DC: American Association on Mental Deficiency.

Kirk, S. A., & Gallagher, J. J. (1989). *Educating exceptional children* (6th ed.). Boston: Houghton Mifflin.

Patton, J. R., Beirne-Smith, M., & Payne, J. S. (1990). *Mental retardation* (3rd ed.). Columbus, OH: Merrill.

Polloway, E. A., Patton, J. R., Payne, J. S., & Payne, R. A. (1989). *Strategies for teaching learners with special needs.* (4th ed.). New York: Merrill.

Reschly, D. J. (1993). Special education decision making and functional/behavioral assessment. In E. L. Meyen, G. A. Vergason, & R. J. Whelan, *Challenges facing special education* (pp. 227–240). Denver: Love.

Valletutti, P. J., & Bender, M. (1982). *Teaching interpersonal and community living skills: A curriculum model for handicapped adolescents and adults.* Baltimore: University Park Press.

Valletutti, P. J., & Bender, M. (1985). *Teaching the moderately and severely handicapped: Curriculum objectives, strategies, and activities. Vol. 2: Communication and socialization.* Austin, TX: PRO-ED.

Valletutti, P. J., & Dummett, L. (1992). *Cognitive development: A functional approach.* San Diego: Singular Publishing Group.

Wheeler, J. (1987). *Transitioning persons with moderate and severe disabilities from school to adulthood: What makes it work.* Menononie: University of Wisconsin Materials Development Center.

Self-Care Skills

Programming in the area of self-care skills is essential for many individuals with disabilities. Skills such as toilet training (Anderson, 1982; Azrin & Foxx, 1974; Honig, 1993; Wilson, 1986), cleaning and grooming (Dreith & Kreps, 1975; Redmond, Bennett, Wiggert, & McLean, 1993), dressing and undressing (Adelson & Sandow, 1978; Dever, 1988; Edgar, Maser, & Haring, 1977), personal safety (Boone, 1992), and drinking and eating (Barnerdt & Bricker, 1978; Edwards & Bergman, 1982; Morris & Klein, 1987; Schloss, Alexander, Hornig, Parker, & Wright, 1993) are skills of daily living that need to be mastered if the student is to become an accepted and functioning member of society. In addition, individuals with disabilities must learn how to manage emergency situations and act safely as they perform these life skills. The following reasons have been offered as a rationale for priority programming in self-care skills:

1. The student who is physically and developmentally capable of being toilet trained, but for some reason has not been trained, will be excluded from many social and community interactions.

2. The student who is not functionally independent in drinking and eating will require supervision that may become burdensome to some parents, teachers, and staff. Furthermore, required care may not be available as the student becomes older. Moreover, he or she will be greatly limited in opportunities for positive social interaction, leisure, and productive work experiences.

3. The student who is not functionally independent in dressing and undressing skills will require significant amounts of attention from parents, staff, and teachers. Attention to the mechanics of self-care, if it continues for many years, will take time away from teaching those higher-level skills involved in functional academics (see Vol. III [Valletutti, Bender, & Sims-Tucker, in press]), communication, and social interaction. The development of social interaction skills will be restricted if inordinate attention must be given to personal care experiences.

4. The student who lacks essential cleaning and grooming skills invariably will be denied or excluded from many interpersonal and social experiences.

5. The student who acts in an unsafe manner will create problems for him- or herself, parents, and teachers, resulting in reduced opportunities for independence, inclusion, and integration into less restrictive programs.

Proficiency in self-care skills helps students with disabilities develop responsibility for their personal needs and enhances their self-esteem. It also increases the likelihood that others will view them as acceptable friends, co-workers, peers, acquaintances, and mates. Individuals with disabilities can gain control over their immediate environment through the acquisition of specific self-care skills. Utilizing this curriculum to facilitate the development of these skills can enrich the lives of the students in the educational setting as well as in their home environment. This curriculum provides activities for individuals at different ages and in multiple settings, including the school, the home, and the community.

The objectives and activities suggested in this area of the curriculum were developed after extensive reviews by master teachers, physical and occupational therapists, nutritionists, psychologists, pediatricians, and nurses. In addition, parents with young, as well as older, children were surveyed for their comments as to what should be included in this third edition.

As teachers and staff use this curriculum, they may soon see that students gain in self-confidence as they begin to master basic self-care skills. Mastery of the environment is perhaps the greatest joy of the developing person. The self-concept of the student will also be enhanced if he or she is enthusiastically praised for growth in specific areas. Functional independence contributes to successful participation in the home, neighborhood, and society, and, hopefully, to a greater level of financial independence.

Although self-care skills must get early attention in school, they should not be given unique or prolonged emphasis at the expense of other curricular areas. Repeated concentration on these fundamental skills can result in monotonous school days for students and teachers alike. A variety of instructional experiences is important, especially when teachers are programming in the area of self-care. Burnout, an increasing problem in high-stress teaching assignments, is a less likely result of instructional programming that is multidimensional and varied.

The Suggested Readings at the end of this unit provide a review of some current as well as past self-care information, techniques, and programs. The reader may also wish to review the Selected Materials/Resources section at the end of this unit for additional information on specific resources in this area.

General Goals of This Unit

I. The student will be functionally independent in toileting, provided there are no physical or developmental reasons for not being trained.

II. The student will be functionally independent in drinking and eating skills in a manner that allows for optimal performance in diverse situations.

III. The student will be functionally independent in dressing and undressing skills in a manner that allows for optimal performance in diverse situations.

IV. The student will be functionally independent in personal cleanliness and grooming in a manner that allows for optimal performance in diverse situations.

GOAL I.

The student will be functionally independent in toileting, provided there are no physical or developmental reasons for not being trained.

It is important that the teacher or parent who is working in the area of toilet training first consider whether the student is ready to be toilet trained (after he or she has been medically evaluated as able to participate in such a program). Readiness is usually indicated when the student

1. Is ambulatory and can walk to the toilet or is able to be assisted.

2. Has enough vision to see where the toilet is and to see gestures or is able to follow auditory instructions.

3. Has enough motor control to undress below the waist.

4. Has sufficient receptive language skills to understand simple commands.

SPECIFIC OBJECTIVES

The student:

☐ A. When requiring supervision or assistance, indicates in an acceptable manner the need to go to the bathroom.

☐ B. When independent in toileting, closes the bathroom and/or stall door for privacy.

☐ C. Removes, lowers, unfastens, and/or opens appropriate clothing before toileting.

☐ D. When appropriate, either raises the toilet seat for voiding or uses a urinal.

☐ E. Sits on the toilet seat for eliminating or for voiding.

☐ F. Wipes appropriately after voiding or eliminating.

☐ G. Flushes the toilet after wiping, or flushes the urinal after voiding.

☐ H. Washes and dries hands after toileting.

☐ I. Dresses and/or arranges clothing after toileting.

☐ J. Locates and uses a bathroom or public restroom independently and safely.

SUGGESTED ACTIVITIES

 ### Specific Objective A

The student, when requiring supervision or assistance, indicates in an acceptable manner the need to go to the bathroom.

Teacher Interventions

Infant and Toddler/Preschool Level. Wait for the student to be engrossed in an activity. Wave your hand directly in his or her line of vision until the student's eyes fix on either your hand or your eyes. If the student looks in your eyes, offer your hand to him or her.

When the student is dry and not demonstrating negative behaviors, place him or her on the toilet or potty.

Record the frequency of the student's urination and bowel movements. Take the student to the bathroom to toilet on this schedule. Share this schedule with the student's parents and request that they continue to record times at home. If a specific time or times during the school day (e.g., before recess or during free time) has not been set, select a time when the student is free to go to use the potty or toilet and you know that there is a need to go to the bathroom. Use verbal clues.

Make a time chart for the student. Chart each time the student indicates a need to go to the bathroom (see Figure 1.1). Discuss timing with the toddler's parents. Use a point system for each time the child uses the toilet and explain the reward the child will get for each five points.

Make maintenance checks for those students who are being trained to stay dry and reinforce them if they are dry. Say "No" if their pants are wet or indicate displeasure in some other way. Do this check at intervals and later at intermittent intervals. Make a maintenance check chart for each student (see Figure 1.2).

Family Interventions

Infant and Toddler/Preschool Level. When the toddler wakes from a nap or a night's sleep dry and the toddler can sit, voluntary training of the bladder can begin. Parents should be encouraged to observe their toddlers clutching themselves. Some children are capable of control at 18 months, whereas others may not be ready until 4 years.

Ask the parents if they notice time patterns when their child is wet. Have the parents use a chart to record these times. Tell them to remind the child to use the potty 10 to 15 minutes before these times occur. Use a potty chair that sits firmly on the floor and fits the toddler. (Note: Use a gesture that is socially acceptable and as widely recognized as possible.)

When the child begins to use the potty, the parents can explain the difference between urination and bowel movements. The parents can use the name that the child already may be using to distinguish between them. Parents can note the differences in physical feelings that may precede the bowel movement from those that precede urination.

 ## Specific Objective B

The student, when independent in toileting, closes the bathroom and/or stall door for privacy.

Time Chart—Student's Name _____

	7-8	8-9	9-10	10-11	11-12	12-1	1-2	2-3	3-4	4-5	5-6	6-7	7-8	8-9
Monday		8:15	9:20		11:15		1:30							
Tuesday		8:10	9:00		11:10									
Wednesday		8:15	9:30		11:15		1:15							
Thursday														
Friday														
Saturday														
Sunday														

FIGURE 1.1. Time chart for toileting.

Maintenance Check Chart—Student's Name

	7-8	8-9	9-10	10-11	11-12	12-1	1-2	2-3	3-4	4-5	5-6	6-7	7-8	8-9
Monday	7:30 dry	8:30 dry	9:30 wet	10:30 dry	11:30 dry	12:30 dry	1:30 dry							
Tuesday	wet	dry	dry	dry	dry	dry								
Wednesday	dry	dry	dry											
Thursday														
Friday														
Saturday														
Sunday														

FIGURE 1.2. Maintenance check chart for toileting.

Teacher Interventions

Infant and Toddler/Preschool Level. Explain to the child that he or she can get a star or a point if he or she goes to the bathroom at specified intervals without asking. (Note: The child should be completely toilet trained at this point because voluntary control is an important component of the child's cooperating with the teacher.)

Primary Level. Set specific times during the school day (e.g., before or after lunch and during recess) when the student is free to go to the bathroom. Chart if the student remembers to close the door after entering the bathroom. If not, remind the student. At toileting time, indicate through gesture and/or words that toileting takes place only in the bathroom, and students in other rooms should not be able to see us or we see them. Indicate that closed doors stop others from seeing into the bathroom. (Note: Locks should be placed on bathroom doors only after the student has developed the cognitive and fine motor skills involved in unlocking a door. At all times, doors should be capable of being opened from the outside in case of emergency.

Family Interventions

Primary Level. Ask the parents to observe whether or not their child closes the bathroom door when the child goes to the toilet. If the child fails to close the door, encourage the parents to remind him or her as they close the door.

When possible, go for a walk through the child's immediate community or go to a community event (e.g., a ball game, the movies, or a puppet show). Encourage the student to gesture appropriately or tell you when there is a need to go to the bathroom. Assist the child in finding a safe public restroom. Have the child enter the restroom, locate the stall, and close the door.

Before taking the child on an outing or community visit, check to see what bathroom facilities are available, clean, and operable (e.g., public restrooms in a movie theater or individual bathrooms in a private residence). Observe to see if the student closes the bathroom or stall door during toileting. If he or she forgets, encourage him or her to close the door.

 ## Specific Objective C

The student removes, lowers, unfastens, and/or opens appropriate clothing before toileting.

Teacher Interventions

Infant and Toddler/Preschool Level. During bathroom time(s), observe how the students removes, lowers, unfastens, and opens his or her clothing. If the student is having difficulty, demonstrate how to pull down the clothes, assisting him or her while explaining orally and/or through gestures what you are doing. Practice dressing and undressing with oversize clothing worn over the student's regular clothes. Use clothing that can be easily removed, lowered, unfastened, and/or opened.

Primary Level. Plan a visit to a store or event in the community. Before the trip, provide time for the student to practice (in a bathroom) removing, lowering, unfastening, and/or opening specific clothing that would interfere with or restrict the student from going to the bathroom. If this part of the activity is successful, proceed to the community event, allowing time for at least one community restroom stop.

Family Interventions

Infant and Toddler/Preschool Level. Ask the parents to monitor whether their child is having difficulty lowering, removing, fastening, or opening clothing before going to the bathroom. If difficulties exist, provide suggestions (e.g., loose clothing, fewer buttons, and the use of Velcro fasteners) about ways the parents can help to improve the situation. Also, use clothing that is age appropriate (e.g., avoid elastic waistbands for older children).

Encourage the parent to have the child adjust his or her clothing prior to leaving the bathroom. Have the parent work with the child using dolls and discussing the need for all toileting to be completed, including the securing of all clothing. Have the parent provide a bell in the toilet for the child to use if he or she has a problem while toileting.

Primary Level. Encourage the parents to provide independence to the child in selecting appropriate clothing by limiting the options available and making clothing accessible.

 ## Specific Objective D

The male student, when appropriate, either raises the toilet seat for voiding or uses a urinal.

Teacher Interventions

Infant and Toddler/Preschool Level. During toilet time, take the student to the bathroom. Point out the toilet seat and explain that it should be down when someone is going to sit on the toilet and raised when someone is going to urinate in the standing position. When the boy can stand, determine where he should stand and direct his penis.

During bathroom times, remind the male student to lift the toilet seat before voiding. (It is important that this reminder be made privately to avoid any embarrassment for the student.) If the student continues to forget to lift the toilet seat, place a picture by the toilet (i.e., a picture showing the actions of lifting the seat, flushing, and lowering the seat). Ask him to recite the process before he goes to the bathroom. Include in the rules the use of good health habits after going to the bathroom (i.e., washing and drying hands).

Primary Level. Assist the student in selecting the restroom for the correct gender by taking the student to an unfamiliar setting and observing whether he selects the appropriate restroom.

Observe whether the male student raises the seat when appropriate and provide a verbal reward or additional instructions, depending on whether the student chooses the urinal or raises the toilet seat.

Family Interventions

Infant and Toddler/Preschool Level. Assist the child to stand at the toilet or urinal to void. Assist the child with his balance, for safety as well as to protect clothing and the floor. Demonstrate how to excuse oneself to use the toilet and how to ask for the location of the appropriate facility.

Primary Level. Enlist the help of the parents in monitoring whether their male child lifts the toilet seat before voiding when at home. Tell the parents to demonstrate to their child how to lift the toilet seat before voiding. Remind them to emphasize lowering the toilet seat slowly after voiding.

When on a community outing or activity, set a specific time to go to the bathroom. Select a place that has restrooms with urinals as well as toilets (e.g., theaters, department stores, recreation parks, or shopping malls or centers). Encourage the male student to use the urinal correctly. It may be necessary for a male teacher to demonstrate how to stand in front of a urinal, how to flush, and, in certain instances, how to decide which size urinal is appropriate.

Encourage student awareness of typical public restroom situations, such as when other people are waiting to use the same toilet or urinal (e.g., at ball games, theaters, and department stores), the avoidance of deodorizers or screens placed in urinals, and the use of appropriate behavior when using urinals and toilets (e.g., not putting in excessive paper, flushing unnecessarily, or discarding foreign objects).

 ## Specific Objective E

The student sits on the toilet seat for eliminating or for voiding. (Note: Female teachers should implement activities with female students and male teachers with male students whenever possible.)

Teacher Interventions

Infant and Toddler/Preschool Level. Place the student on the potty or toilet (with appropriate adaptation) and reward the student every time elimination occurs. If the student does not eliminate, reward the student every few minutes for sitting.

Primary Level. During bathroom time, observe how the student sits on the toilet seat. Provide some stability if the student is having difficulty. Gradually decrease assistance until the student appears at ease when sitting on the toilet seat. (Note: Adaptive equipment should be used when necessary.)

During bathroom time, but only when necessary, monitor to see that the student is sitting correctly on the toilet seat. Because the privacy of the student is very important, observe only if there is a need to monitor this behavior.

If the student appears to be having difficulty sitting on the toilet seat, hold him or her so that he or she feels secure. When the student appears steady, remove your hands. Never leave the student alone until he or she has mastered the procedure. Support the student whenever he or she appears afraid or uncertain of his or her balance.

Family Interventions

Infant and Toddler/Preschool Level. Have the parent sit with the child and provide fluids, rewarding the child with hugs, praise, and other predetermined rewards each time the child eliminates. A footstool may be used to assist the child to get on and off the toilet.

Primary Level. Enlist the help of the parents to monitor how their child is sitting on the toilet seat. Provide suggestions and/or help if they are experiencing difficulties. Use adaptive equipment when necessary.

When the student has to go to the bathroom, provide him or her with experience sitting on a variety of toilet seats that are typically found in community restrooms (i.e., split seat, round, and oval). Avoid restrooms that are not clean or that are in unsafe areas.

 Specific Objective F

The student wipes appropriately after voiding or eliminating. (Note: If the student is a boy, tell him to practice wiping himself with toilet paper. Boys may wipe from front to back or back to front. If the student is a girl, tell her to practice wiping herself with toilet paper, always wiping from front to back.)

Teacher Interventions

Infant and Toddler/Preschool Level. Instruct the student as to the toilet paper procedures in the early intervention setting, assisting the child to get enough toilet paper. Praise the student and use verbal instructions (e.g., "Wipe yourself"), observing and correcting during the process.

Primary Level. Observe to see whether the student is wiping him- or herself thoroughly, using the proper movement.

Develop a checklist for bathroom objectives. Include on this list an objective on wiping oneself after using the toilet. Post this chart on or near the bathroom door. If more privacy is preferred, give each student his or her own checklist. At specific times, observe to see if he or she is using the checklist.

Family Interventions

Infant and Toddler/Preschool Level. The parent should paste stickers on each fifth or sixth sheet of rolled toilet paper. Have the child unroll the paper until the sticker and tear the roll at the sheet with the sticker. Assist the child with wiping, correcting for wiping direction. Have the child put the tissue in the toilet.

Primary Level. Set up a time each month, or, if necessary, more often, to call the student's parents or caregivers. Ask them to monitor whether their child is remembering to wipe him- or herself after using the toilet. Send a note home as a reminder for those parents or caregivers who cannot be reached by phone.

Ask the parents to remind their child of appropriate bathroom behaviors before the child visits a community restroom. Ask the parents to monitor how well the child uses the bathroom, wipes him- or herself, and flushes the toilet. Select public restrooms that are clean and have an ample supply of toilet paper, as well as toilet seats of the appropriate size.

 ### Specific Objective G

The student flushes the toilet after wiping, or flushes the urinal after voiding.

Teacher Interventions

Infant and Toddler/Preschool Level. Instruct the student to drop the paper into the toilet after wiping, helping the child to release the paper. Tell the student to flush by guiding the hand to the handle and pushing firmly to flush.

Primary Level Randomly check to see that the toilet has been flushed after the student has used it. When necessary, if the child is only partially flushing the toilet (i.e., does not put enough pressure on the handle or flusher), demonstrate the correct way to flush the toilet.

Once the student has acquired the motor skills needed to flush the toilet, remind him or her (verbally or nonverbally) to flush. If he or she completes the act, reward him or her immediately. (Note: Activities involving flushing should be limited to those that are purely functional so that flushing for fun is not encouraged or reinforced.)

Family Interventions

Infant and Toddler/Preschool Level. After the child has eliminated, assist the child to flush if he or she is not frightened of the flushing toilet. Praise the child for flushing.

Primary Level. Call the parents and ask them to unobtrusively monitor whether their child flushes the toilet after using it. Suggest that they not interfere with the child's privacy when the child is able to use the toilet independently.

Visit a variety of public restrooms so that the student has experiences with the various kinds of flushing mechanisms. (Note: Certain restrooms now come equipped with sensors that flush the toilet automatically, which may frighten children. Find out in advance whether the restroom is sensor-operated, and explain the flushing mechanism to the child.)

 ## Specific Objective H

The student washes and dries hands after toileting.

Teacher Interventions

Infant and Toddler/Preschool Level. Have the student face the sink and verbally instruct the student in the process of turning on the water, using the soap, rubbing the hands gently, and thoroughly rinsing the hands. Encourage the student to look at his or her hands and observe the sudsing process, telling the student to cover the entire hand.

Tell the student to dry his or her hands. If the student is having difficulty, take his or her hands and the towel in yours and work the towel until the hands are completely dry, explaining the process verbally. Have the student hang the towel up or throw paper towels in the trash.

Primary Level. Ask the parents to help you provide each student with his or her own grooming aids, including his or her own bar of soap. These items can be kept in a special place in the student's "cubby," desk, locker, or learning area. Initially remind the student to check his or her area for any grooming aids he or she may need before toileting. Congratulate the student when he or she appropriately washes and dries his or her hands after using the toilet.

Tape a 3-by-5-inch index card with the student's name on it next to the bathroom. Each time the student appropriately washes and dries his or her hands after using the toilet, tell him or her to record it by using a check mark or star.

Family Interventions

Infant and Toddler/Preschool Level. Use a footstool for the child and stand behind the child with your hands on the child's. Assist the child in turning on the water, using the soap and rubbing the hands gently, rinsing, and drying. Have the child replace the towel.

Primary Level Send home a checklist on bathroom behaviors to the student's parents or caregivers. As part of this checklist, list several behaviors that require the parents to observe whether their child is washing and drying his or her hands after toileting. If this behavior is not occurring, provide suggestions to the parents, such as leaving a bar of soap or a liquid soap dispenser near the sink. The soap and/or dispenser can be in the child's favorite color.

After a community activity and/or when there is a need to go to a community restroom, observe to see if the child washes and dries his or her hands after using the toilet. It may be necessary to demonstrate how to use some of the soap dispensers typically found in public restrooms. When the child appropriately and correctly washes and dries his or her hands, record it. Later, review the trip and praise the child for his or her appropriate social behaviors. Be sure to specify the behaviors for which you are praising him or her.

(Note: Select bathrooms that are clean, have operating sinks and basins, have identifiable hot/cold faucets, and have a variety of faucets and drying mechanisms, such as those that are single-lever action, automatically turn off after being used or released, or are activated by pressing oversize button switches, such as hot air hand blowers. Also, it is important to demonstrate how to regulate water temperature: Turn on cold water first, and gradually turn on hot water. Also stress the importance of not using bars of already used public restroom soap and continuous cloth towel machines.)

 ## Specific Objective I

The student dresses and/or arranges clothing after toileting.

Teacher Interventions

Infant and Toddler/Preschool Level. Using a large clown doll, have the student undo the clown's pants, using pants with a button and zipper. If the student is a girl, have her practice with a skirt and pants. Young children frequently have elastic-waist pants. Practice with whatever the student typically wears.

Tell the student to go to the bathroom and use the potty or toilet, observing how the student handles his or her own clothing. Assist the student if there are problems, demonstrating with verbal cues if necessary.

Primary Level. After the student has voided or eliminated and wiped him- or herself, indicate through gesture and/or words that he or she must dress before leaving the bathroom and returning to class.

Place an unbreakable mirror on the inside of the bathroom door. Instruct the student to check his or her appearance before he or she leaves the bathroom, making sure his or her clothing is arranged properly (i.e., tucked in, zipped, buttoned, snapped, or closed).

Family Interventions

Infant and Toddler/Preschool Level. Take the child to the bathroom and demonstrate how to pull down the necessary clothing, sitting or standing, as appropriate, and pulling up the clothing. Young children should be in loose clothing that can be easily removed by the child to facilitate self-help in the toileting process.

Primary Level. On trips to public restrooms and at home, encourage the child to use bathroom mirrors to arrange his or her clothes properly. Use appropriately fitting clothing and avoid snaps and fasteners that are difficult to open and close. Remind boys to check to see that their fly is closed.

   As part of a community outing, set aside time to go to a public restroom. Ask parents or caregivers to observe how their child's clothing looks after the child has used the bathroom. If the appearance is inappropriate, they should take the child aside privately and tell him or her to correct the problem. When possible, ask the child to look in a mirror to verify what you are saying. Select bathrooms that are well lit, are in safe areas, and are clean.

 Specific Objective J

The student locates and uses a bathroom or public restroom independently and safely.

Teacher Interventions

Primary Level. Check to see how independent the student is in finding the school bathroom. Provide opportunities to use bathroom(s) that are in or near the student's room as well as in different parts of the school. Check to see that the student uses the appropriate bathroom. Provide help when needed.

   If the student might be transferred to another school in the district, visit the school with the student and ask him or her to locate the restrooms there.

Family Interventions

Primary Level. Ask the student's parents if their child knows where the bathroom(s) are located in his or her home. If the child has difficulty in finding the bathroom, provide suggestions to the parent on how to achieve this objective (e.g., placing a rebus or symbol outside the bathroom and developing a toilet schedule that includes going to each bathroom in the house if there is more than one).

Have the child's parents review the various signs and symbols found on public restrooms. Parents should make a chart of these signs and locate them in the community. Remind parents to avoid public restrooms in unsafe areas. Have parents tell their child about using toilet facilities on interstate buses, planes, or trains. Have them remind their child that other people may be waiting to use the same facilities.

GOAL II.

The student will be functionally independent in drinking and eating skills in a manner that allows for optimal performance in diverse situations.

Feeding skills range from sucking and swallowing of liquids to the consumption of regular foods without assistance. Initially, control of the muscles involved in the eating/drinking processes (sucking, swallowing, and chewing) must be evaluated. The utensils used in feeding continue to change and should be assessed in terms of type of material, strength, size, and appropriateness (plastic utensils are usually not recommended). Initial feeding stages, such as grasp of utensil, plate-to-mouth movement patterns, and scooping of food all occur normally between the ages of 12 and 18 months, but vary considerably in students with disabilities.

Positioning of children during drinking and eating, as well as using appropriate types and textures of food, are other considerations that need to be reviewed. Consultation with drinking and eating specialists (e.g., occupational therapists, speech pathologists, nutritionists) is necessary before the objectives are incorporated into instructional experiences in the home, school, or community.

Teachers, parents, early intervention personnel, and others utilizing this section should continually chart the progress of the student. This ongoing assessment should include his or her appearance as he or she eats, as this is an important social aspect of the feeding program, particularly as the child matures.

SPECIFIC OBJECTIVES

The student:

❏ A. Drinks from a bottle or cup.

❏ B. Drinks through a straw.

❏ C. Drinks from a glass.

❏ D. Drinks from a container.

❏ E. Drinks from a water fountain.

❏ F. Eats with a spoon in an appropriate manner.

❏ G. Eats with a fork in an appropriate manner.

❏ H. Uses a knife appropriately during eating activities.

❏ I. Uses a napkin appropriately.

❏ J. Eats in a safe and socially acceptable manner.

SUGGESTED ACTIVITIES

 Specific Objective A

The student drinks from a bottle or cup.

Teacher Interventions

Infant and Toddler/Preschool Level. If the young student is not able to hold the bottle, hold the student during feeding and support the head. When the student wants to hold the bottle, hand him or her the bottle to drink from on his or her own. By 7 months, infants are usually sitting independently and have increased motor control. At this age, children are usually fed in a high chair or infant chair. Children who walk should be encouraged to sit while using the bottle for safety purposes and to insure that bottles are not exchanged by younger children.

Give the child a small amount of preferred liquids in a cup. Assist the child in bringing the cup to his or her mouth and tip it gently. As the child shows an interest, pause with the cup several inches from the child's mouth until he or she leans forward to close his or her lips around the cup.

During snack or lunchtime, observe how the student uses his or her cup. Provide assistance if he or she appears to be unstable in handling the cup or if there is excessive spilling by holding the cup to the student's mouth with the head level or slightly forward. Be patient if this is a messy process. Practice with a variety of sizes and types of cups, ranging from a cup with 1 or 2 handles, spill proof, to those typically found in restaurants.

Primary Level. Assign a peer who can successfully drink from a cup to sit next to the student when in the cafeteria or lunchroom. Ask the peer to provide assistance to the student when appropriate. Emphasize the use of safety precautions appropriate for drinking hot beverages. (Note: Children with visual or motor disabilities may require special adaptions such as training in techniques to determine liquid levels in the cup or drinking only from a straw.)

Family Interventions

Infant and Toddler/Preschool Level. During feeding periods, the parent should hold the bottle to the child's mouth to encourage sucking from the bottle, gently rubbing the mouth with the nipple and moving the bottle between the lips. Once the child is sucking on the bottle, have the parent place the child's hands on the bottle. After a period of time the child will firmly grip the bottle.

To encourage independence in bottle holding, have the parent hold the bottle a small distance from the child's mouth and observe if the child reaches for it. As the child's reaching and holding skills increase, the parent can allow the child to hold the bottle. Caution parents to never leave a child propped with a bottle and to check frequently to see if the child has dropped the bottle.

To encourage swallowing, the parent should place liquid in the child's mouth with the head level or slightly forward, holding his or her hand on the throat to feel the swallow motion.

Parents can begin the training of using the cup with fluids with a thicker texture to assist the child in learning to identify when the fluid is in the mouth and with lip closure. Remind the parent of the child with motor problems to position the child with his or her head slightly flexed and to use language in the approach of the cup and cues to get the child prepared to drink the liquids from the cup.

Primary Level. When possible, have the parents take their child to a sporting or recreational event where the child is a spectator. Have them bring the child's favorite drink or juice. At an appropriate interval, have them ask the child if he or she is thirsty and if so, offer the cup of drink. Ask the parents to assist only when necessary and encourage good grooming habits while the child is drinking from the cup (i.e., wiping the mouth).

 Specific Objective B

The student drinks through a straw.

Teacher Interventions

Primary Level. At snack or lunchtime and when appropriate, encourage the student to drink his or her beverages through a straw. Use a variety of straws for this lesson. When possible, use juice or drink boxes that come with straws.

Conduct a beverage-tasting party where all beverages are suitable for drinking with a straw (e.g., water, milk, soda, lemonade). Emphasize acceptable health and safety habits for drinking with a straw (e.g., not sharing the straw with others).

Family Interventions

Primary Level. Ask the parents to observe how well their child uses a straw. If the child is having trouble, ask the parents to describe what problem the child is having. Offer specific suggestions according to the problem cited (e.g., cut size of the straw, increase the diameter of the straw, and/or change material of the straw).

Ask the parents to take their child to a fast-food restaurant. Have them model appropriate drinking from a straw (e.g., no slurping, dribbling, or pinching of straw).

 Specific Objective C

The student drinks from a glass.

Teacher Interventions

Primary Level. During lunch, practice with the student who is just learning to drink from a glass. You may wish to fill the student's glass to a certain point, help the student lift the glass, and/or show him or her ways of tipping the glass so that a minimum amount of liquid comes to his or her mouth. Also, emphasize the use of good health habits for drinking from a glass (e.g., not sharing someone else's glass).

Conduct a safety lesson on drinking glasses. Bring in a variety of glasses and ask the student to identify which ones are the most fragile (easily broken and/or difficult to hold). Also, emphasize the use of good safety habits for drinking from a glass (e.g., selecting the right size and weight of glass and not using a glass that is chipped).

Family Interventions

Primary Level. When appropriate, ask the parents to use drinking glasses during their child's meals. Suggest that they may initially use a plastic or unbreakable glass. Ask them to monitor how well their child uses the glass and provide suggestions when necessary.

Ask the parents to take their child out to eat for the child's birthday or a special occasion. Ask them to observe how well the child uses a glass.

Ask the parents to tell their child places where glasses should not be taken (e.g., near a swimming pool or at public events such as ball games).

 ## Specific Objective D

The student drinks from a container (e.g., can, juice box, soft drink bottle).

Teacher Interventions

Infant and Toddler/Preschool Level. Bring juice boxes for snack time and assist the student in finding and unwrapping the straw. Instruct the student on holding the juice box with one hand and inserting the straw into the juice box through the hole.

Primary Level. Serve drinks from a container during special times at school (e.g., parties and school events). Observe how well the student drinks from the container and provide assistance when necessary. Always select containers that are safe, appear to have no sharp edges, and are easily opened.

Plan a beverage-tasting party where the students have to taste beverages that come in containers (e.g., soda cans or bottles, juice boxes). Monitor how well the student drinks from the container and praise the student when he or she does well. Emphasize good health habits for using containers (e.g., not sharing a can and making sure the top of the container is clean). Also emphasize the need to discard used containers in an appropriate place.

Family Interventions

Infant and Toddler/Preschool Level. Encourage parents to provide the child with a range of drink containers in the home, particularly juice boxes and half-pint milk cartons, which are frequently used in group settings. Encouraging the child's use of a range of container types will foster his or her independence.

Primary Level. Encourage the parents to purchase a drink from a vending machine while out shopping with their child. Ask them to observe the child drinking from the container. Have them emphasize using caution in opening aluminum cans and safely disposing of any metal strips or rings.

 Specific Objective E

The student drinks from a water fountain. (Note: For younger individuals and/or those with physical disabilities, the water fountain may need to be adapted.)

Teacher Interventions

Primary Level. Plan breaks during the day that allow the student to go for a drink from the school's water fountain. Monitor how well the student drinks, how courteous he or she is in allowing others to drink, and how careful he or she is in not spilling water.

When visiting other schools or places, observe the location of the water fountains. Point these places out to the student. When he or she is thirsty, direct him or her to one of these places.

Family Interventions

Primary Level. Encourage the student's parents to visit places that have water fountains. Suggest that they direct their child to the fountain when he or she is thirsty and assist him or her when necessary. Have them select fountains that are in safe places, are properly working, and are clean and well maintained. Ask the parent to monitor whether the child puts his or her mouth on the apparatus and encourage the parents to caution the child against this practice.

Ask the parents to locate water fountains in the community that have a variety of mechanisms for turning on the water (e.g., push buttons, pedals, turn mechanisms). Have them provide their child with opportunities to try a variety of these mechanisms.

 ## Specific Objective F

The student eats with a spoon in an appropriate manner.

Teacher Interventions

Infant and Toddler/Preschool Level. Place food in the student's mouth; place your fingers on the cheek and under the jaw to feel the movement of the mouth muscles due to tongue movement.

Introduce finger feeding to the student by using a variety of foods such as cereals and crackers, as well as foods such as pudding, which can be licked from the fingers. Initially, use foods that will not require finger release and graduate to cereal and other items that can be grasped and released.

Show the student a variety of spoons, including those with looped handles for children who have difficulty grasping a utensil. Ask the student to hold and try each spoon as if he or she were eating some food. Help the student select the most appropriate size and shape of spoon. Avoid wooden spoons, which can splinter, and thin plastic spoons, which can break and cause injury with their sharp edges.

If a child has a bite reflex, biting down on the spoon may be a problem. Wait a few seconds for the child to release the bite. Do not attempt to force the spoon from the child's mouth, because this will cause the child to tighten the reflex and could damage the child's mouth and teeth.

During snack or lunchtime, prepare appropriate foods that can be eaten with a spoon (e.g., Spaghettios, applesauce, and pudding). Praise the student for appropriate use of spoons. At first the student may need assistance, and you can provide added arm support or wrist guidance. (Note: Students with visual impairments can be instructed to hold the plate with one hand and feed with the dominant hand. Children with a bite reflex should be provided with unbreakable plastic-coated metal spoons.)

Family Interventions

Infant and Toddler/Preschool Level. Encourage the parent to provide the child with a variety of foods to provide for chewing, observing rotary jaw movements and the movement of food from side to side. The child should swallow in between bites. Young children frequently reach for the spoon during feeding, and as the child develops motor control, this should be encouraged.

Ask the parents to place their hand over the child's to arrange the grasp of the spoon, lift up the hand with the spoon, and praise the child. Have the parent guide the spoon to assist in the process of getting food on the spoon and rotating the wrist to dip down and scoop up.

Parents should have the child use finger foods and use the spoon to practice scooping. Remind the parents to praise the child even if there is spillage. Some children will continue to mouth the spoon even though food may no longer be on it. These children will need to be reminded to remove the spoon from their mouths. Other children may tend to shovel food into the mouth and may need to be reminded to chew and swallow.

Primary Level. Ask the parents to provide their child with a variety of spoons during different meals. Tell the parents to demonstrate to the child how to use each spoon with a variety of foods. If necessary, have them consult with specialists involved with feeding, if their child has specific feeding problems. Also, when necessary, have them modify the spoon for maximum comfort and utility by wrapping tape around the handle or bending the spoon (see Figure 1.3).

When parents dine out with their child, have them order foods that are eaten with spoons. Have them praise their child if he or she eats appropriately and with good manners.

 ## Specific Objective G

The student eats with a fork in an appropriate manner. (Note: The use of a fork should not be taught unless the teacher has made the judgment that the student will be able to use it safely. Students who are destructive to others and themselves should be carefully monitored during these activities.)

Teacher Interventions

Infant and Toddler/Preschool Level. Provide a lunch that requires the student to use an appropriately sized fork. The student may need assistance. Provide foods such as apple chunks to assist the student to piece foods. The use

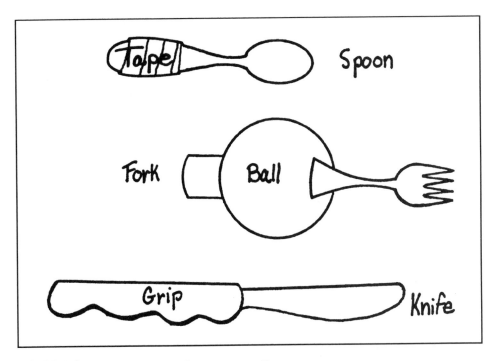

FIGURE 1.3. Modifications of eating utensils.

of a fork should be introduced only after the student has learned to use a spoon successfully.

Look through magazines for pictures of foods that can be eaten with a fork. Paste these pictures on index cards. Next, ask the student to select foods that are difficult or impossible to eat with a fork. Ask the student to paste these pictures on index cards. Mix up both series of cards and ask the student to pick out the cards that show pictures of foods that are eaten with a fork.

Family Interventions

Primary Level. Encourage parents to serve food their child likes and that is easy to handle with a fork (e.g., french fries, string beans, and sliced cucumbers). Tell them to gradually include other foods that are more difficult to handle with a fork, such as spaghetti, noodles, and pie. When necessary, have the parents seek advice from feeding specialists on how to modify forks for ease of handling (see Figure 1.3).

Ask the parents to dine out with their child, ordering food that requires eating with a fork. Have them praise their child for eating correctly, safely, and appropriately with a fork.

Specific Objective H

The student uses a knife appropriately during eating activities. (Note: Do not engage in the following activities if the student is not ready for this type of activity, is self-injurious or injurious to others, or has motor impairments, e.g., spasticity, which would make these activities dangerous.)

Teacher Interventions

Primary Level. Show the student a variety of knives (e.g., bread, table, butter, steak, and carving knives) and demonstrate their use. Always emphasize safety procedures and use a cutting board to avoid marking or cutting tables or work areas. When necessary, and with the advice of feeding specialists, modify the knife so it feels comfortable to the student (see Figure 1.3).

Allow the student to imitate the motions of spreading and cutting using a plastic knife. Provide the student with a table knife and fork, placing them in the student's hands correctly. Provide the student with a variety of textured foods.

Using a sharp knife, demonstrate (with caution) how to cut a slice of Italian or French bread as part of preparing a class breakfast. Help the student to cut a slice of margarine from a stick and then ask him or her to use a butter knife to spread it on the bread. Tell the student to eat the buttered bread. If he or she has trouble spreading the butter, use soft tub margarine, which is easier to spread.

Family Interventions

Primary Level. Encourage the parents to allow their child to make his or her lunch on certain occasions. Suggest that they encourage him or her to make peanut butter and jelly or similar sandwiches that require the use of a knife for spreading purposes. Ask the parents to carefully monitor how their child uses the knife and to praise the child when he or she does it safely and correctly.

Ask the parents to take their child to a pizza restaurant, order a pizza, and, when it arrives, have their child recut the slices and give everyone a piece.

Specific Objective I

The student uses a napkin appropriately.

Teacher Interventions

Infant and Toddler/Preschool Level. During meals, provide the child with a napkin for his or her own use, even if the child is not self-feeding. Children often imitate adult behaviors and will slowly begin to wipe at their mouth if a napkin is available.

Primary Level. Show the student a variety of napkins (paper, cloth, and the type found in holders in fast-food restaurants) and demonstrate their use.

Demonstrate wiping your mouth with a napkin. During snack time and lunch, tell the student to imitate your actions and practice wiping his or her mouth after every few bites of food and sips of milk or juice, and at the completion of the meal or snack. Emphasize the use of appropriate social skills for using a napkin (e.g., using a clean napkin and discarding a dirty one in an appropriate receptacle) and the identification of when one may need more than one napkin (for foods such as chicken, melon, and foods eaten with the hands).

Family Interventions

Infant and Toddler/Preschool Level. Encourage parents to model wiping their mouth and cueing their child to the behavior as the child's feeding skills improve. Alert the parents to the need to have a napkin available for the child and to assist the child to wipe his or her mouth, particularly when eating textured foods, so the child learns to recognize the sensation of food on his or her mouth and face.

Primary Level. Suggest that the parents serve food that requires the use of more than one napkin during the meal (chicken, ribs, melon). Ask them to monitor how well their child uses his or her napkin.

Ask the parents, the next time they take their child to a fast-food restaurant, to point out the different types of napkin holders. Ask them to order a meal and observe if their child retrieves a napkin from a holder before he or she starts to eat. If he or she appropriately retrieves a napkin and uses it, praise the child. If the child doesn't, remind him or her.

Specific Objective J

The student eats in a safe and socially acceptable manner.

Teacher Interventions

Infant and Toddler/Preschool Level. During snack or lunchtime, encourage the young student to pull food off of the spoon, closing the lips and swallowing after each bite. Demonstrate cleaning the lower lip with the tongue.

Primary Level. Model appropriate eating behavior, such as eating small mouthfuls of food, taking small sips of liquid, chewing with the mouth closed, and using a napkin.

At lunch or snack time, show the student how to pass requested food or condiments to another person and how to request food to be passed. Praise him or her when this is done correctly.

Prepare and serve a potluck dinner and invite the student's family to attend. Praise the student when he or she eats in a socially acceptable manner.

Family Interventions

Infant and Toddler/Preschool Level. Encourage the parents to expect their toddler to eat with utensils and wipe his or her mouth with a napkin. Young children need to be frequently reminded to use utensils and may need a guided hand to assist them. Modifications to assist the child's grip may be necessary, as well as modified drinking assistance.

Because young children can be picky eaters, remind the parents to change the foods that are fed to the child daily to insure that the child can tolerate varying textures and tastes.

Primary Level. Ask the parents to demonstrate socially acceptable eating habits by eating with their child and pointing out acceptable ways of eating. Have them follow up this activity by dining out at a family-style restaurant.

Suggest that the parents provide opportunities at the dinner table for their child to serve his or her own food, learning to scoop or pierce food as appropriate. Instruct the child to pour from a pitcher and pass foods when requested.

Ask the parents, when appropriate, to make a reservation at a restaurant that requires special attire (e.g., suits, ties, and jackets). Monitor how well the child eats in terms of being socially acceptable. Ask the parents to select restaurants that serve food in a variety of ways and styles.

Also, have them emphasize that their child should eat the food that is on his or her plate while discouraging him or her from tasting food from someone else's plate.

GOAL III.

The student will be functionally independent in dressing and undressing skills in a manner that allows for optimal performance in diverse situations.

Young infants do not have control over their movements and require total care in dressing. Reaching and kicking is frequently without purpose. Initially, infants will utilize the whole-hand grasp. Their body movements will need to be directed to assist in the dressing process. As infants develop, they gain limited control over their movements, and, by interacting with their environments, they attain and refine new skills.

By 1 year of age, many infants have obtained some head control and can use their hands at the midline. Cooperation with dressing has increased, as well as balance. For infants with disabilities, these skills may be delayed, so they may require assistive devices to facilitate dressing.

Tasks related to dressing and undressing can be easily woven into an integrated curriculum of living skills. The intent should be to provide activities that promote independence. In selecting clothing for children, parents should be encouraged to be consistent with the child's degree of motor facility, yet creative in insuring the age appropriateness of clothing.

SPECIFIC OBJECTIVES

The student:

- ❐ A. Puts on and removes clothing with no fasteners.
- ❐ B. Puts on and removes clothing with zippers.
- ❐ C. Puts on and removes clothing with snaps.
- ❐ D. Puts on and removes clothing with buttons.
- ❐ E. Puts on and removes clothing with hooks and eyes.
- ❐ F. Puts on and removes clothing with Velcro fasteners.
- ❐ G. Adjusts clothing when necessary.

    ❐ H. Chooses clothing appropriate for the weather.

    ❐ I. Chooses clothing appropriate to the time of day, situation, and occasion.

SUGGESTED ACTIVITIES

 ## Specific Objective A

The student puts on and removes clothing with no fasteners.

Teacher Interventions

Infant and Toddler/Preschool Level. Some young children with tactile sensitivity need to learn to tolerate outer clothing; place the clothing on the student and observe whether the student resists or pulls at the clothing. Work with the child by using large clothing, making sure that sleeves, waistbands, and pant legs are loose, until the clothing can be put on and removed without resistive behaviors.

Provide the child with a pullover garment and provide verbal instructions while placing arms and head into the clothing and assisting in pulling it down. Iron or sew colored felt or yarn around the armholes of garments. Show the child the armholes and encourage him or her to put his or her arms in through the holes.

Primary Level. (Note: Many primary-level activities listed under the General Goals of This Unit are also appropriate for toddlers and preschoolers.)

When it is time to go outside, put on a poncho or other sleeveless article without armholes and then assist the student in putting his or her head through the opening of a poncho or other sleeveless item. Use a mirror throughout so that the student may carefully observe your dressing and then monitor him- or herself throughout his or her imitation of the activity. Encourage him or her to check on the way he or she looks when the item is completely on.

Practice putting on and removing garments and reward the student for a job well done. Always select clothing that is in style, age appropriate, well made, and not easily torn.

Put on an article of clothing with sleeves, such as a sweater or a blouse with no fasteners of any kind. Use an oversize garment to begin with. Assist the student in identifying front/back and top/bottom. Help him or her when necessary to put his or her arms through the armholes and the garment over his or her head and onto his or her body.

Use a mirror and tell the student to practice putting on and removing garments. Engage in dressing and undressing activities during actual dressing and undressing periods.

Put on a pair of oversize socks or stockings. Assist the student in identifying heel, toe, and sock opening. Help the student to put his or her toes into the opening and then to pull the sock over the foot with the heel of the sock over the heel of the foot. Help the student to straighten the body and top of the sock. Reward the student and repeat the procedure with his or her own socks.

Family Interventions

Infant and Toddler/Preschool Level. Ask the parents to provide the child with clothing that is roomy and that will provide a comfortable dressing experience. Suggest that a variety of over-the-head garments and front-opening clothing be selected for the child to assist in varied experiential opportunities.

Demonstrate techniques for the parents to support the child while pushing arms through sleeves or pulling garments over the head. Encourage the parent to use a variety of stimuli so the child will reach through the sleeve to get the surprise or see a puppet when the garment is pulled over the head.

As the child develops, ask the parent to remove top and bottom outer garments upon request or with assistance. Suggest dress-up with the toddler and provide parents with instructions to assist the child to choose and put on the clothes. Encourage the parents to take instant pictures and share them with child, showing off the outfit and offering praise.

As the child is able to grasp, have the parent provide the child with oversize socks and gloves with animal felt designs, and have the child remove them to practice pulling with the hand.

Primary Level. Ask the parents to assist their child in putting on and removing articles of clothing that have no fasteners. Caution parents to be patient, as many young children easily get frustrated or become scared when clothing does not easily go over their head.

Ask the parents to take their child to an indoor event, such as a movie or museum. Have the child dress in a sweater. While there, have the parents ask the child if he or she is hot and would like to remove his or her sweater. Parents should assist only when necessary.

 Specific Objective B

The student puts on and removes clothing with zippers.

Teacher Interventions

Infant and Toddler/Preschool Level.   If the child has clothing with small zipper tabs, hook a novelty zipper pull or a large key chain to the tab. Demonstrate how the zipper operates, zipping it up, then asking the child to pull the zipper down. For children with problems with grasp, attach a cord to the tab and assist the child to insert his or her hand in the cord and pull the zipper down.

Primary Level.   Bring in or borrow several coats with zippers of different sizes. Ask the students to pick coats they like and see how quickly they can zip them up. If they are having difficulty, assist them and eliminate the time criterion. Avoid very small zippers that get caught easily or are poorly made, and zippers that are decorative and difficult to start. When necessary, use adaptive zippers or ones that have been modified.

Engage in zipping and unzipping activities during actual dressing and undressing periods. Always emphasize safety procedures during zipping, such as being careful to avoid getting one's skin caught in pants zippers.

Help the student practice using zippers on nonclothing items such as handbags, carrying cases, makeup kits, and portfolios. Take the student on outings that require the use of these accessories.

Family Interventions

Infant and Toddler/Preschool Level.   Encourage parents to practice with the child to unzip clothing when the child arrives home or is undressing. Have the parent assist the child with zipping as the child is able. Make sure the parent has the necessary modifications for the child to provide the maximum support necessary. Have the parent fade out supports when these are no longer needed.

Primary Level.   Ask the parents to prepare their child for putting on a zippered coat by first having the child zip an oversize coat. Ask parents to practice with their child in front of a mirror. When the child is successful, the parents should gradually phase out the oversize coat and use the child's regular zippered coat. When success is achieved, parents should reward their child.

Ask the parents to assist their child in putting on clothing with zippers that do not require starting when it is time for the child to go out. Male children can begin with pants and female children can begin with pants, dresses, slacks, and skirts.

Ask the parents to use oversize clothing first and then tell their child to practice with his or her actual clothing. Suggest to the parents that they help dress their child in front of a mirror so the child can monitor zipping, or help a female child with reaching behind her back to zip up a dress or blouse.

Specific Objective C

The student puts on and removes clothing with snaps.

Teacher Interventions

Infant and Toddler/Preschool Level.   For young children, Velcro is an alternative to snaps on clothing. Velcro provides the child with the maximum opportunity for independence. However, as the child is able, secure a jacket or other clothing item with large snaps.

Demonstrate how the snaps open and close. After the child is able to open the snaps, have the child practice closing the snaps with the garment in a comfortable position. Have the child use the thumb on one side and forefinger on the other side. Assist the child to line up the two sides and to press firmly together. Children with physical impairments may rely solely on Velcro closures.

Primary Level.   Make cardboard and felt pictures with snaps (e.g., an apple tree with snap-on apples, a clown with snap-on facial features). Encourage the student to work with this during free-time activities.

Assist the student in snapping and unsnapping snaps, first on oversize clothing and then on his or her actual clothing. Practice this activity in front of a mirror. Select a variety of snaps on different types of clothing, and use larger snaps if small snaps present difficulty.

Family Interventions

Infant and Toddler/Preschool Level.   Encourage the parent to practice the process of snapping and unsnapping a jacket with large snaps that operate easily. Be sure the parent understands that children with physical limitations who need Velcro and other adaptations can still achieve modified levels of independence.

Primary Level.   When appropriate, have parents use toys with snaps that help teach snapping (e.g., dolls, stuffed animals, snapping blocks). It is very important that this activity be age appropriate; that is, it would not be recommended for children who normally would be too old for such toys.

Ask the parents to plan a community trip. Have them select clothing that has snaps. Ask them to have their child put on and remove this clothing at appropriate times and assist only when necessary.

Specific Objective D

The student puts on and removes clothing with buttons.

Teacher Interventions

Infant and Toddler/Preschool Level. When children have the ability to grasp small objects that lay flat, they can begin to pick up such objects and place them through a slot into a container. This activity helps to develop the child's understanding of vertical and horizontal alignment. Using a button board covered with sturdy fabric and large buttons can provide practice activities for the preschool child.

Primary Level. Ask the parents to send in a coat with buttons. When the student is dressing to go outside, put the student's finger on a button and then immediately put that finger in the buttonhole to develop the understanding that a button goes into a buttonhole. Next, put your finger on the button and grasp the button and push it through the hole. Take the student's finger and put it on the button and assist him or her in buttoning.

Play dress-up in costumes or oversize clothes with buttons for Halloween parties, class plays, or other class events. Assist the student in lining up shirt, jacket, coat, or sweater so that the appropriate button is adjacent to its corresponding buttonhole. Select clothing with quality buttons and use modified or large buttons when necessary.

Family Interventions

Infant and Toddler/Preschool Level. The parents can be provided with information on creating a button board to work with their child. In addition, the parents can play with the child's doll, demonstrating buttoning and encouraging the child to button and unbutton the doll's clothing.

Primary Level. Ask the parents to practice with their child how to put on and remove clothing during dressing time. Suggest that they use large buttons to begin with and gradually work down to shirt-size or blouse-size buttons. Use oversize clothing if necessary and avoid decorative buttons that are hard to use and serve little functional purpose.

Specific Objective E

The student puts on and removes clothing with hooks and eyes.

Teacher Interventions

Primary Level.   Plan a dress-up party where everyone has to dress in different types of clothing. Include in the clothing selection some items that require the fastening of hooks and eyes. Praise the student if he or she uses hooks and eyes while dressing. Avoid clothes that have hooks and eyes solely for decorative purposes.

Plan a Halloween or costume party. Gather a collection of inexpensive outfits that require fastening by hooks and eyes. Ask the student to select an outfit and monitor how well he or she uses its fasteners. Provide assistance when necessary.

Family Interventions

Primary Level.   Ask the parents to plan a clothes-shopping trip with their child. Suggest that they shop for clothes that include hook-and-eye fasteners. Ask them to observe how well their child dresses when he or she tries on clothing using these fasteners. Ask them to assist only when necessary.

Specific Objective F

The student puts on and removes clothing with Velcro fasteners.

Teacher Interventions

Infant and Toddler/Preschool Level.   Young children can obtain a higher level of independence in managing their clothing and their shoes if Velcro is used to secure the closures. Velcro attachments can be practiced on doll clothing; encourage the child to line up the two pieces and press firmly.

Primary Level. Plan an exhibit that shows all the types of fasteners used for clothing. Ask the student to include clothes with Velcro fasteners. Ask the student to demonstrate how to use all the fasteners, paying special attention to how he or she uses the Velcro fasteners.

Ask the student to bring in any clothes he or she has that have Velcro fasteners. If he or she does not have any, provide some. Ask the student to demonstrate how he or she uses the fastener as part of getting dressed. (Note: Because the privacy and wishes of the student should always be kept in mind, this activity should be closely monitored for possible causes of embarrassment.)

Family Interventions

Infant and Toddler/Preschool Level. Parents should be encouraged to purchase shoes or adapt clothing as necessary to provide easily manipulated closures for the young child. Many parents are concerned that a child will not learn to tie his or her shoes. Reassure the parents that when the child is developmentally ready and physically able, these other skills will be taught to the child.

Primary Level. When parents are asked to purchase or make a costume for a class play or a party, ask them to select items with Velcro fasteners. Ask them to demonstrate how to use these fasteners with their child.

Ask the parents to take their child clothes shopping to see if the child can find any clothes that have Velcro fasteners. Stores or shops that sell exercise clothes are an example where they might start.

 ## Specific Objective G

The student adjusts clothing when necessary.

Teacher Interventions

Infant and Toddler/Preschool Level. With the younger child, modeling clothing adjustment should be implemented in all applicable situations. If the child needs assistance, verbally explain to the child what is being done and why, such as zipping pants or securing buttons. When the child removes his or her jacket and the sleeve is inside out, assist the child to reach through the sleeve, grasp the cuff, and pull.

Primary Level. Wait until the student's clothes need adjusting, as when buttons are unbuttoned, zippers are unzipped, a pant cuff is down, underwear is showing, or the shirt or blouse is out. Take the student to a full-length mirror and indicate in some way what is wrong.

Assist the students in adjusting their clothing. Comment on the fact that they look better, and reward them. Emphasize the use of appropriate social skills for adjusting clothes (e.g., adjustment is done in privacy and at appropriate times).

Wear your own clothes in a way that needs adjusting. Look in a full-length mirror. Comment that your clothes need adjusting. Adjust your clothes and praise yourself for looking better. Use clothes that require minimum care and adjust quickly.

Family Interventions

Infant and Toddler/Preschool Level. Encourage the parents to instruct the child as they assist the child in adjusting clothing. Have the parents practice complete dressing and clothing manipulations with a doll, indicating when the process is complete. Describe a game to the parents where the child has to identify which items are not complete in the dressing process. Remind the parents to praise the child.

Primary Level. Provide the parents with a chart on dressing skills for their child (see Figure 1.4). Ask them to encourage their child to use this chart and to look in the mirror to make sure clothes are adjusted correctly. Emphasize the use of these skills following toileting.

Ask the parents to plan a trip into the community with their child. Before the parents are ready to go, have them ask their child to check his or her appearance in the mirror. If the child looks good, the parents should praise him or her. If he or she needs to have his or her clothing adjusted, have parents assist.

 ## Specific Objective H

The student chooses clothing appropriate for the weather.

Teacher Interventions

Infant and Toddler/Preschool Level. During arrival time, discuss the current weather with the class and have the children observe their clothing. Discuss why the children are wearing these clothes and the relationship of clothing to the weather.

Have pictures of various weather conditions available. Discuss each picture and ask the child to describe the weather conditions in each pic-

STUDENT'S PICTURE (for younger students)	I can dress myself!	STUDENT'S NAME (for older students)							
Buttons	😊	✦							
Snaps		✦							
Zips									
Puts on shoes	✓								
Puts on socks	✓	✓							
Puts on underwear	✓	✓							
Puts on slacks	✓	✓							
Puts on shirt	✓	✓							
Puts on coat	✓	✓							
Puts on hat	✓	✓							
Puts on mittens		😊							

Key: Smiling faces, stars, decals, or checkmarks indicate when a student is able to do dressing skill

FIGURE 1.4. Dressing skills chart.

ture. Have the child match pictures of the types of clothing that would be appropriate to wear.

Primary Level. Take the student on trips outside the building you are in during the following types of weather conditions, wearing the articles of clothing listed below:

> a. Snow or cold weather: rubbers or boots, hat or head scarf, neck scarf, mittens or gloves, heavy or insulated coat or jacket, sweaters, and insulated or thermal underwear (optional).
>
> b. Rain: clear umbrella for better visibility, rubbers or boots, rain hat or scarf, and raincoat, slicker, or poncho.
>
> c. Warm and hot weather: for male children, lightweight pants, shirts, jackets, coats, and suits; for female children, light coats, lightweight dresses, slacks, and blouses.
>
> d. Cool or fall weather: Transitional cottons or blends.

Discuss with the student what might happen if inappropriate clothing were worn. Demonstrate what would occur if someone wore clothes unsuitable to the weather (provided it does not present a health hazard). For example, the student could put on heavy clothes when the weather is hot. When the student begins to feel uncomfortable, assist him or her in changing his or her clothes while indicating that he or she was dressed inappropriately for that day.

Family Interventions

Infant and Toddler/Preschool Level. Encourage the parents to discuss the types of clothing the child is wearing in relation to the day's weather. Remind the parents to ask the child to name the item and ask the child to describe why it is being worn.

Primary Level. Ask the parents to encourage their child before he or she gets dressed to check the weather in some way: looking out the window, listening to the television or radio, looking at an outdoor thermometer, or calling the weather service. Ask the parents to assist their child in finding the way he or she is most capable of using.

Ask the parents to plan to go shopping with their child on a day when the weather is calling for showers. Ask them to check and see if their child brings a raincoat. If the child does, the parents should praise him or her. If the child does not, have the parents review why it is important to be prepared for weather changes, especially when inclement weather is being forecast.

Specific Objective I

The student chooses clothing appropriate to the time of day, situation, and occasion.

(Note: The four categories to be chosen from are (a) everyday clothes, (b) work clothes, (c) recreation [regulation gym suits, swimsuits, or tennis shoes], and (d) special events [attendance at church, temple, weddings, bar mitzvahs, etc.].)

Teacher Interventions

Primary Level. Discuss a scheduled activity. Ask the student to indicate in some way what he or she should wear. Reward him or her for selecting appropriate clothes. When the student is dressed for the activity, take a picture of him or her and post it on a bulletin board or in a display case. Promise him or her another similar activity and follow through soon.

Match situation pictures from magazines with pictures of appropriate clothing. Take pictures with a self-developing camera of the student dressed for each of the four categories noted above. Make a chart of the student's pictures so that he or she can refer to it as a model at all times (see Figure 1.5).

Family Interventions

Primary Level. Ask the parents, when necessary, to assist their child in dressing appropriately for a specific activity by actively preparing the child for that activity: for example, work clothes for gardening (work pants, work shirt, gardening gloves), recreational clothes for a picnic, and special events clothes for a school or birthday party.

Ask the parents to plan an activity outside the school that requires semiformal attire (e.g., attending a concert and/or visiting a museum). Ask them to check to see if their child is aware of how he or she should dress. If he or she is not aware, they should suggest options (e.g., relationship of sportswear to semiformal events). Emphasis should also be placed on clothing that is well made, in style, and clean.

GOAL IV.

The student will be functionally independent in personal cleanliness and grooming in a manner that allows for optimal performance in diverse situations.

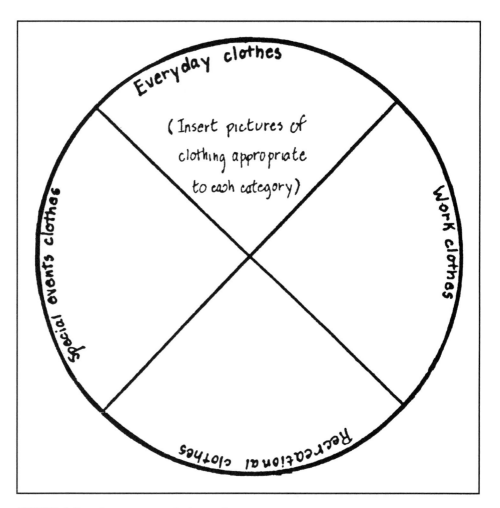

Everyday clothes

(Insert pictures of clothing appropriate to each category)

Special events clothes

Work clothes

Recreational clothes

FIGURE 1.5. Appropriate clothing chart.

Grooming is an important component in providing children with the opportunities for inclusion and independence. For young children, these activities are self-help skills and are modeled or assisted by parents and other caregivers. Grooming encompasses many activities and changes as individuals mature and their bodily needs change.

If a child has disabilities, certain tasks may require assistance. The young adult, particularly, should be afforded as many adapted grooming opportunities as possible to provide the maximum level of independence. It is always important to explain the need for certain grooming activities, and, when appropriate, the individual should be provided with choices (e.g., hairstyle, toothpaste, use of perfume or aftershave).

SPECIFIC OBJECTIVES

The student:

☐ A. Controls drooling when physically able.

☐ B. Controls the water flow or adjusts the water temperature for washing hands and face.

☐ C. Washes and dries hands and face.

☐ D. Washes underarms and uses a deodorant.

☐ E. Brushes and flosses teeth and rinses mouth.

☐ F. Cleans and cares for nails.

☐ G. Wipes and blows nose.

☐ H. Takes a sponge bath.

☐ I. Bathes in a tub.

☐ J. Takes a shower.

☐ K. Washes and dries hair.

☐ L. Combs, sets, and/or styles hair or has it done professionally.

☐ M. Shaves face or body hair when appropriate.

☐ N. Uses facial blemish treatments when needed.

☐ O. Applies makeup when appropriate.

☐ P. Uses and cares for eyeglasses, hearing aids, and prosthetic devices when appropriate.

☐ Q. Cares for herself during menstruation.

SUGGESTED ACTIVITIES

 ### Specific Objective A

The student controls drooling when physically able. (Note: It is important that specialists in this area be consulted to insure that activities are reasonable and within the limits of the specific student.)

Teacher Interventions

Infant and Toddler/Preschool Level.   As the student will tolerate, the teacher can secure a cloth material under the chin and gently wipe the drool. As the student becomes able, the teacher can place the cloth in the student's hand and wipe the drool.

   The student can be placed in front of the mirror and verbal directions provided to "swallow" and "wipe" while the teacher guides the student's hand.

Primary Level.   (Note: Many primary-level activities listed under the General Goals of This Unit are also appropriate for toddlers and preschoolers.)

   At appropriate intervals, the teacher should remind the student to swallow. Place the student in front of a mirror when he or she is not drooling and point this out. Indicate your pleasure and reward the student appropriately for not drooling.

Family Interventions

Infant and Toddler/Preschool Level.   Parents can be encouraged to provide an easily available soft cloth to assist the child in learning to wipe away drool. Some children respond to being reminded to swallow or close the lips. A physician can be consulted to determine if drooling is related to teething, diet, or development. If parents are concerned about clothing, encourage them to obtain plastic-backed terry bibs, which should be changed when they become saturated.

Primary Level.   Ask the parents to remind their child verbally and nonverbally to close his or her mouth to prevent drooling. They can touch the child's jaw as a reminder to keep his or her mouth closed.

   Ask the parents to give their child a sip of his or her favorite beverage during meals. Parents should then encourage their child to close his or her lips and then to swallow while not allowing the liquid to escape from the mouth.

 ## Specific Objective B

The student controls the water flow or adjusts the water temperature for washing hands and face.

Teacher Interventions

Infant and Toddler/Preschool Level. Initially, it is important to get the young child to cooperate in the process of handwashing. Before snack and lunch time are opportunities to have the child wash his or her hands. If a child cannot reach the sink, provide a basin with water.

After the child cooperates in handwashing and is able to reach the sink, have the child turn on the hot water if available. Certain bathroom facilities do not provide hot water or have separate faucets. Adjust the activity depending on the options. If the child can only control the flow, have the child observe the process, discussing why it is important to have a gentle flow and how a gentle flow is accomplished.

If the child can control the temperature with two faucets, have the child wait until the hot water flows and then have him or her turn on the cold water to lower the temperature. Demonstrate how the child can feel the mist for temperature without plunging his or her hand into the flow. If the sink has one faucet, demonstrate how to turn it on so as to be in the middle and adjust the temperature. (Note: Always surpervise young children in the bathroom.)

Primary Level. Before the student washes his or her hands, demonstrate how to turn the faucets on and off. Ask the student to imitate your actions and praise the student when he or she does it correctly.

Tell the student to touch hot and cold faucets when they are not being used. You can color-code the faucets (red = hot, blue = cold) as they appear in public restrooms and indicate verbally and nonverbally which faucet is hot and which is cold.

Family Interventions

Infant and Toddler/Preschool Level. Encourage the parents to utilize the proper method to have the child learn to control the flow and temperature. See Teacher Interventions above. Remind parents that household hot water temperatures should be lowered for safety purposes when young or developmentally delayed children are in the home.

Primary Level. Ask the parents to make certain that their child knows how to regulate water temperature safely by putting the cold water on first. Tell the parents to demonstrate the temperature of both the water flow and the water in the basin. Always have the parents demonstrate that hot water is always turned off first, for safety reasons.

Ask the parents to encourage their child to wash hands before and/or after eating in a restaurant. Have them observe how he or she adjusts the water temperature. Have them praise the child if he or she does it correctly, or show him or her the correct way if he or she does not do it safely. Ask the parents to eat at different restaurants as a way of exposing their child to a variety of different sinks and faucets.

 ## Specific Objective C

The student washes and dries hands and face.

Teacher Interventions

Infant and Toddler/Preschool Level.   Provide opportunities for the child to wash hands before a meal or after a messy classroom activity. Announce that it is time to wash hands and ask the child to go to the sink in the classroom or take the child to the bathroom. If the child can reach the sink and faucets, have the child set the water and instruct him or her to use soap. Remind the child to rinse thoroughly. Decrease the verbal instructions until the child is able to wash independently.

Primary Level.   When the student needs to wash his or her hands and face, show him or her a bar of soap. Demonstrate the use of the soap. For ease in handling, you may initially want to use hotel-size soap or break a regular-size bar in half. Assist the student in using the soap to wash his or her hands and face. Try to avoid using soap that someone else has used and encourage using disposable paper towels.

After daily school activities such as toileting, eating, play activities (pasting, finger painting, etc.), indicate to the student that his or her hands should be washed and assist him or her in washing them.

Introduce commercial soap dispensers and home soft soap and liquid dispensers. Show the student how to push down on a plunger to release some soap. Have the student use the dispenser when the washing of face and hands is needed.

Use a chart on good grooming on a daily basis to record all washing activities (see Figure 1.6).

Family Interventions

Infant and Toddler/Preschool Level. Remind the parents of the importance of modeling and the need to provide opportunities for the child to wash his or her hands on a routine basis. The parents can always take the child to wash hands before meals in the home, providing a star on a chart for each time the child reminds the parents that his or her hands need washing.

Grooming Chart—Student's Name

Skill	S (or date)	M	T	W	Th	F	S	S	M	T	W	Th	F	S
Washes face	✓	☺												
Dries face	✓	☺												
Washes hands	✓	☺												
Dries hands	✓	✓												
Washes underarms	☺	☺												
Uses deodorant	☺	☺												
Brushes teeth	✓	✓												
Cleans nails														
Showers														
Bathes	✓	☺												
Washes hair	✓	✓												
Dries hair	✓	✓												

Key: ☺ means skill was performed
✓ means skill was attempted

FIGURE 1.6. Good grooming chart.

Primary Level. Ask the parents to encourage, and when necessary assist, their child in washing and drying hands and face. Ask the parents to introduce a face cloth when appropriate. Have them emphasize safety procedures, which include avoiding soap in the eyes and monitoring water, which can quickly become too hot.

Ask the parents to encourage the washing and drying of hands before the meal arrives while they are eating in a restaurant. Have them take their child to the restroom and point out the type of faucet and type of dispenser, as well as the system for drying hands (e.g., paper towels, continuous cloth towel, hand blower). If necessary, have the parents assist their child in using the faucets or in drying hands.

Specific Objective D

The student washes underarms and uses a deodorant.

Teacher Interventions

Primary Level. When the student needs to wash under his or her arms (e.g., after strenuous play), assist the student by demonstrating wetting and rinsing out a washcloth. Have the student imitate this action and use the washcloth to wash under his or her arms.

As part of a grooming lesson and if the student is motorically able to use a roll-on or environmentally safe spray deodorant, demonstrate deodorant application. Explain the use of nonallergenic deodorants as well as those that are geared toward specific genders.

Use a chart on good grooming to reward the student with check marks for washing and drying the underarms and using a roll-on deodorant (see Figure 1.6).

Family Interventions

Primary Level. Ask the parents to demonstrate to their child the use of a roll-on deodorant as part of being well groomed.

Ask the parent to encourage their child to use deodorant during morning washing.

Specific Objective E

The student brushes and flosses teeth and rinses mouth.

Teacher Interventions

Primary Level. Reward the student for brushing by saying, "Good," "Great," or some other word that indicates enthusiastic pleasure and by charting his daily brushing on a chart on good grooming (see Figure 1.6).

Use special materials and procedures the dentist would use (e.g., tablets that leave a harmless dye on teeth not brushed well, giant set of teeth and toothbrush) to demonstrate appropriate brushing procedures.

Demonstrate the use of the different types of toothpaste dispensers (squeeze tube, hinged cap, push-top, etc.) and help the student decide which type of dispenser is most appropriate. Also, emphasize that it is necessary to use only a small amount of toothpaste on a brush, and to clean up after brushing.

Family Interventions

Infant and Toddler/Preschool and Primary Levels. Ask the parents to assist their child in his or her grooming by helping him or her brush his or her teeth. Suggest that the parents stand in front of a mirror and place their hands over their child's as he or she holds and uses the toothbrush.

Ask the parents to enlist the help of their dentist during the child's scheduled visit in demonstrating how their child should use dental floss. Ask them to practice with their child using the dental floss at home on a regular basis.

 ## Specific Objective F

The student cleans and cares for nails.

Teacher Interventions

Infant and Toddler/Preschool and Primary Levels. After engaging in a work activity that is likely to lead to dirty nails (e.g., gardening), require the student to clean his or her nails. If necessary, demonstrate how to do the task and praise the student if he or she attempts to do it.

During grooming activities, discuss the need to have clean nails and hands. Emphasize the safety factors involved in cleaning nails (e.g., not using knives, paper clips, or other inappropriate materials as tools to clean nails, and observation of water temperature when getting ready to soak hands or nails in water).

Family Interventions

Infant and Toddler/Preschool and Primary Levels. Ask the parents to call their child's attention to the cleanliness and good appearance of clean nails. If possible, ask them to use their nails as a model.

Ask the parents to demonstrate using a nail brush to clean nails. Tell them to schedule clean nail checkups.

 ### Specific Objective G

The student wipes and blows nose.

Teacher Interventions

Infant and Toddler/Preschool and Primary Levels. During class, call the student's attention to his or her nose when it needs blowing or wiping. Do this verbally or nonverbally, or have the student view his or her appearance in the mirror before wiping or blowing his or her nose.

When the student is sniffling or appears to have a cold, show him or her a box of tissues. Demonstrate removing a tissue from the box. Tell the student to imitate your actions and remove some tissues from the box and use them to wipe his or her nose. Include in your demonstration procedures for appropriately disposing of used tissues.

Family Interventions

Infant and Toddler/Preschool and Primary Levels. Suggest that the parents demonstrate to their child in front of a mirror how they wipe and blow their nose. Ask them to tell the child to imitate their actions and to practice blowing and wiping his or her nose. Remind the parents to praise their child for wiping and blowing his or her nose at appropriate times.

Ask the parents to make sure their child is reminded to carry tissues with him or her at all times, especially when he or she has a cold. Have the parents plan a trip into the community and see if their child brings tissues. Have them praise the child if he or she does.

If tissues are not available, ask the parents to give their child a handkerchief. Have them stress that a handkerchief is not to be shared and should be used only when tissues are not available.

Specific Objective H

The student takes a sponge bath.

Teacher Interventions

Primary Level. During grooming time or discussions about health, discuss sponge baths. Indicate that they are convenient to use when one is sick or in a hurry.

Show the film *Learning About Health—Questions About Health,* put out by Encyclopaedia Britannica.

Provide an opportunity for the student to sponge bathe, when necessary, during class time (for example, following recess, physical education, work, or toilet accidents).

Family Interventions

Primary Level. Ask the parents to explain to their child how to use a sponge and take a sponge bath. Tell them to practice with the child wetting a sponge and taking a sponge bath. Have them emphasize that the child should begin washing his or her body by starting with the face and working down. Have the parents observe privacy considerations whenever possible.

Ask the parents to initially monitor any safety considerations involved with taking a sponge bath, such as regulating the water temperature, using clean bathing materials, and cleaning up any spilled water.

Specific Objective I

The student bathes in a tub.

Teacher Interventions

Infant and Toddler/Preschool and Primary Levels. Discuss what is needed to take a bath in a tub. Emphasize the safety considerations of appropriate water temperature and clean bathing materials. If the student requires adaptive equipment such as hand rails, discuss how to use them.

Family Interventions

Infant and Toddler/Preschool Level. If age appropriate, ask the parents to use a doll to demonstrate taking a bath. Tell them to point out the parts of the body that require special cleaning attention.

Primary Level. Ask the parents to assist their child in taking a tub bath when he or she needs to bathe. Tell them to provide supervision always and assistance only when needed or if safety is involved, and to observe any privacy requested whenever possible.

Ask the parents to include in any bathing instructions procedures for placing dirty clothes in a hamper or clothes basket.

 ### Specific Objective J

The student takes a shower. (Note: This activity is only for those students who will not require supervision for safety reasons.)

Teacher Interventions

Infant and Toddler/Preschool and Primary Levels. When appropriate, work with the parents in providing information to the student about showering. Emphasize safety procedures involved in taking a shower (e.g., standing on a rubber mat, getting in and out of a shower stall or tub, using hand rails when necessary).

Ask the student to list and describe the type of materials he or she needs to gather before taking a shower (e.g., soap, washcloth, towels, shower cap).

Instruct the student in how to turn on and use a shower, how to adjust water temperature, and how to decide on a reasonable amount of time to spend in a shower.

Family Interventions

Primary Level. Ask the parents to encourage their child to shower as well as to take sponge and tub baths. Suggest that the parents provide maximum supervision until they feel certain that the child can safely take a shower.

Suggest that the parents encourage their child to wash his or her body from head to toe while standing in a shower. Have them caution their child that water temperature sometimes quickly changes (if someone has flushed a toilet or uses water somewhere else in the house), and have them tell the child how to get out of the stream of the shower quickly while adjusting the temperature.

 ## Specific Objective K

The student washes and dries hair.

Teacher Interventions

Infant and Toddler/Preschool and Primary Levels. In preparation for going out to dinner, or after a strenuous activity, discuss with the student the need to wash his or her hair. Show him or her pictures of peers with dirty hair and clean hair and ask the student to say which appearance looks better.

When a student comes in with clean hair, ask him or her if he or she has washed it, and if so, place a mark on his or her good grooming chart (if age appropriate) or praise him or her for having clean hair.

Family Interventions

Infant and Toddler/Preschool and Primary Levels. Ask the parents to assist their child in washing his or her hair on a regular basis and at special times when the hair needs washing (e.g., after swimming, after strenuous activities, and after working in dirty or dusty environments).

Ask the parents to emphasize basic precautions for washing hair, such as avoiding getting shampoo in the eyes and making sure the water is not too hot or cold.

 ## Specific Objective L

The student combs, sets, and/or styles hair or has it done professionally.

Teacher Interventions

Primary Level. Encourage the student to use grooming time to practice combing and brushing hair. Assist him or her when necessary and appropriate.

As part of an art activity, take "before" and "after" snapshots and make a display board of the pictures. During grooming time, discuss beauty salons and barber shops. Talk about what constitutes appropriate behavior in public settings.

Read (at an appropriate level) a story about a student and his or her trip to the barber or beauty shop. Discuss and demonstrate what goes on in these places.

Family Interventions

Primary Level. Ask the parents to look through magazines with the student and help him or her decide on an appropriate hairstyle.

Ask the parents to take their child to a shopping mall. While there, have them ask their child to identify places where they may get their hair cut and/or styled.

Ask the parents to visit a beauty or barber shop. Ask the parents to point out to their child some of the dangers and cautions to exercise when in these places (e.g., avoidance of prolonged exposure to hair-setting chemicals, use of scissors and razors).

 ## Specific Objective M

The student shaves face or body hair when appropriate. (Note: Because of safety problems associated with a blade razor, the activities presented and suggested use an electric or battery-operated shaver.)

Teacher Interventions

Primary Level. As part of daily activities involving grooming, schedule time for the student to demonstrate his or her ability to take care of grooming aids. For example, take the student to a wastebasket. Demonstrate opening and cleaning the electric shaver over the basket. Have the student practice using the small cleaning brush supplied with the shaver.

After shaving, ask the student to make sure that he or she has put the protective cap on the shaver and returned the shaver to its base or storage place. For electric shavers, have the student make sure they are unplugged and safely put away.

Family Interventions

Primary Level. Ask the parents to practice with their child who needs to shave, turning on and off an electric or battery-operated shaver. For a female student (when appropriate), ask the parents to assist the child in shaving body hair (legs) in very gradual and safe steps. Have them allow the child to compare a shaved leg with an unshaved leg. This activity can be repeated for underarm hair.

Ask the parents to demonstrate how to prevent and/or treat razor burn.

Specific Objective N

The student uses facial blemish treatments when needed.

Teacher Interventions

Primary Level. As part of a grooming lesson, show the student pictures of people with clear skin and contrasting pictures of adolescents with acne. Indicate in some way that the people with acne can be helped to look better. Before-and-after pictures of the same individual or of a peer might be shown to demonstrate this.

During lunch, help the student differentiate between foods that contribute to facial blemishes (check with a physician, if necessary) and those that do not.

Construct a chart or checklist of skin care activities (see Figure 1.7), and indicate with a check mark, sticker, or symbol those skin care activities the student observes. If the student decides to use a skin blemish or cover-up treatment, make sure its ingredients are approved and safe. If necessary, consult your physician or pharmacist.

Family Interventions

Primary Level. Ask the parents, as part of daily grooming, to supervise their child in washing his or her face appropriately and regularly.

Ask the parents to reward their child for substituting nongreasy and nonspicy foods for those that are acne producing. Provide the parents with a preferred foods chart (see Figure 1.8), to help them offer the child healthy foods.

	M	T	W	T	F	Comments
Skin Care—Student's Name						
Washes face	✓	✓	✓	✓	✓	
Treats blemishes				✓	✓	
Removes make-up					✓	
*						
*						
*						
*						

Key: Place stars/pictures/ happy faces next to each activity when student completes it.

* Add specific activities for each student's particular skin problem

FIGURE 1.7. Skin care chart.

 Specific Objective O

The student applies makeup when appropriate.

Teacher Interventions

Primary Level. Discuss social events that include young women who are adolescent or older. Discuss the use of makeup as part of dressing for these events. In the discussion, point out that, just as there are different clothes, there are different types of makeup.

As part of grooming activities, show the student pictures of a made-up clown. Tell the student that the use of a lot of makeup is funny, but just the right amount of makeup can make someone look better. Look through magazines with the student for pictures of the well-made-up face of an everyday girl or woman. Ads for lipsticks, blusher, face powder, or cold cream usually have good pictures for this purpose.

```
┌─────────────────────────────────────────────────────────┐
│  PREFERRED FOODS CHART                                   │
│                                                          │
│         MILK                │        MEATS               │
│  milk                       │  hamburgers  salmon        │
│  cheese                     │  hot dogs    eggs          │
│  yogurt                     │  ham         liver         │
│  cottage cheese             │  bologna                   │
│  ice cream                  │  lamb chops                │
│  pudding                    │  pork chops                │
│  custard                    │  tunafish                  │
│          (4 cups per day    │  chicken  (2 servings      │
│           for teenagers)    │  turkey    per day)        │
│ ─────────────────────────── │ ────────────────────────── │
│     VEGETABLES/FRUITS       │  BREADS AND CEREALS        │
│  apples     asparagus       │  white bread               │
│  bananas    carrots         │  rye bread                 │
│  oranges    beets           │  whole wheat bread         │
│  grapefruit celery          │  saltines                  │
│  pears      lettuce         │  oatmeal                   │
│  peaches    tomatoes        │  Cream of Wheat            │
│  apricots   cucumbers       │  Corn Flakes               │
│  fruit juices potatoes      │  Granola                   │
│              spinach        │                            │
│         (4 servings         │       (4 servings          │
│          per day)           │        per day)            │
└─────────────────────────────────────────────────────────┘
```

FIGURE 1.8. Preferred foods chart.

Family Interventions

Primary Level. When makeup is age appropriate and acceptable to the parents, ask them to demonstrate its use to their child. Have them emphasize that too much makeup may draw inappropriate attention, and that their child should select only nonallergenic and safe makeup.

Ask the parents to demonstrate removing makeup. The parents should tell their child to imitate the parent's actions and remove makeup before going to sleep. The parents should reward the child for completely cleansing the face before going to bed.

 ## Specific Objective P

The student uses and cares for eyeglasses, hearing aids, and prosthetic devices when appropriate. (Note: The parent and teacher should work together on the activities listed below. Also, when dealing with special aids and devices, it is important to consult and work cooperatively with appropriate medical personnel.)

Teacher/Family Interventions

Care. Show the student pictures of others, especially classmates or peers, who use the same devices as those used by the student. Point out persons around the student, including the teacher, who use such devices because they need them and because these devices help.

Assist the student in putting on glasses and/or a hearing aid (teachers and parents need to make sure they know the correct way to do this). Have them use a mirror when necessary and if the use of a mirror is not disturbing to the student. Comment on the help it is giving him or her.

Cleaning. Demonstrate cleaning eyeglasses to the student. Assist him or her in using a tissue or Sight Saver.

Assist the student in identifying when his or her glasses are dirty. Show him or her pairs of clean and dirty glasses. Help him or her to distinguish between the clean and dirty pairs. Join him or her in cleaning the dirty glasses.

Demonstrate removing glasses and putting them in a slip-in case. Assist the student to do so. Help him or her identify a safe and suitable storage place for his or her glasses. In a similar fashion, remove other aids and store them in safe and suitable places.

 ## Specific Objective Q

The student cares for herself during menstruation.

(Note: The activities below typically start at the intermediate and secondary levels. The activities can be modified for home, school, or community settings.)

Intermediate and Secondary Levels.   For the female student who has not yet begun to menstruate, prepare her for its eventuality by showing videos, films, or books on menstruation.

When appropriate, show her pictures, read to her about menstruation, demonstrate with a mannequin or science model, and discuss the topic.

Tell the student that, when menstruation begins, it is something to feel good about because it means that she is growing up and becoming a woman. Assure the student that there is nothing to be afraid of, that it happens to all women.

Practice putting on a sanitary napkin according to package directions. Also, show the student how to wrap up a used sanitary napkin and how and where to dispose of it properly.

Assist the student in identifying signs that menstruation is beginning.

If helpful, put the student on a napkin-changing schedule, perhaps every other time she goes to the bathroom to void.

Discuss the need for the student to be prepared by keeping a napkin with her at all times. Check first at regular, then irregular, intervals to see that she has one available.

Tell the student that she should not announce her menstrual period or discuss it with everyone. Help her select someone whom she should discuss it with in case she needs help and for record-keeping purposes.

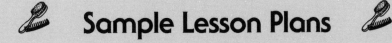

Sample Lesson Plans

Sample Lesson Plan 1

Topic Area: Self-Care Skills

Designed by: Samantha Whitehorse

Time Recommended: 30 Minutes

Student Involved: Oscar (Primary Special Class)

Background Information:

> The student has limited reading ability. He does appear to identify letters and symbols. He also appears to identify a limited set of sight words, for example: (a) he looks at a red stop sign and will identify the sign by saying "Stop," (b) when an object is named he will look at that object, and (c) he responds appropriately to simple oral directions. He cannot read words independently, but relies on prompts, both verbal and visual.

General Goal *(Self-Care Skills I):*

> The student will be functionally independent in toileting, provided there are no physical or developmental reasons for not being trained.

Specific Objective *(Self-Care Skills I-J):*

> The student locates and uses a bathroom or public restroom independently and safely.

Lesson Objective:

> When the student is asked to locate the correct bathroom (men's or women's) on a field trip, the student will request the information if unsure or independently select the appropriate restroom.

Materials and Equipment:

> - Set of visual symbols for the bathroom symbols for men's and women's restrooms

- Flashcards for the words *Men* and *Women*
- Alternative language spellings (e.g., Buoys–Gulls)

Motivating Activity:

Plan a trip to a local television station in conjunction with a unit on the weather. Many stations have a weather school program and schedule class trips to the meteorological center at the station.

Instructional Procedures:

Initiation—Tell the student that the class will be going on a field trip to a local television station and that each student will need to locate the appropriate restroom independently because the station will provide group guides who may break the class into small groups. Each student will need to select the correct bathroom to use (the men's or women's).

Guided Practice—Use the basic symbols or words for the bathrooms on flashcards (e.g., Boys/Girls, Men/Women) to familiarize the student with the variability in styles on restroom doors. Review these with the student until he or she is familiar with them and can correctly identify the word or symbol upon request. Select pictures or take pictures of bathroom doors that display alternative styles of identification and discuss these with the student.

In the school setting, point out the words and symbols on the doors of the bathrooms. Have the student look at the door of the appropriate bathroom prior to entering.

Take the student to an unfamiliar area of the school or to a nearby building. Go to the bathroom area and ask the student to select the appropriate bathroom. Discuss with the student the importance of using the same-sex bathroom and the need to request assistance if the student is unsure.

Independent Practice—Ask the student to take a younger classmate to the correct bathroom in the school. Go with the student to insure that the student can correctly identify the appropriate bathroom.

Closure—Ask the student to help you sort the flashcards into piles for boys and girls. Ask the student to independently identify which doors he or she could enter.

Assessment Strategy:

Observe the student to determine whether he or she correctly and quickly selects the appropriate restroom at school and during flashcard activities.

Follow-Up Activity or Objective:

If the student achieves the lesson objective, proceed to a lesson involving writing the words as spelling words.

Sample Lesson Plan 2

Topic Area: Self-Care Skills

Designed by: Seth Whyster

Time Recommended: 30 Minutes

Student Involved: Teddy (Preschool Class)

Background Information:

The student has learned to use a spoon successfully. He has the physical ability to hold a fork and to track eye-hand coordination. He also appears to tolerate a variety of textured foods. The student can chew food sufficiently to avoid choking when swallowing. The student's food allergies, if any, are known. The student does not have any aggressive or uncontrolled physical behaviors that would be dangerous to himself or others.

General Goal (Self-Care Skills II):

The student will be functionally independent in drinking and eating skills in a manner that allows for optimal performance in diverse situations.

Specific Objective (Self-Care Skills II-G):

The student eats with a fork in an appropriate manner.

Lesson Objective:

When the student is asked to use his fork to eat, he picks it up, pierces food, and places it in his mouth.

Materials and Equipment:

- Fork made from a hard plastic that cannot be broken by biting and with prongs that are sharp enough to pierce food; the fork should have a handle thick enough to be held in an inverted fist

- Plastic bowls with handles for grabbing with one hand
- Marshmallows, apple pieces, small chunks of hot dogs
- Napkins

Motivating Activity:

During snack time, progressively introduce foods that can be pierced by a fork. Encourage the children who are using forks by complimenting them on their eating with the appropriate utensil. Use a fork yourself and discuss the types of foods that are best eaten with a fork. Suggest that the student may be ready to eat with a fork.

Instructional Procedures:

Initiation—Tell the student that during the next snack period you will be giving the student a fork and ask the student to select some favorite foods that can be eaten with a fork. Explain the types of foods that can be pierced. Experiment with the student to identify the student's hand strength and which grip is most comfortable. Start with marshmallows in a bowl and have the student pierce them, remove them, and pierce them again until accuracy is obtained in identifying the object to be pierced and the eye-hand coordination necessary for piercing the selected food object.

Guided Practice—Use food items with progressively firmer textures until the student can easily pierce the food. Continue to involve the student in self-correcting strategies for piercing in the center of the food and biting off the items without hurting lips or tongue.

Provide the student with a bowl of his favorite food to have at snack time with the class. Be sure the student is ready to utilize a fork with little verbal instruction so the student may enjoy the eating activity within the group.

Let the parent know that the student is eating with a fork during school and provide the parent with a description of the fork.

Independent Practice—Give the student the choice of snack items that can be eaten with a fork and have the student eat with the group, using the fork.

Closure—Ask the student to set the table with the appropriate eating utensils and the snack food. Have the student sit at the table and eat his snack with the other children.

Assessment Strategy:

Provide the student with a snack requiring the use of a fork. Observe the student eating his snack to determine whether he correctly uses the fork.

Follow-Up Activity or Objective:

If the student achieves the lesson objective, proceed to a lesson involving eating several different foods that require the student to select a fork or a spoon, depending on what one is eating.

References

Adelson, N., & Sandow, L. (1978). Teaching buttoning to severely–profoundly multi-handicapped children. *Education and Training of the Mentally Retarded, 13,* 178–183.

Anderson, D. M. (1982). Ten years later: Toilet training in the post-Azrin-and-Foxx era. *Journal of the Association for the Severely Handicapped, 7,* 71–79.

Azrin, N. H., & Foxx, R. M. (1974). *Toilet training the retarded.* Chicago: Research Press.

Barnerdt, B., & Bricker, D. (1978). A training program for selected self-feeding skills for the motorically impaired. *American Association for the Severely and Profoundly Handicapped Review, 3,* 222–229.

Boone, C. (1992). Independence: To have and to hold. *Future Reflections, 11* (3), 15–19.

Dever, R. B. (1988). *Community living skills: A taxonomy.* Washington, DC: American Association on Mental Retardation.

Dreith, R., & Kreps, A. (1975). *Community living skills guide—Wardrobe II: Selection and buying of clothing.* Denver: Metropolitan State College, The College for Living.

Edgar, E., Maser, J. T., & Haring, N. G. (1977). Button up! A systematic approach for teaching children to fasten. *Teaching Exceptional Children, 9,* 104–105.

Edwards, G., & Bergman, J. S. (1982). Evaluation of a feeding training program for caregivers of individuals who are severely physically handicapped. *Journal of the Association of the Severely Handicapped, 7,* 93–100.

Honig, A. S. (1993, Fall). Toilet learning. *Day Care and Early Education,* pp. 6–9.

Morris, S. E., & Klein, M. D. (1987). *Pre-feeding skills: A comprehensive resource for feeding development.* Tucson, AZ: Therapy Skill Builders.

Redmond, N. B., Bennett, C., Wiggert, J., & McLean, B. (1993). Using functional assessment to support a student with severe disabilities in the community. *Teaching Exceptional Children, 25* (3), 51–52.

Schloss, P. J., Alexander, N., Hornig, E., Parker, K., & Wright, B. (1993, Spring). Teaching meal preparation vocabulary and procedures to individuals with mental retardation. *Teaching Exceptional Children, 25* (3), 7–12.

Valletutti, P., Bender, M., & Sims-Tucker, B. (in press). *A functional curriculum for teaching students with disabilities: Functional academics* (Vol. III, 2nd ed.). Austin, TX: PRO-ED.

Wilson, L. C. (1986). *Infants and toddlers curriculum and teaching.* Albany, NY: Delmar.

Suggested Readings

Azrin, N. H., & Foxx, R. M. (1971). A rapid method of toilet training the institutionalized retarded. *Journal of Applied Behavior Analysis, 4,* 88–89.

Bettison, S. (1978). Toilet training the retarded: Analysis of the stages of development and procedures for designing programs. *Australian Journal of Mental Retardation, 5,* 95–100.

Bredekamp, S. (Ed.). (1986). *Developmentally appropriate practice.* Washington, DC: National Association for the Education of Young Children.

Bromwich, R. (1981). *Working with parents and infants: An interactional approach.* Austin, TX: PRO-ED.

Calkin, G. B., Grant, P. A., Bowman, M. M., & Gollop, D. F. (1978). *Toilet training: Help for the delayed learner.* New York: McGraw-Hill.

Caplan, T., & Caplan, F. (1983). *The early childhood years: The 2 to 6 year old.* New York: Perigree Books.

Comer, D. (1987). *Developing safety skills with the young child.* Albany, NY: Delmar.

Crnic, K. A., & Pym, H. A. (1979). Training mentally retarded adults in independent living skills. *Mental Retardation, 17,* 13–16.

Dever, R. B. (1989). A taxonomy of community living skills. *Exceptional Children, 55,* 395–404.

Dixon, J. W., & Saudargas, R. A. (1980). Toilet training, cueing, praise and self-cleaning in the treatment of classroom encopresis: A case study. *Journal of School Psychology, 18,* 135–140.

Gallender, D. (1979). *Eating handicaps: Illustrated techniques for feeding disorders.* Springfield, IL: Thomas.

Gallender, D. (1980). *Teaching eating and toileting skills to the multihandicapped in the school setting.* Springfield, IL: Thomas.

Honig, A. S. (Ed.). (1993). *The Eriksonian approach: Infant-toddler education* (2nd ed.). Columbus, OH: Merrill.

Horner, R. D., & Keilitz, I. (1975). Training mentally retarded adolescents to brush their teeth. *Journal of Applied Behavior Analysis, 8,* 301–309.

Johnson-Martin, N. M., Jens, K. G., Attermeier, S. M., & Hacker, B. J. (1991). *The Carolina curriculum for infants and toddlers with special needs* (2nd ed.). Baltimore: Brookes.

Klein, M. D. (1983). *Pre-dressing skills.* Tucson, AZ: Communication Skill Builders.

Kramer, L., & Whitehurst, C. (1981). Effects of button features on self-dressing in young retarded children. *Education and Training of the Mentally Retarded, 16,* 277–283.

Lovaas, O. I. (1981). *Teaching developmentally disabled children: The me book.* Austin, TX: PRO-ED.

Mack, A. (1989). *Dry all night: The picture book technique that stops bedwetting.* New York: Little, Brown.

Matson, J. L. (1988). Teaching and training relevant community skills to mentally retarded persons. *Child & Youth Services, 10,* 107–121.

Matson, J. L., Marchetti, A., & Adkins, J. (1980). A controlled group comparison of procedures for training self-help skills to the mentally retarded. *American Journal of Mental Deficiency, 84,* 113–122.

Moyer, I. D. (1983). *Responding to infants.* Minneapolis: T. S. Denison.

Neely, R. A., & Smith, M. (1977). *Program for feeding training of developmentally delayed children.* Memphis: University of Tennessee, Child Development Center.

Perske, R., Clifton, A., McLean, B., & Stein, J. I. (Eds.). (1977). *Mealtimes for severely and profoundly handicapped persons.* Baltimore: University Park Press.

Smith, P. S. (1979). A comparison of different methods of toilet training the mentally handicapped. *Behavior Research and Therapy, 17,* 33–43.

Snow, C., & Tabors, P. (1993). Home: Where children get ready for school. *Harvard Graduate School of Education Alumni Bulletin, 12,* 7–9.

Stainback, S., & Stainback, W. (1988). Educating students with severe disabilities in regular classes. *Teaching Exceptional Children, 21,* 16–19.

Swain, J. J., Allard, G. B., & Holborn, S. W. (1982). The Good Toothbrushing Game: A school-based dental hygiene program for increasing the toothbrushing effectiveness of children. *Journal of Applied Behavior Analysis, 15,* 171–176.

Thinesen, P. J., & Bryan, A. J. (1981). The use of sequential pictorial cues in the initiation and maintenance of grooming behaviors with mentally retarded adults. *Mental Retardation, 19,* 247–250.

Trott, M. C. (1977). Application of Foxx and Azrin toilet training for the retarded in a school program. *Education and Training of the Mentally Retarded, 12,* 336–338.

Turnbull, A. P., & Turnbull, H. R. (1990). *Families, professionals and exceptionality: A special partnership* (2nd ed.). Columbus, OH: Merrill.

Van der Zande, I. (1986). *1, 2, 3 . . . The toddler years: A practical guide for parents and caregivers.* Santa Cruz, CA: Santa Cruz Toddler Care Center.

Walls, R. T., Crist, K., Sienicki, D. A., & Grant, L. (1981). Prompting sequences in teaching independent living skills. *Mental Retardation, 19,* 243–246.

Selected Materials/Resources

KITS/CURRICULAR MATERIALS

- *Activities for Developing Pre-Skill Concepts in Children with Autism*
  PRO-ED, Inc.
  8700 Shoal Creek Boulevard
  Austin, Texas 78757-6897

- *First Start: Care of Infants and Toddlers with Disabilities and Chronic Conditions, 1988–1991*
  First Start Programs
  University of Colorado Health Sciences Center, School of Nursing
  4200 East 9th Avenue, Box C-287
  Denver, Colorado 80262

- *Giant Teeth and Brush*
  Kaplan School Supply Co.
  600 Jonestown Road
  Winston-Salem, North Carolina 27103

- *Model of Interdisciplinary Training for Children with Handicaps: A Series for Caregivers of Infants and Toddlers (MITCH)*
  Educational Materials Distribution Center
  Florida Department of Education
  B-1 Collins Building
  Tallahassee, Florida 32399-0400
  (904) 488-7101

- *Personal Care Skills*
  PRO-ED, Inc.
  8700 Shoal Creek Boulevard
  Austin, Texas 78757-6897

- *Self-Help Skills Instructional Kit #8700*
  EBSCO Curriculum Materials
  Box 278
  Chelsea, Alabama 35043-0278

- *The Walker Social Skills Curriculum: The ACCEPTS Program*
  PRO-ED, Inc.
  8700 Shoal Creek Boulevard
  Austin, Texas 78757-6897

VIDEOS

- *All About Babies: A Guide for the First Two Years of Life. 4 Months to 12 Months: Reaching Out*
  Churchhill Films
  662 North Robertson Boulevard
  Los Angeles, California 90069

- *Brigance for the Early Years*
  Curriculum Associates, Inc.
  5 Esquire Road
  North Billerica, Massachusetts 01862-2589

- *Day by Day: Raising the Child with Autism/PDD*
  Guilford Publications, Inc.
  72 Spring Street
  New York, New York 10012

- *Good Life Videotapes*
  PRO-ED, Inc.
  8700 Shoal Creek Boulevard
  Austin, Texas 78757-6897

ASSISTIVE DEVICES

- *Adjustable Bath Seat*
  Arista Surgical Supply Company
  67 Lexington Avenue
  New York, New York 10010
  (800) 223-1984

- *Assistive Technology Sourcebook*
  Special Needs Project
  1482 East Valley Road
  Santa Barbara, California 93108
  (800) 333-6867

- *Clear Food Guards*
  Therafin Corporation
  3800 South Union Avenue
  Steger, Illinois 60475
  (312) 755-1535

- *On the Rise*
  Clothing for Special People with Special Needs
  2282 Four Oaks Grange Road
  Eugene, Oregon 97404
  (503) 687-0119

Gross Motor Skills

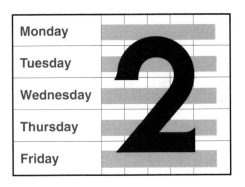

Monday
Tuesday
Wednesday
Thursday
Friday

This unit presents goals, objectives, and activities involving the student's gross motor skills, with emphasis on the use of the lower extremities. The student who is to function optimally, travel within his or her working, living, or learning environment, and participate in diverse community, recreational, and leisure activities will need to possess these skills, particularly those involving ambulation and movement in space and time (Geralis, 1991; Presland, 1982).

Educators are in agreement that individuals with disabilities can make substantial gains in motor proficiency if they are provided with learning experiences that are functionally relevant and that occur in natural environments. Too often, gross motor programs isolate skills that have been identified as developmentally significant, but that occur infrequently during everyday situations. Thus, although the student with disabilities may become proficient in specific motor skills, a limited repertoire or a program that disregards cognitive and affective dimensions may restrict him or her from taking part in many work, social, and leisure-time activities and may limit his or her becoming a successful participant in community life. With this in mind, this revised curriculum presents a wide range of functional gross motor objectives and activities that concentrate on those skills that the student needs to perform in everyday situations (Kriegsman, Zaslow, & D'Zmura-Rechsteiner, 1992).

In this unit, preambulation skills are presented as the first general objective. Many students will require lengthy programming in this area, especially if they are developmentally young or are confined by assistive devices. These skills may serve as building blocks to higher-level skills and are often omitted from educational programs that promote gross motor development. We suggest that teachers and school teams carefully consider whether their students need educational programming and/or therapeutic intervention in this area before they consider programming for more advanced skills.

Many individuals with disabilities have been denied educational, recreational, social, and work experiences because of their dependency on others for transportation or movement within their environment (Gruber, Reeser, & Reid, 1979). The use of assistive devices such as walkers, crutches, canes, and wheelchairs has enabled such persons to become more independent and has allowed them to participate more fully in society. Therefore, one of the major goals (II) of this unit addresses the use of assistive devices. At all times, teachers should consult with occupational and physical therapists for additional information, especially in light of new technological advances, which continue to occur at a rapid pace.

It should be noted that goals, objectives, and activities for nonambulatory students have been included in this unit because a significant number of individuals with severe disabilities are motorically impaired. This area has often been neglected in gross motor programs that hold ambulation as the minimum performance level before programming for gross motor skills development. Many of the activities used with ambulatory students may be successfully applied to nonambulatory students.

The locomotion skills necessary within the home, school, and community have been determined after consultation with clients, teachers, parents, and professionals working in group homes and alternate living units/apartments for individuals with disabilities. The specific objectives presented involve travel within the community. Too often, individuals with severe disabilities have been prevented from traveling because of their inability to navigate curbs, follow routing and detour signs, walk through automatic or revolving doors (Cipani, Augustine, & Blomgren, 1982), and negotiate stairways, elevators, or escalators (Cipani et al., 1982).

The teaching of gross motor skills pertinent to recreational and leisure activities is also highlighted because of the significant amount of nonworking hours available to individuals with disabilities (Adil, 1994). Unfortunately, employment options continue to be scarce for many individuals with disabilities, and those that do find work are often *underemployed,* leaving increased amounts of free time.

I. The student will acquire those basic gross motor skills that will facilitate the later development of ambulation.

II. The student who requires assistive devices as an aid to ambulation will be able to use such assistive devices as canes, crutches, walkers, and wheelchairs to a degree that will allow him or her to function optimally.

III. The student will be able to move or walk, with or without assistive devices, to a degree that will allow him or her to function optimally in diverse settings.

IV. The student will acquire those gross motor skills that are an integral part of recreation and leisure activities.

GOAL I.

The student will acquire those basic gross motor skills that will facilitate the later development of ambulation.

Physical development begins with the infant having reflexive responses and progressing to activities such as lifting the head in a prone position, sitting, standing, walking, and using imitative motor skills. In any gross motor program, the normal developmental sequences are part of the process of (a) developing a program to address atypical motor patterns and (b) reinforcing the strengths of the student.

The term *ambulatory* is used to describe any student who walks, either independently or with the assistance of canes, crutches, or walkers. The term *nonambulatory* is used to describe any student who uses a wheelchair. The teacher should seek the consultation of appropriate medical and allied health personnel, especially physical and occupational therapists, for advice, approval, and programming suggestions for developing these skills.

SPECIFIC OBJECTIVES

The student:

- ❏ A. Lifts and turns head.
- ❏ B. Steadies head.
- ❏ C. Rolls over.
- ❏ D. Pulls self to a sitting position.
- ❏ E. Sits without support.
- ❏ F. Extends legs.
- ❏ G. Supports self on one arm.
- ❏ H. Crawls and creeps.
- ❏ I. Pulls self to a standing position.
- ❏ J. Stands with or without support.
- ❏ K. Cruises from object to object.

SUGGESTED ACTIVITIES

Specific Objective A

The student lifts and turns head.

In designing instructional activities and plans, emphasize the following elements: (a) facilitation of lifting and turning the head to visual stimuli; (b) facilitation of lifting and turning the head to sound stimuli; and (c) development of strength, control, and duration of response.

Teacher Interventions

Infant and Toddler/Preschool Level. Place the student on his or her stomach on a mat. Encourage head lifting by placing objects on the mat and moving the object to attract the student's attention. Continue to provide motivation by varying the object and introducing sounds.

Primary Level. Ask the student to practice head rolls. Demonstrate how it should be done. Ask the student to roll his or her head to one side, focus on a target (favorite toy or object), and then roll his or her head the other way.

Show the student large picture cards or pictures from a magazine. Use a level commensurate with the student's level of abilities and interests. Ask the student to turn his or her head to look at or identify the pictures of familiar objects.

Family Interventions

Infant and Toddler/Preschool Level.   Ask the parents to observe when their child lifts and turns his or her head. Tell them to assist their child when necessary by placing a hand or arm under his or her neck and head.

Ask the parents to place a picture, mobile, or other interesting object at the foot of their child's bed or crib. They should ensure that the object cannot be seen by the child while he or she is lying flat on the bed. Ask the parents to tell their child that there is a surprise at the foot of the bed and encourage the child to lift his or her head to see it. Tell them to change the object often to keep the child's interest.

Encourage the parents to play games with the child by placing him or her on their chest and raising the child by arching their back and raising their shoulders.

Specific Objective B

The student steadies head.

In designing instructional activities in this area, it is important to emphasize the following elements: (a) facilitation of head control in response to visual and auditory stimuli; (b) development of strength, control, and duration of response; and (c) development of head control as a means of surveying the environment.

Teacher Interventions

Infant and Toddler/Preschool Level.   When the student can raise his or her head, assist him or her to utilize elbows for support. Provide toys and other stimulation to encourage the student to strengthen the neck and steady the head.

Ask the student to practice steadying his or her head. Tell the student to lift his or her head and steady it while looking at his or her toes.

Tell the student to hold this position for a few seconds. Gradually increase the length of time the student is expected to hold his or her head steady.

Tell a simple story using a flannel board. Place the flannel board in a position that requires the student to lift and steady his or her head to watch as you add flannel cutouts to the board.

Family Interventions

Infant and Toddler/Preschool Level. Ask the parents to invite visitors or friends into their child's room. Suggest that the parents ask these visitors to stand so that the child has to lift and steady his or her head to see them.

Place toys in a circle on either side of the child's head. Encourage the child to reach for the toys. Move the toys to keep the child's attention.

Specific Objective C

The student rolls over.

Teacher Interventions

Infant and Toddler/Preschool Level. Place the student at the very edge of a mat. Tell him or her you are going to roll him or her over. Pick up the edge of the mat and roll the student over. Encourage the student to roll the rest of the length of the mat on his or her own. Help the student if he or she gets stuck before the end of the mat.

Gently roll the student by assisting movement at the shoulders or hips. As the student understands these movements and can begin to move independently, dangle toys to the side and back of the student.

Primary Level. Ask the student to roll while music is being played in the background. Play music and encourage the student to roll first to one end of the mat and then back to the other end of the mat.

Family Interventions

Infant and Toddler/Preschool Level. Ask the parents to assist their child in rolling over onto blankets that have been placed on the floor. Tell them to place one hand on the child's shoulder and one on his or her hips, say "Roll over," and help the child to roll over.

Suggest that the parents practice until the child can roll independently. Tell the parents to remind the child that his or her arms and legs should be used to help him or her roll over and to have him or her practice rolling over on both sides. This activity can be used as a physical exercise as well as a play activity.

Parents can place their child on a blanket or mat across from a favored object or musical toy. Ask them to tell their child to roll over to the object or toy. Have them allow the child to play with the toy if he or she rolls over to it or attempts to move in the appropriate direction.

 ## Specific Objective D

The student pulls self to a sitting position.

Teacher Intervention

Infant and Toddler/Preschool Level. When appropriate and in a safe manner, assign helpers to the student who is beginning to pull up to a sitting position. Instruct them to help the student pull him- or herself up to a sitting position.

Use an inner tube to assist the student in pulling him- or herself to a sitting position. Hold the inner tube and assist the student in locking his or her arms around the inner tube. Encourage the student to use it as a support as he or she pulls him- or herself to a sitting position.

Family Interventions

Infant and Toddler/Preschool Level. Ask the parents to assist their child in pulling him- or herself to a sitting position. Tell them to extend their fingers to the child so that he or she may grasp them while he or she lies in a bed and to help him or her pull him- or herself to a sitting position.

Ask the parents to help their child in a crib to come to a sitting position. The parents should start by assisting the child to roll to one side. Next, they should have the child grasp the crib rail with one arm while pushing up with the other arm. Tell the parents to place a mirror beside the crib or bed so the child can see his or her progress.

 ## Specific Objective E

The student sits without support.

Teacher Interventions

Infant and Toddler/Preschool Level. After the student is placed in a sitting position, push him or her gently to one side. Check to see if the child puts his or her hands out to his or her side to brace him- or herself. (This bracing to avoid falling is called a "parachute reaction.") If the child does not brace him- or herself, assist him or her in doing so. Repeat activity, this time gently pushing the child to the alternate side and then backward.

(Note: Be aware that many students with severe and moderate disabilities often have restrictions in leg movements, making it difficult to sit on flat surfaces.)

At music time, place the student in a sitting position on a mat. Sing songs that he or she enjoys and encourage him or her to sing along and clap to the music. Place the student who is at a beginning stage of sitting between two students who are able to sit independently.

Family Interventions

Infant and Toddler/Preschool Level. Ask the parents to place their child in a sitting position on a mat or in his or her crib or bed. Suggest that the parents do a finger play or show the child an interesting plaything such as blocks or small toys to keep him or her interested in remaining in the sitting position.

Ask the parents to assist their child in sitting without support. If the child starts to lose his or her balance, the parents should use some pillows to prop him or her up.

 ## Specific Objective F

The student extends legs.

Teacher Interventions

Infant and Toddler/Preschool Level. Seat the student on a mat on the floor. Ask him or her to extend his or her legs as far as possible. Place a toy, game, or favorite object on the mat within reach of the student's extended legs. If the student's toes touch the object, give it to him or her to play with.

Seat the student on the floor. Place a ball on the floor so that the student will be able to move the ball by extending his or her legs. Sit across from the student and encourage him or her to tap the ball toward you.

Tape a balloon or punching bag to the floor. Seat the student on the floor and tell him or her to extend his or her legs to bounce or move the punching bag or balloon back and forth.

Family Interventions

Infant and Toddler/Preschool Level. Ask the parents to assist their child in extending his or her legs. If he or she sits in a chair, wheelchair, or other chair, tell the parents to lift the child's legs gently until they are extended in front of him or her. The parents should practice until their child can extend his or her legs as independently as possible, commensurate with his or her physical abilities and medical oversight (children in wheelchairs may be unable to do this independently).

Again, with medical clearance, ask the parents to put a picture on the foot board of their child's bed. Ask them to tell the child to extend his or her legs and touch the mark or picture. This is a good way to exercise cramped legs.

 Specific Objective G

The student supports self on one arm.

Teacher Interventions

Infant and Toddler/Preschool Level. Give the student a box or container of wooden blocks. Tell the student to support him- or herself with one arm and dump the container of blocks with the other. Allow him or her to play with the blocks.

Ask the student to look through magazines or picture books while supporting him- or herself on one arm as he or she lies on a mat, in a crib, or in a bed. Use pop-up books as an added incentive.

Do exercises requiring the student to support him- or herself on one arm. Tell the student to lie on his or her side and support him- or herself with one arm. First, ask the student to raise his or her leg. Then ask the student to raise the leg a certain number of times. Finally, ask him or her to lie on the other side and raise the other leg. If the student cannot lift his or her leg independently, help him or her.

Family Interventions

Infant and Toddler/Preschool Level. Ask the parents to ask their child, while he or she is lying on a mat, in a crib, or in bed, to support him- or herself on one arm. Tell them to demonstrate what they want him or her to do and encourage him or her to imitate their movements.

Ask the parents to place a toy, game, or favorite object within reach of their child as he or she lies in a prone position on a mat, in a crib, or in bed. Tell them to encourage him or her to support him- or herself with one arm and reach for the toy or game with his or her free hand. Ask the parents to utilize this behavior to increase the child's ability to manipulate objects in the environment.

Specific Objective H

The student crawls and creeps.

Teacher Interventions

Infant and Toddler/Preschool Level. Tape cutout hand prints on the floor and connect them with yarn or masking tape. Ask the student to place his or her hands on the cutout hand prints and to crawl along the trail.

Construct an obstacle course of desks, chairs, and other large articles found in the classroom. Appoint a leader, and tell the students to crawl or creep through the obstacle course while following the leader.

Family Interventions

Infant and Toddler/Preschool Level. When the child is able to rock back and forth on his or her knees, have the parents place a toy beyond the child's reach. The child is now ready for floor activities that have him or her creep on a carpet.

Ask the parents to assist their child in crawling and creeping by demonstrating crawling to him or her. Tell them to help him or her to imitate them by moving his or her hands along or by giving him or her a gentle push. Suggest that they continually use verbal, facial, and gestural reinforcement.

Ask the parents to put a pillow under their child and place him or her on the floor (the pillow must allow his or her hands and feet to reach the floor). Tell the parents to gently move the pillow forward while encouraging the child to creep.

Have the parents place objects one step up and assist the child to reach for the objects. Parents should withdraw physical assistance as the child gains confidence and the parents feel comfortable that the child has the necessary balance.

Specific Objective I

The student pulls self to a standing position.

Teacher Interventions

Infant and Toddler/Preschool Level. Place the student on a stable chair. Assist him or her to a standing position from the chair.

Conduct a "roll call." Seat the students on mats on the floor next to pieces of furniture. When you call each student's name, tell the student to pull him- or herself to a kneeling position first, and then to a standing position. Use a variety of furniture that aids or helps the standing process.

Family Interventions

Infant and Toddler/Preschool Level. Once the child is able to sit independently, encourage the parents to assist the child to develop upper body strength by placing toys just outside of the child's reach and playing games to have the child rotate and reach. Children should be placed in a sitting position as frequently as possible to facilitate development of hip and trunk muscles. When the child is able to free his or her hands, the child can be encouraged to pull him- or herself to a standing position.

Ask the parents to seat their young child in a crib or playpen, facing the crib bars or playpen netting. Tell them to place the child's hands on the bars or netting and encourage him or her to gradually pull him- or herself to a standing position. Make sure all equipment and furniture are safe according to the most recent safety standards.

Ask the parents to assist their child in pulling him- or herself to a standing position. When the child is sitting, the parents should offer their hands to him or her and help him or her pull him- or herself to a standing position.

 ## Specific Objective J

The student stands with or without support.

Teacher Interventions

Infant and Toddler/Preschool Level. Play games that require the student to stand. For example, ask the student to pretend that he or she is a tree blowing in the wind and encourage him or her to bend his or her body in different directions. If the student needs support in standing, place him or her near a sturdy table or chair so he or she can grasp it for support. Use a variety of equipment that aids and/or helps the standing process.

Play Simon Says, with required standing movements. For example, say, "Simon says, 'Stand up straight.' Simon says, 'March in place.'"

Family Interventions

Infant and Toddler/Preschool Level. Ask the parents to tell their child to pull him- or herself to a standing position. Tell them to assist their child in standing with or without support.

Ask parents to play music and encourage their child to stand and sway in time to the music. Tell them to modify the tempo and intensity of the music as the child becomes more independent in the activity.

 Specific Objective K

The student cruises from object to object.

Teacher Interventions

Infant and Toddler/Preschool Level. Construct cruising paths in the classroom. Arrange the furniture so that the student may cruise from one interest area to another (e.g., toy shelves to table, and back, and from desk to bathroom). Avoid furniture that has sharp edges or is not stable. Also, select cruising paths that are safe and free of hazards.

During class activities, ask the student to do things that require him or her to cruise (e.g., "John, will you please close the door?"). Be sure there is a cruising path to the door. Gradually increase the distance between objects along the cruising path. Select cruising paths that are safe and free of hazards.

Family Interventions

Infant and Toddler/Preschool Level. Ask the parents to assist their child as he or she cruises from object to object. Suggest that the parents initially use a long table for the child to hold onto and show him or her how to hold onto the table and cruise from one end to the other. Tell the parents to encourage imitation. When possible, they should select places for cruising that have rugs or carpeting to cushion any falls.

Ask the parents to arrange furniture in the room so that their child may cruise from one object to another and travel around the room. The furniture should be close enough so that the child does not lose his or her balance. The parents should show the child large picture cards or pictures from a magazine, using a level commensurate with the student's level of abilities and interests. The parents should ask the child to turn his or her head to look at or identify the pictures of familiar objects.

GOAL II.

The student who requires assistive devices as an aid to ambulation will be able to use such assistive devices as canes, crutches, walkers, and wheelchairs to a degree that will allow him or her to function optimally.

The objectives and activities in this section are written from the viewpoint that the teacher and parents may be the major providers of services in teaching the use of assistive devices to the student. It is important that activities taught in the Teacher Interventions be shared with the parents so carryover, progress, and reinforcement can be enhanced. Consultation with medical personnel, physical therapists, and allied health personnel is necessary for prescription, measurement, appropriateness, and monitoring of activities using assistive devices. Safety considerations, in all cases, should help determine the appropriate times and places for activities.

SPECIFIC OBJECTIVES

The student:

❑ A. Uses a walker.

❑ B. Uses crutches.

❑ C. Uses a cane.

❑ D. Opens, closes, and uses a wheelchair.

SUGGESTED ACTIVITIES

 ## Specific Objective A

The student uses a walker.

There are several major types of walkers. The infant walker (see Figure 2.1) is usually designed for children from 1½ to 4 years of age. It is adjustable in height from 18 to 24 inches. The child walker (see Figure 2.2) is for children from 2 to 8 years of age who are not expected to be ambulatory in the future. Many of these walkers have a padded body ring with an inside diameter of 10 inches. Many adjustable and select models are equipped with brakes. A walker that many adults and children use for functional ambulation is illustrated in Figure 2.3. It usually has adjustable handrails and wheels.

Teacher Interventions

Infant and Toddler/Preschool Level. Place a rattle or toy on a chair in the corner of a room. Tell or gesture to the student who is in an infant walker to move across the room and retrieve the toy. Then ask the student to bring it to you. Only use infant walkers that have been approved by appropriate safety agencies, and supervise their use closely.

Tell or gesture to the student in an upright walker to follow a group of cardboard arrows that have been placed on the floor. Show the student how to move the walker forward and then move his or her body in the same direction. Include in the lesson curves or the turning of corners.

Tape three weighted balloons to the student's walker. Place three empty cartons or baskets in different parts of the room. Tell the student to drop the specific colored balloon in the box with the corresponding color on the outside.

Set up a wastebasket in a corner. Give the student a small beach ball or volleyball and help him or her to move toward the basket. When possible, tell the student to throw it in the basket. For older students, play a basketball-type game and reward the student when he or she scores a basket.

Family Interventions

Infant and Toddler/Preschool and Primary Levels. Ask the parents to plan a trip in the community that requires their child to use his or her walker when mov-

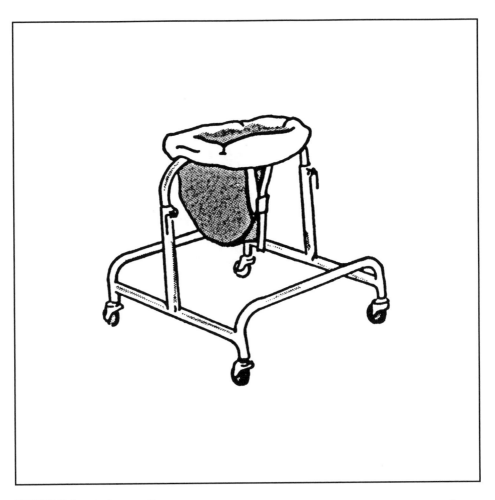

FIGURE 2.1. Infant walker.

ing from place to place and up and down inclines. Have them assist the child when necessary.

Ask the parents to take their child shopping at a store that has large aisles. Plan a time to do this shopping when there are minimal crowds. The parents should have the child use the walker to go down the aisles, assisting him or her when necessary.

 ## Specific Objective B

The student uses crutches.

FIGURE 2.2.   Child walker.

As with all assistive devices, crutches should be used only after the appropriate medical and related health personnel have been consulted. During evaluations, the student's muscle, joint, and pain status can be ascertained and a determination made as to whether or not he or she can manage successfully with crutches. Crutches are used to increase balance and stability as well as to reduce or eliminate stress on weight-bearing joints. Basically, crutches compensate for a loss of muscle control. The major type of crutch, the axillary, has an underarm rest (see Figure 2.4). Sometimes crutches are adapted for use within specific parts of the country or on different terrains. Figure 2.5 pictures a tip of a crutch specifically developed for walking in icy conditions.

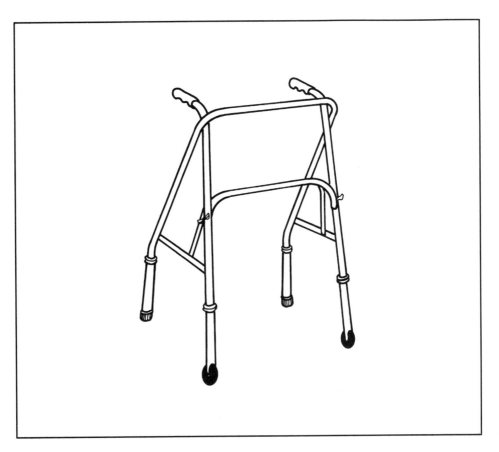

FIGURE 2.3. Adult walker with wheels.

Teacher Interventions

Toddler/Preschool Level. Show the student the "four-point gait." This gait offers maximum support because there are always three points of contact with the ground. The cycle for the student to follow is: (1) right crutch forward, (2) left foot forward, (3) left crutch forward, and (4) right foot forward. Assist the student in practicing this gait pattern. Tell the student to walk from one end of the room to the other employing this gait.

For the student with a severe unilateral involvement of a lower extremity that needs to be protected from stress, practice a "three-point gait." This is a weight-bearing type of gait. Tell the student to follow this cycle: (1) bring involved leg and both crutches forward at the same time and (2) bring unaffected leg forward.

When appropriate, tell the student to practice going from one end of the room to the other using a "two-point gait." This gait requires the student to be able to balance on one leg and involves a significant amount of skill. There is usually a progression from a four-point to a two-point

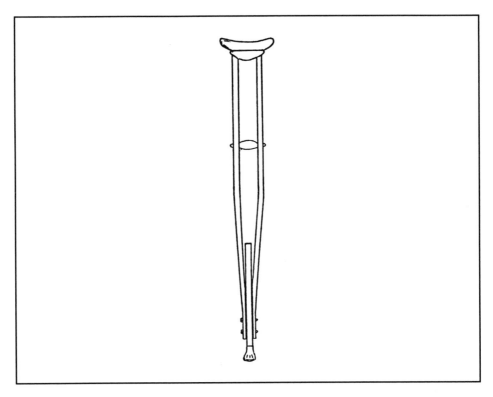

FIGURE 2.4. Axillary crutch.

gait. Show the student how to bring the right crutch and left foot forward at the same time and then bring the left crutch and right foot forward. Reward the student when he or she moves appropriately.

Family Interventions

Toddler/Preschool Level. Ask the parents to take their child to a community event such as a ball game or concert. Suggest that they arrive early so the child will be able to use his or her crutches without feeling the pressure of being in a crowd. Have them assist their child when necessary.

Suggest to the parents that they plan trips in the neighborhood that require their child to use his or her crutches on a variety of surfaces.

 ## Specific Objective C

The student uses a cane.

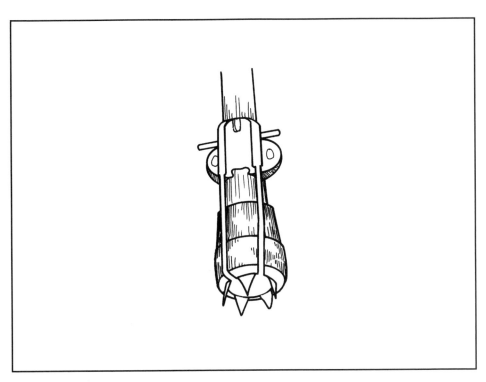

FIGURE 2.5.   Crutch/cane tip adaptation for walking on ice.

Canes provide less support than crutches. Some canes are weighted to provide added stability, but most are not. Some have molded handles that have been developed to fit the contours of the hand. The tips of canes can vary from the traditional rubber ones to built-up ones that provide a wider base of support. Various tips have been developed for walking on different surfaces. There are several major types:

- Single-point canes, which can be made of wood and are usually 36 inches long with a curved handle. These can be cut down to the appropriate length. Telescopic aluminum canes are another example; this type of cane is usually adjustable from 22 to 38 inches (adjustability allows for the child's growth).

- Tripod canes, which are three-legged canes that allow for an ankle-type action to grasp the ground (thus providing additional support).

- Quad canes, which are four-legged canes that provide maximum support with four points of contact with the ground.

- Loftstrand canes, which are single-point canes with additional forearm support.

Teacher Interventions

Toddler/Preschool and Primary Levels. Indicate to the student, by gesture and/or speech, that he or she should walk toward you using his or her cane. Indicate that the student should bring the cane and affected leg forward simultaneously and then bring the unaffected limb forward. Practice with the student and correct him or her when this sequence is not followed. If necessary, move him or her through the activity.

Place taped "X" marks at different intervals in the room. Ask and/or gesture to the student who uses a quad cane or tripod cane to walk to these marks. Once he or she is there, reward him or her for a job well done.

Ask the student with a single-point telescopic or wooden cane to walk to the base of a set of stairs. Tell him or her to slowly climb the stairs by stepping up with the unaffected leg first. (It may be necessary to tap the student's leg to indicate the one to move.) Tell him or her by gesture and/or speech to then bring up the cane and the affected leg. Carefully supervise this activity. Reverse this procedure for coming down the stairs. Emphasize that the affected leg and cane should come down first.

Family Interventions

Toddler/Preschool and Primary Levels. Ask the parents to take their child who is using a cane for a walk in the community. Have them bring the child to a street where there is a high curb. Have them tell their child that stepping up on the curb is similar to the way he or she steps up when he or she climbs stairs, that is, the unaffected leg first followed by the cane and then the affected leg. The child should practice stepping up on a curb.

Suggest that the parents take their child who uses a cane shopping, preferably during hours when stores are least busy. Ask the parents to help their child practice walking over thresholds, up stairs leading to stores, and in and out of elevators. Caution the parents to emphasize safety considerations when using store elevators (i.e., avoiding the crack in the floor, in which the cane could get caught).

 ## Specific Objective D

The student opens, closes, and uses a wheelchair.

(Note: Many individuals with moderate and severe disabilities may not be able to open or close a wheelchair but should be able to move the chair.)

When wheelchairs are prescribed by the medical team, they should be measured for their durability, strength, size, and weight. Additionally, they should fold easily and have replaceable parts and accessories (see Figure 2.6). The earliest age at which a child may be placed in a wheelchair varies. A child's wheelchair should be used with a seating system to meet the needs of the child. Armrests and footrests are usually removable and adjustable for height. Wheels are frequently removable for ease in transport. Seating systems usually have a removable seat and back, trunk and hip supports as necessary, and a tray attached to the wheelchair with clamps to provide a working surface or eating surface for the student. A seat belt, anterior trunk support, and head support should be used if the child will be transported in the wheelchair or on the school bus. Additionally, power chairs and scooters are becoming more popular because they allow children to keep up with their peers and exert less energy. Their compact size and tight-turning radius also allows navigation through narrow halls and doorways.

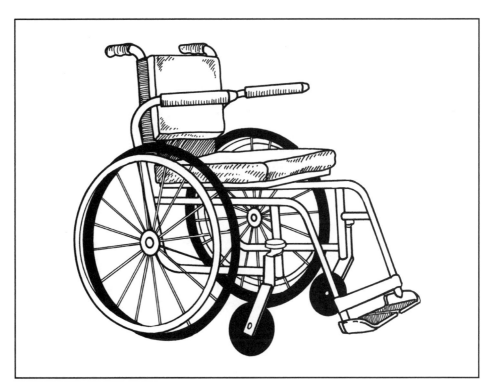

FIGURE 2.6. Wheelchair.

Teacher Interventions

Toddler/Preschool and Primary Levels.   First, practice how to open and close a wheelchair. Try various types of chairs until you are proficient. Demonstrate to the student how to open a folded wheelchair. Practice until the student is comfortable with the process.

Similar to the above activity, practice closing a wheelchair. Make sure that the arms (if removable) are locked and the footrests are folded up. Ask the student to make a fold in the seat from above or below. If above, pull up, closing the chair. Practice this procedure with the student.

Plan lessons that use different components of the wheelchair that the student should be proficient in using. These include using the seat belt, locking and unlocking brakes, putting foot plates up, and using the hand rims of the chair.

Show the student how to transfer from his or her wheelchair to a chair. Assist the student in placing the right front wheel of the wheelchair against the left front leg of the chair. Then assist him or her in placing his or her right knee close to the chair's right front leg. Require the student to lock his or her brakes, put his or her foot plates up, and put his or her hand on the seat of the other chair. Assist the student in pushing up and sliding from the wheelchair to the seat of the other chair.

For the student who is in bed and wants to transfer to his or her wheelchair, supervision is required. Assist the student in removing one arm of the wheelchair (if possible) and moving the chair next to the bed. Make sure the bed and wheelchair are on a horizontal plane whenever possible. Assist the student in making the transfer.

Find a bathroom that has been made accessible for individuals with disabilities. Help the student transfer to a toilet by first removing the appropriate arm(s) of the wheelchair. Assist the student in wheeling into the bathroom and holding onto the L-shaped bar placed there for "handicapped" access. Show the student how to lift and transfer to the toilet seat using the L-bar as a support. Practice.

Family Interventions

Toddler/Preschool Level.   Ask the parents to take their child who is in a wheelchair to a department store that has an elevator. The parents should point out the grooves in the front of the elevator doors. The parents should tell the child to approach the elevator at a right angle and from a short distance, making sure the student enters the elevator backward, so the larger back wheels will not get caught in the door grooves.

Ask the parents to help their child transfer into their car. Have them park their car so that their child can transfer as close to the curb as possible. Transfer is handled best when the level of the wheelchair and the car seat are the same. Have them assist the child in standing up, supported by his right hand, right armrest, and right foot. Have them turn the child a little to the right and then tell him or her to support him- or herself with the right hand on the left armrest of the wheelchair or the car door frame. The child can now do a push-up and carry him- or herself over to the car seat.

GOAL III.

The student will be able to move or walk, with or without assistive devices, to a degree that will allow him or her to function optimally in diverse settings.

The specific objectives and activities that follow include activities for non-ambulatory students as well as those who are ambulatory. Activities have been selected to reflect how a student moves or walks in his or her living and learning areas, how he or she travels within the community, and how he or she uses public or private transportation. Because all children, especially those with developmental disabilities, may develop these skills at varying ages, a wide range of activities that support moving and walking needs to be provided.

SPECIFIC OBJECTIVES

The student:

☐ A. Walks or moves in a wheelchair on a flat surface, including sidewalks.

☐ B. Walks or moves in a wheelchair over thresholds and up and down curbs.

☐ C. Walks or moves in a wheelchair through doorways.

☐ D. Walks or moves in a wheelchair in a line.

☐ E. Avoids ruts, holes, and other uneven surfaces.

☐ F. Walks or moves in a wheelchair up and down hills, inclines, and ramps.

☐ G. Walks or moves in a wheelchair in aisles and around stationary objects and other obstacles.

☐ H. Walks or moves in a wheelchair safely on icy surfaces in inclement weather.

❏ I.   Turns corners when walking or using a wheelchair.

❏ J.   Follows routing and detour symbols when walking or using a wheelchair.

❏ K.   Crosses streets when walking or using a wheelchair.

❏ L.   Walks or moves in a wheelchair into and out of home and public restrooms.

❏ M. Steps or moves in a wheelchair into and out of elevators.

❏ N.   Gets into and out of cars or transfers into and out of cars from a wheelchair.

❏ O.   Walks up and down stairways.

❏ P.   Steps on and off buses, trains, planes, and other public transportation vehicles.

 ## Specific Objective A

The student walks or moves in a wheelchair on a flat surface, including sidewalks.

Teacher Interventions

Toddler/Preschool and Primary Levels.   Play Follow the Leader, telling the leader to do things that require the student to move in his or her wheelchair around the room or on a hard-topped playground.

Tape cutouts of feet on the floor, making various pathways. Tell the student to follow the footprints to a hidden prize or favorite object.

Play Musical Chairs using very slow music. Wheelchair students may claim a seat by placing their hand on the back or seat of the chair.

Family Interventions

Toddler/Preschool and Primary Levels.   Ask the parents to assist their child if he or she has difficulty walking on a flat surface. Suggest that they tell him or her to hold onto them for support and encourage him or her to let go and to try a few steps on his or her own. Tell the parents to gradually increase the number of steps until the child can walk independently.

Ask the parents to encourage their child to walk or move safely in his or her wheelchair throughout the house and community. Tell them to give the child directions that require him or her to walk or move in the room (e.g., "John, shut the door, please"). Tell them to walk beside the child in case he or she loses his or her balance or the control of his or her wheelchair while on the street. The parents should tell him or her to walk by the walls because he or she may want to lean against them if he or she feels unsteady, loses his or her balance, or loses control of the wheelchair.

Specific Objective B

The student walks or moves in a wheelchair over thresholds and up and down curbs.

Teacher Interventions

Toddler/Preschool and Primary Levels. Assist the student in walking or moving in a wheelchair over thresholds. As a student approaches a threshold, call his or her attention to it. Demonstrate lifting first one foot and then the other to step over the threshold. Practice and praise his or her efforts.

Place threshold-height pieces of wood or blocks on the floor. Play Follow the Leader and walk over the blocks. Encourage the student to follow you. As the student becomes more sure of this activity, ask him or her, if capable, to walk backward and at an angle over the thresholds. Move backward and forward with the student who is in a wheelchair over the pieces of wood or blocks.

Family Interventions

Toddler/Preschool and Primary Levels. Ask the parents to help their child practice walking or moving in and out of stores in the community that have different types of thresholds.

Practice walking up and down curbs in the community when crossing streets. Also use inclined curbs that have been adapted for access whenever possible.

Specific Objective C

The student walks or moves in a wheelchair through doorways.

Teacher Interventions

Toddler/Preschool and Primary Levels.   Take the student around the building in which he or she is being taught. Practice walking or moving in a wheelchair through various types of doorways (single doors, double doors, swinging doors, and doors with an "in" and "out" side, such as in a cafeteria where one group is entering as another is leaving through the same doorway).

On the floor, place a masking tape line that passes from the room through the doorway and into the corridor. Tell the student to line up on the tape and walk or move in a wheelchair through the doorway, utilizing the line as a guide.

Family Interventions

Toddler/Preschool and Primary Levels.   Ask the parents to send their child on errands within the home that require him or her to go in and out of doorways. Examples are returning materials to another room and eating in a special area of the house.

Suggest that the family eat at restaurants in the community that are clearly identified as being accessible to people with disabilities. While there, have them point out the doorways, ramps, or other adaptations their child should look for when dining out in the community.

 ## Specific Objective D

The student walks or moves in a wheelchair in a line.

Teacher Interventions

Toddler/Preschool and Primary Levels.   Assist the student in walking or moving in a line. Form a line with peers who are able to walk or move in a wheelchair and ask them to demonstrate to other students.

Play games in a line such as Follow the Leader or marching in line to music. In addition, ask the students to line up for daily activities such as washing hands, going to lunch, going to gym, or being dismissed.

Family Interventions

Toddler/Preschool and Primary Levels.   Ask the parents to go food shopping with their child. While there, have them ask their child to wait in line at the checkout counter when he or she is through making purchases. Have the parents assist the child when necessary and point out any safety factors involved in walking or moving in a wheelchair in a line.

As part of a family leisure outing, the parents should plan a trip to the local movie theater, telling the child he or she may have to wait in line to purchase tickets. Have the parents provide help, if necessary, and see the movie. Initially, it may be easier if this activity is tried during a time when the ticket line is not very crowded.

 ## Specific Objective E

The student avoids ruts, holes, and other uneven surfaces.

Teacher Interventions

Toddler/Preschool and Primary Levels. In the classroom, construct uneven surfaces. Place mats on the floor and put balls or blocks of wood under them to produce uneven surfaces. Also, place boxes or large pieces of wood on top of mats. Lead the student over the mats. Encourage the student to step or move over small bumps or uneven areas and around larger uneven areas. Ask the student to practice traveling over the mats independently. Explain that, when he or she is outdoors in the community, he or she should avoid similar uneven surfaces.

Get large sheets of foam rubber and place them in the classroom or on the playground. Cut holes and large ridges in the foam rubber to simulate potholes and ruts. Demonstrate stepping or moving over holes and ridges and avoiding them. After this activity, take the students on a trip to an area that has ruts and holes where they can practice what they have learned in the natural environment.

Family Interventions

Toddler/Preschool and Primary Levels. Ask the parents to take their child on trips in their neighborhood where the child can practice avoiding ruts and holes. This can include trips down uneven sidewalks, to a park, or to a playground. As the parents walk or move along the street, have them point out the curbs, holes, and ruts, and how to avoid them.

When possible, suggest that the parents take their child to different types of areas around his or her home and neighborhood. Have them include areas with rocks and rough terrain, sandy areas, and areas that have some debris or branches down on the path or sidewalk. Have the parents practice with their child navigating these different surfaces and obstacles.

Specific Objective F

The student walks or moves in a wheelchair up and down hills, inclines, and ramps.

Teacher Interventions

Toddler/Preschool and Primary Levels.   Construct or borrow ramps for short stairways (two or three steps) or place wide, heavy pieces of ½-inch plywood (4 × 8 feet) safely over the stairs. If necessary, place two wooden poles or rails at each end of the ramp. String clothesline rope between the rails to make a rope railing. Demonstrate how to walk or move over the ramp. Encourage the student to practice walking or moving up and down the ramp. Use ramps to enter and leave the building, whenever possible.

Practice walking up and down ramps found in the school, especially those at entrances and exits.

Family Interventions

Toddler/Preschool and Primary Levels.   Suggest that the parents occasionally bring their child with them when they go shopping. Have them frequent stores that have ramps and inclines and practice entering and exiting these stores with their child.

Ask the parents to take their child to places with varying terrains such as a playground with a hilly area, woods with inclines, or a beach. Ask them to show their child how to navigate these areas. In some instances, the parents may need to show their child how to overbalance (i.e., lean forward going uphill and backward going downhill, to avoid losing balance).

Specific Objective G

The student walks or moves in a wheelchair in aisles and around stationary objects and other obstacles.

Teacher Interventions

Toddler/Preschool and Primary Levels.   Arrange classroom furniture in aisles. Assist the student in walking or moving in aisles, between furniture, and around stationary objects.

Tell the student to stand or sit in his or her wheelchair behind you. Ask the student to follow you as you walk up and down the classroom aisles. As he or she feels more confident about negotiating the aisles, ask him or her to walk or move in his or her wheelchair up and down the aisles independently.

Family Interventions

Toddler/Preschool and Primary Levels.   Ask the parents to rearrange the furniture at home or in the living areas periodically, and to require their child to walk or move in a wheelchair around the pieces of furniture.

Suggest that the parents go shopping with their child in places that have numerous aisles, such as large discount stores. Have them help the child maneuver around these aisles.

Specific Objective H

The student walks or moves in a wheelchair safely on icy surfaces in inclement weather.

Teacher Interventions

Toddler/Preschool and Primary Levels.   Demonstrate to the students the slippery characteristics of ice by using ice cubes. Tell the student to run his or her fingers over ice cubes and feel how slippery they are. Then wrap the student's finger in different materials (e.g., velvet, sandpaper) or put on a rubber finger and ask him or her to note how some materials slide smoothly over the ice and others seem to grip it. Explain that rubber, as found on rubber-soled shoes or rubber boots, helps to resist the slipperiness. Explain that sandpaper has a similar effect and that is why we throw sand on icy ground or roads.

Discuss safety on ice. Explain to the student that he or she should never go on frozen ponds or rivers unless he or she has been told by parents or park police that it is safe. Stress that the student should always be accompanied by a responsible adult. In addition, the student should be taught to avoid areas that present hazards because of icy surfaces.

Family Interventions

Toddler/Preschool and Primary Levels.   Have the parents utilize times when the ground is icy to assist their child in learning how to walk or move on ice.

Ask the parents to take their child to an indoor ice rink during off hours. After permission is granted from the owner, the parents should demonstrate how to actually walk on ice with regular shoes first, then rubber shoes. The parents should continually emphasize the hazards of falling on ice and the need to be extremely cautious. If appropriate, the child should initially wear a safety helmet for these activities.

 ## Specific Objective I

The student turns corners when walking or using a wheelchair.

Teacher Interventions

Toddler/Preschool and Primary Levels. Assist the student in turning corners when walking or using a wheelchair. Tell the student to walk or use a wheelchair to go down the hallways of the school. As he or she approaches a corner, demonstrate turning the corner. Ask the student to follow you. The student who has trouble turning the corner may need additional practice.

Construct a maze using large portable desks, tables, and other large pieces of furniture. Be sure the maze corridors are wide enough to accommodate wheelchairs. Tell the student to move through the maze, turning the various corners.

Family Interventions

Toddler/Preschool and Primary Levels. Ask the parents to take their child grocery shopping. Have them go up and down each aisle so that the student will have to turn corners at each end.

Suggest that the parents clear aisles and passageways in the home so the child can move his or her wheelchair freely in these areas. Ask the parents to tell him or her at different times of the day or evening to do specific chores. Ask the parents to observe if he or she is moving around corners appropriately. They should provide assistance when necessary.

 ## Specific Objective J

The student follows routing and detour symbols when walking or using a wheelchair.

Teacher Interventions

Toddler/Preschool and Primary Levels.   In the hallways of the school, use directional arrows to indicate the way to the cafeteria, playground, and other special areas. Place a representative picture next to the directional arrow. Explain to the student that the sign means that the direction of the arrow leads to the place portrayed by the picture.

Construct an obstacle course on the playground or in the classroom. Place detour signs at various places along the course. Walk through the course with the student, stopping at each sign. Ask the student to show you where the sign is telling him or her to go. Offer help if he or she needs it. Tell the student to use the obstacle course to practice following the detour signs. Explain to him or her that he or she should also follow signs in the community.

Family Interventions

Toddler/Preschool and Primary Levels.   Ask the parents to take their child on a trip where there is construction going on requiring the taking of detours. Have the parents point out the signs and explain that the arrow or message tells them which way to go. Demonstrate following the direction of the arrow on the detour sign.

Suggest that the parents take their child on a field trip within the neighborhood. Point out crosswalks. Explain that crosswalks guide pedestrians across the street. The child should practice using the crosswalks to cross the street, with the parents emphasizing the rules of "Stop, look, and listen" to assure safe crossing.

 ## Specific Objective K

The student crosses streets when walking or using a wheelchair.

Teacher Interventions

Toddler/Preschool and Primary Levels.   Make signs saying "Walk" and "Don't Walk" or obtain commercially made signs. Drill the student until he or she does what the signs are telling him or her to do. Stress that even when he or she sees a "Walk" sign, he or she should still stop, look, and listen before crossing the street.

Tape or purchase a record of traffic sounds. Play this for the student and encourage him or her to identify the sounds. Discuss how these sounds would affect the student preparing to cross the street. Perhaps a horn would cause the student to look and see if the horn was warning him or her not to cross, a siren would warn the student to step back on the curb and wait until the fire engine or ambulance has passed, and a police whistle would tell the student to obey the police officer, regardless of the crossing lights.

Family Interventions

Toddler/Preschool and Primary Levels. Ask the parents to assist their child in crossing streets when walking or using a wheelchair. Have them take the child to a street that is not very heavily traveled. Discuss the safety involved in crossing streets independently. Tell the child to always stop before stepping off the curb, to look all around and both ways to be sure the street is clear, and to listen for the sound of cars and sirens. Tell the child to cross the street when it is safe.

Suggest that the parents take their child on a field trip within their neighborhood as well as to a busy intersection. Have them point out "Walk" and "Don't Walk" signs if they are available. Have them observe their child crossing the street by him- or herself (when appropriate), using the signs as a guide. In addition to the signs, supervision may still be required for some students.

 ## Specific Objective L

The student walks or moves in a wheelchair into and out of home and public restrooms.

Family Interventions

Toddler/Preschool and Primary Levels. Ask the parents to assist their child in using the toilets in the home. Tell them to praise the child when he or she uses the toilet appropriately.

Suggest that the parents provide opportunities for their child to use relatives' bathrooms during visits. Suggest that they visit the bathrooms beforehand to make sure they are accessible.

Ask the parents to locate a coin-operated toilet in a store. Ask them to assist their child in walking or moving in a wheelchair into and out of coin-operated toilets (they may want to secure permission from store personnel first). Ask them to show the door to their child and note the amount of money needed. Have them put the correct coin(s) into the slot, turn the door latch, and push in. Suggest that the parents go into the toilet and close the door behind them. Next, have them open the door and take their child into the stall. Ask them to show their child the knob to turn to lock the door and how to release it to unlock it. Have them practice with their child. (Note: Suggest that the parents exercise caution because some children cannot handle the locking of doors and should use other toilet facilities.)

For the child in a wheelchair, look for toilet stalls that have a wheelchair insignia on the door. If there is no insignia, the wheelchair will probably not fit inside the stall with the door closed.

 ## Specific Objective M

The student steps or moves in a wheelchair into and out of elevators.

Family Interventions

Toddler/Preschool and Primary Levels. Ask the parents to assist their child as he or she steps into elevators. Have them take their child to a building that has elevators (they may want to check initially to see when the elevators are least busy). The parents should ask for permission to use one of the elevators for a 10-minute training period. After permission is granted, the parents should engage the switch or button that stops the elevator at their floor and lock it on stop or hold, so it will not leave the floor while the child is practicing.

Have the parents show and emphasize to their child that the doors are open and that the elevator is level with the floor. Have the parents demonstrate stepping into the elevator by stepping over the grooves where the doors slide open and shut. They should then place their hands on the doorjamb so that it will not accidentally close. They should repeat this movement two or three times so that their child sees what they are doing. Ask them then to practice walking into the elevator with their child. As a final step, have them encourage their child to walk into the elevator independently. Next, have them demonstrate to their child stepping out of the elevator in a similar manner.

Suggest that the parents take their child to a large building with many elevators. Have them show him or her how to enter and leave one of the elevators. If the elevators are crowded, have them make sure the student faces the doors, says "Excuse me" when entering and leaving, and keeps his or her hands by the sides to avoid touching others in the elevator. Tell the parents to remind their child never to use elevators in case of fire.

Specific Objective N

The student gets into and out of cars or transfers into and out of cars from a wheelchair.

The teacher can provide many school activities that simulate getting into and out of cars or transferring into and out of cars from wheelchairs. These activities include arranging chairs in class to simulate car seats and making cardboard cars with seats inside. Although all these activities may have some value, it is strongly suggested that practice occur in the natural environment using real cars. Some activities that can be done by the teacher or parent are discussed below.

Teacher/Family Interventions

Toddler/Preschool and Primary Levels. Take the student to a school parking lot or safe parking area where he or she can use a car to practice getting in and out of. Open the car door and demonstrate to the student how to get in and out. One way is to sit sideways on the seat and then to swing his or her legs into the car. Encourage the student to pretend he or she is on a trip and to get into and out of his or her car to go shopping, to stop for lunch, or to go sightseeing.

For the student who is in a wheelchair, ask for assistance from a physical therapist or someone knowledgeable about wheelchair transfers. It is important that the type of wheelchair the student is using is adaptable and stable enough for transfers.

Always stress safety rules, including (a) never get into a stranger's car; (b) do not practice getting into and out of cars unless you have permission and supervision; and (c) do not put your hands on the car's doorjamb for support as you get into the car because you may get your hands caught.

Specific Objective O

The student walks up and down stairways.

(Note: For the student using crutches, consult medical personnel for specific instructions.)

Teacher Interventions

Toddler/Preschool and Primary Levels. Using flashcards initially, drill the student until he or she identifies the words *stairs* and *stairway.* These are necessary survival words to enable the student to find the stairs in public buildings easily.

If the school has stairways, practice using them during times of low traffic.

Family Interventions

Toddler/Preschool and Primary Levels. Ask the parents to allow their child to use the stairways whenever appropriate. Tell them to carefully monitor this activity because of the dangers that can quickly arise.

Suggest that the parents take their child to a ball game or other recreational event that requires walking up some stairs as one way of entering the facility. Suggest that they arrive early if their child has difficulty with walking up and down steps. They should also plan to leave the event after most of the crowds have left. Whenever necessary, entrances and exits that have stair rails should be selected.

Specific Objective P

The student steps on and off buses, trains, planes, and other public transportation vehicles.

Teacher Interventions

Toddler/Preschool and Primary Levels. Ask the individual in charge of transportation for your school if you may borrow a bus for a short period of time so your students may practice stepping on and off the bus. Take the student to the bus and point out the steps, emphasizing their height, handrails, and folding bus doors. Ask the bus driver to open the door. Demonstrate stepping onto the bus steps and grasping the handrail at the same time. Tell the student what you are doing as you do it slowly. When you reach the top of the bus steps, turn around, and, grasping the handrail, step down the bus steps.

Ask the students to imitate your actions as described in the above activity. If the students are having difficulty stepping on and off the bus, take them by the hand and walk them through the activity. Once they have developed a degree of confidence, encourage them to practice stepping on and off the bus.

Family Interventions

Toddler/Preschool and Primary Levels. Ask the parents to take their child on a trip involving transportation. Many shopping centers, museums, parks, and athletic stadiums are on or near bus lines. Have the parents go with their child as he or she independently steps on and off buses.

If there is a commuter train or light rail in the parents' community, suggest that they take their child on a trip to a nearby destination. Suggest that they go out for lunch or a visit and then return home. Have them praise their child for stepping on and off the train or light rail correctly and safely.

Suggest that the parents call an airport and ask if they can come with their child to take a tour. These tours usually include stepping on and off a plane. Practice with the child walking up the boarding steps by holding the handrail and carefully climbing the boarding steps. Once at the top of the steps, have the child step into the plane, turn around, and descend the steps, grasping the handrail and walking down the boarding steps slowly and carefully.

GOAL IV.

The student will acquire those gross motor skills that are an integral part of recreation and leisure activities.

Whenever possible, nonambulatory students should be encouraged to participate in recreational activities with individuals who do not have disabilities. When possible, materials should be modified or adapted to their individual needs.

Recreation and leisure activities provide a variety of opportunities for students with many levels of gross motor skills. In addition, the entire family of the student can participate in the same activity at their level of ability. Even variations in weather can provide interesting opportunities for families with children of all ages.

SPECIFIC OBJECTIVES

The student:

☐ A. Pulls a wagon or pull toy.

❐ B. Throws balls, beanbags, Frisbees, and other recreational equipment.

❐ C. Hits appropriate recreational equipment.

❐ D. Catches objects used during recreation.

❐ E. Balances his or her body as he or she participates in recreational activities.

❐ F. Marches.

❐ G. Runs.

❐ H. Gallops.

❐ I. Slides.

❐ J. Hops.

❐ K. Jumps.

❐ L. Skips.

❐ M. Dances.

❐ N. Climbs.

❐ O. Rides Big Wheels, tricycles, and bicycles.

 ## Specific Objective A

The student pulls a wagon or pull toy.

SUGGESTED ACTIVITIES

Teacher Interventions

Toddler/Preschool Level. Arrange for relay races using wagons and blocks. Divide the students into teams. Establish a race course and place half of each team at each end of the course. At each end, place a block for each member of the team. Ask one student to pull a wagon from one end of the course to the other and place a block in the wagon. Then the next student pulls the wagon, and the next student takes over. This is repeated until each member of the team has a turn. The first team to finish is the winner.

Family Interventions

Toddler/Preschool Level. Ask the parents to assist their child as he or she pulls a wagon or pull toy. Ask them to demonstrate grasping the handle or string and pulling the wagon or toy. Tell them to ask the child to imitate their actions and practice pulling the toy or wagon on different surfaces.

Tell the parents to ask their child to pull a wagon and place some toys into it at toy clean-up time. Ask the parents to tell their child to return the toys to their proper place. Ask the parents to select toys that are safe and nontoxic and to avoid toys that are very small in size or that have a large number of parts.

 ## Specific Objective B

The student throws balls, beanbags, Frisbees, and other recreational equipment.

Teacher Interventions

Infant and Toddler/Preschool and Primary Levels. Arrange a game of beanbag throw. Place a tire on the floor. Ask the student to stand up or to sit in his or her wheelchair and toss beanbags into the tire. Encourage the student, if appropriate, to practice throwing beanbags overhand and underhand into the tire. Scores can be kept or successful throws can be rewarded.

Start a game of Nerf basketball. Ask the student to practice throwing or "shooting" the Nerf basketball into a wastebasket or plastic laundry basket. Once the student is used to the Nerf basketball, form teams, make rules, and allow the student to play Nerf basketball during free time or rainy day recess.

Primary Level. Show the student how to play horseshoes. For the younger student, a plastic set of horseshoes may be more appropriate. Schedule a tournament that will allow the student to compete, individually or in teams, with his or her peers.

Family Interventions

Infant and Toddler/Preschool and Primary Levels. Ask the parents to assist their child in throwing balls, beanbags, Frisbees, and other recreational training equipment in an area that has been cleared of breakable objects. Tell the parents to show the child the above-mentioned equipment and demonstrate the appropriate use of each type. Tell the parents to give the child time to practice.

Ask the parents to play catch with their child using a variety of balls. Have them start with a soft rubber or cloth ball and eventually use a rubber or tennis ball. Suggest they use balls of different sizes and colors.

Specific Objective C

The student hits appropriate recreational equipment.

Teacher Interventions

Toddler/Preschool and Primary Levels. Demonstrate and assist the student as he or she hits appropriate recreational equipment (e.g., hitting a ball with a bat or tennis racket). Set aside time for the student to practice these activities. Modify recreational equipment when necessary.

Set up a croquet game on the playground. Demonstrate how to play the game, emphasizing how sometimes it is important to hit the ball very gently. Tell the student to imitate your actions. Schedule a tournament, allowing for team and individual play.

For the student who is having difficulty hitting a ball with a bat, play a modified version of baseball using a bat and a beach ball. This can be fun for all students and will encourage those having difficulty hitting smaller balls.

Explain to the student the rules or instructions required for specific recreational equipment. When necessary, break the instructions down into as few steps as possible.

Family Interventions

Toddler/Preschool and Primary Levels. Ask the parents, whenever possible, to practice at home the games or skills taught at school. Caution them to use recreational equipment that is safe, age appropriate, and within the motor abilities of their child.

Specific Objective D

The student catches objects used during recreation.

Teacher Interventions

Infant and Toddler/Preschool and Primary Levels.   Using the Time Bomb toy, encourage the students to pass it back and forth to each other. When the bomb goes off, the student holding it is eliminated from the game.

Seat two students on the floor or a mat facing each other. Ask one student to roll the ball and the other to catch it. Tell them to take turns rolling and catching the ball.

Assist the student in catching balls, beanbags, or other recreational equipment. Demonstrate ways to catch: with two hands, with one hand, or by trapping the object against the body. Show the student how to estimate the space needed to catch the object.

Family Interventions

Toddler/Preschool and Primary Levels.   Ask the parents to demonstrate bouncing a large ball and catching it. Ask them to encourage their child to practice bouncing and catching. The child should begin by using two hands to bounce and catch, gradually switching to one hand as he or she becomes more skillful in catching the ball.

Ask the parents to demonstrate bouncing balls in time to music. Tell them to have their child stand in a large marked circle. Tell them to play popular music, marches, or familiar tunes and ask their child to bounce a ball to the beat of the music. Suggest that the parents stand at the center of the circle and demonstrate bouncing a ball to establish a rhythm to the bouncing and to provide a model.

 ## Specific Objective E

The student balances his or her body as he or she participates in recreational activities.

Teacher Interventions

Toddler/Preschool and Primary Levels.   Assist the student in maintaining balance during recreational activities. Demonstrate balancing using arms, hands, and upper body as well as legs and feet. Ask the student to imitate your actions and practice balancing.

Play Simon Says. Include commands requiring the student to balance (e.g., "Simon says, 'Hop on one foot'").

Do balancing activities to music. Ask the student to balance on one foot with eyes closed, on tiptoes with eyes closed, and with arms extended in various directions.

Family Interventions

Toddler/Preschool and Primary Levels. Ask the parents to do exercises as part of their child's daily schedule. Tell them to include things such as hopping or standing on one foot and bending forward, backward, and sideways from the waist. Be sure to include upper body exercises that would be suitable for children in wheelchairs.

Ask the parents to construct a Twister game by pasting cutout footprints on an old shower curtain. Ask them to show their child how to play Twister by placing his or her feet on the footprints. Tell the parents to supervise closely because this type of balancing activity may be difficult.

 ## Specific Objective F

The student marches.

Teacher Interventions

Toddler/Preschool and Primary Levels. Play marching music. Ask the student to join you as you march to music. Use a variety of music for marching.

Give the student rhythm band instruments. Play marching music and encourage the student to march as he or she plays the rhythm band instrument.

Chant a cadence and ask the student to march to it. Emphasize the identification of the child's left and right foot.

Family Interventions

Toddler/Preschool and Primary Levels. Ask the parents to take their child to see a parade. There are often parades on various holidays or half-time shows at football games that the student might enjoy.

Ask the parents to make arrangements to watch a school or other marching band practice.

Specific Objective G

The student runs.

Teacher Interventions

Toddler/Preschool and Primary Levels. During physical exercise, model running in place and ask the student to imitate you. Ask the student to run short sprints. Time the student and chart his or her time.

Form a race course with tires as markers so the student can run around the tires and back in a figure-8. Divide the students into teams; the first team to complete the race is the winner.

Family Interventions

Toddler/Preschool and Primary Levels. Review with the parents the type of footwear needed for running and proper foot care, should problems arise. Remind the parent that exercise is necessary and that running can be healthy.

When appropriate, ask the parents to assist their child as he or she runs. Tell them to demonstrate running and encourage the child to imitate their actions. Suggest that they walk with the child, gradually going faster until the child is running, and say, "Now we are running!"

Tell the parents to include running as part of the child's daily exercise during good weather. Emphasize that they use judgment as to when and where to run.

Specific Objective H

The student gallops.

Teacher Interventions

Toddler/Preschool and Primary Levels. Assist the student in galloping. Demonstrate galloping and ask the student to imitate your actions. Practice.

Play the "William Tell Overture" and ask the student to gallop to the music.

Beat a galloping rhythm with wooden blocks. Ask the student to gallop to the rhythm. Change the tempo and ask the student to adjust his or her galloping to match the change in tempo.

Family Interventions

Toddler/Preschool and Primary Levels. Ask the parents to supervise games with their child that may include galloping. Ask them to avoid games or activities that appear unsafe.

 ## Specific Objective I

The student slides.

Teacher Interventions

Toddler/Preschool and Primary Levels. Show the student how to do some simple square dancing that requires him or her to slide (e.g., the "Virginia Reel"). You may wish to modify the difficulty and number of steps involved to suit the student's abilities.

Place large gym mats on the floor. Ask the student to remove his or her shoes and to run and slide on the mat.

Use special exercising sliding mats and shoes as part of an exercise program. Show a videotape, which usually comes with this type of equipment and shows you how to properly slide to music.

Family Interventions

Toddler/Preschool and Primary Levels. When appropriate, have the parents, coach, or physical education teacher show the child how to properly and safely slide into a base during a baseball game. Have them provide supervision while practicing this skill or activity.

Ask the parents to take their child to a square dance where he or she can observe and have the opportunity to slide during the dance routine.

 ## Specific Objective J

The student hops.

Teacher Interventions

Toddler/Preschool and Primary Levels.   Assist the student as he or she hops. Demonstrate hopping and encourage the student to imitate your actions. Practice.

Play the music for the "Bunny Hop." Demonstrate and ask the student to join you in doing the "Bunny Hop."

Play Simon Says. As one of the commands, say, "Simon says, 'Hop on one foot.'" Develop the student's ability to hop on both the left and right foot.

Family Interventions

Toddler/Preschool and Primary Levels.   When age appropriate, ask the parents to read their child a story about rabbits (e.g., "Peter Rabbit"). Tell them to ask the child to pretend he or she is a rabbit and to hop around the room.

Ask the parents to use masking tape (indoors) or marking chalk (outdoors) and mark out a hopscotch court. Tell them to show their child how to play hopscotch.

 ### Specific Objective K

The student jumps.

Teacher Interventions

Primary Level.   Assist the student as he or she jumps. Demonstrate jumping and encourage the student to imitate your actions.

Place a box with low sides on the floor. Show the student how to jump into and out of the box. Assist him or her in doing so.

Show the student how to jump over a rope. Ask two students to hold the end of the rope flat on the floor. Tell the student to jump over it; then raise it a little. Raise it gradually so that the student must jump a little higher at each turn. Be sure there are mats under the rope, and be aware of any safety factors involved in jumping.

Family Interventions

Toddler/Preschool and Primary Levels.   Ask the parents to supervise their child in activities that involve jumping, such as jumping rope, exercises, and broad jumping.

Specific Objective L

The student skips.

Teacher Interventions

Primary Level. Demonstrate skipping and encourage the student to imitate your actions. Practice.

Play "A Tisket, a Tasket" and ask the student to skip as he or she acts out the song. One student can carry a letter or object. The other students sit on the floor in a large circle. The student with the letter or object skips around the circle and drops it behind one person. That person picks it up, skips after the other, and tries to catch the student before he or she gets to the other student's place in the circle.

Play "Skip to My Lou" and other folk dances that require or suggest skipping.

Family Interventions

Toddler/Preschool and Primary Levels. Ask the parents to take their child to the park, perhaps as part of a family outing. Ask them to have their child skip on the grass. Have them check to make sure the area is free of glass and other debris that might be dangerous.

Have the parents repeat the above activity on a beach. Encourage them to plan games or activities that involve skipping.

 ## Specific Objective M

The student dances.

Teacher Interventions

Primary Level. Plan a dance. Invite another class or group of students and ask them to dance to popular music.

Teach the students some simple square dances. Take students individually and in twos through the steps. Do the dances to spoken commands before using the music. Once the students learn a dance or two, arrange for them to perform for others or demonstrate to other classes.

Family Interventions

Primary Level. Ask the parents to assist their child in learning to dance. Tell them to demonstrate different types of dancing.

When available, have the parents take their child to a dance recital or performance. Have them point out the dancing etiquette and rules (e.g., when to switch partners and how to ask someone for a dance).

Have the parents identify types of events that may have dancing, such as weddings, school dances, or birthday parties.

Specific Objective N

The student climbs.

Teacher Interventions

Primary Level. Construct an obstacle course. Include obstacles that may be climbed over. As the student goes through the obstacle course, make sure he or she climbs over things whenever possible.

Take the student to the gym. Demonstrate climbing up a knotted rope. Help the student climb up the rope. Be sure to use mats and spotters for safety during this activity.

Take the student to the school playground and practice climbing (e.g., climbing on a jungle gym).

Family Interventions

Primary Level. Ask the parents to take their child to a playground or neighborhood park. Have them assist their child in climbing on play equipment. Have them point out the safety rules that should be followed when one is climbing.

Specific Objective O

The student rides Big Wheels, tricycles, and bicycles.

Teacher Interventions

Primary Level. When appropriate, seat the student on a Big Wheel, tricycle, or bicycle. Place the student's feet on the pedals and secure them with pedal straps. Move the student's legs in a pedaling motion. Encourage the student to pedal independently. For the student who has difficulty reaching the pedals, construct wooden blocks to affix to the pedals.

Place brightly colored tape on the floor to form a path. Encourage the student to follow the path on his or her tricycle.

Make Big Wheels, tricycles, and bicycles available during free time and encourage the student to ride them in activities such as "Follow the Leader." Use age-appropriate equipment.

Family Interventions

Primary Level. Ask the parents to assist their child in riding Big Wheels, tricycles, and bicycles. Tell them to let the child get on a Big Wheel, tricycle, or bicycle and then gently move until he or she feels safe on the moving vehicle. Ask them to select equipment that is safe, as well as age and size appropriate.

Ask the parents to bring their child to a playground or an area where other children are safely riding their Big Wheels, tricycles, or bicycles. After observing appropriate riding habits, ask them to have their child ride similar equipment.

Sample Lesson Plan 1

Topic Area: Gross Motor Skills

Designed by: Sarabeth Scamper

Time Recommended: 30 Minutes

Student Involved: Daphne (Primary Special Class)

Background Information:

The student has limited receptive language. She appears to comprehend one-step oral directions. She responds to positive verbal and token reinforcements. She enjoys group activities and will model behaviors of other students. She does not participate in activities that require discriminations of several degrees.

Goal *(Gross Motor Skills III)*:

The student will be able to move or walk, with or without assistive devices, to a degree that will allow him or her to function optimally in diverse settings.

Specific Objective *(Gross Motor Skills III-D)*:

The student walks or moves in a wheelchair in a line.

Lesson Objective:

When the student is asked, she will get into a line to move with a group to an activity in another location in the school.

Materials and Equipment:

- Red balls
- Bucket large enough to accommodate several balls
- Tape on the floor in a line leading to the door

Motivating Activity:

Announce a reward system for students getting into line when requested. Provide the students a token for use in a graduated reward system or a food reward when the class lines up to go to a group class activity.

Instructional Procedures:

Initiation—Tell Daphne that she is to put the ball you hand her into a red bucket held by the last student in line. Have each student in the class get in line one at a time. Give Daphne a ball and ask her to place the ball in the bucket held by the student.

Guided Practice—Have another student get in line, then point out the student standing on the tape. Hand Daphne another red ball and walk her to the line to place the ball in the bucket of the last student. Ask the student to get in line and hold the bucket. Give Daphne a ball and have her place it in the last student's bucket. Repeat this activity, pointing to the line each time; have Daphne stand on the line and put the red ball in the bucket held by the next student. Give Daphne verbal instructions to go to the line each time.

Independent Practice—Have Daphne go to stand on the line behind the student with the bucket. Repeat this activity until Daphne will go to the last student without the prompt of the ball and bucket.

Closure—Ask the class to get in line to visit another classroom in the building. Have Daphne take a red ball while she gets in line behind another student.

Assessment Strategy:

Observe the student to determine whether she correctly and quickly responded to the instruction to get in line.

Follow-Up Activity or Objective:

If the student achieves the lesson objective, proceed to a lesson involving the student in a game of Follow the Leader.

Sample Lesson Plan 2

Topic Area: Gross Motor Skills

Designed by: Dwight Eisen

Time Recommended: 30 Minutes

Student Involved: Candace (Preschool Special Class)

Background Information:

The student is able to stand and has full use of both arms. The student understands simple directions and responds positively to food rewards and verbal praise.

Goal (Gross Motor Skills IV):

The student will acquire those gross motor skills that are an integral part of recreation and leisure activities.

Specific Objective (Gross Motor Skills IV-B):

The student throws balls, beanbags, Frisbees, and other recreational equipment.

Lesson Objective:

When the student is asked, she throws an object toward a target, hitting it or getting it into the object.

Materials and Equipment:

- Beanbags
- Tire
- Hula hoop
- Nerf balls
- Scorekeeper

Motivating Activity:

Have several students sit in a small circle around the hula hoop. Demonstrate throwing the beanbag into the center of the hula hoop. As each student throws the bag into the circle, have the group applaud.

Instructional Procedures:

Initiation—Demonstrate the bag toss into the hula hoop. Assist the student to throw the bag by standing behind her and assisting her.

Guided Practice—Then say, "Let's have you throw the bag and get it into the hoop." Have the student toss the bag and reward the student with praise for each successive approximation until the student can throw the bag into the hula hoop at least once.

Independent Practice—Ask the student to throw the beanbags into the hula hoop. Record each successful throw on the scorekeeper.

Closure—Ask the student to throw Nerf balls into a tire with one demonstration.

Assessment Strategy:

Observe the student to determine whether she correctly throws the beanbags into the hula hoop and the Nerf balls into the tire.

Follow-Up Activity or Objective:

If the student achieves the lesson objective, proceed to a lesson involving tossing the beanbags into progressively smaller cylinders.

References

Adil, J. R. (1994). *Accessible gardening for people with physical disabilities: A guide to methods, tools, and plants.* Bethesda, MD: Woodbine House.

Cipani, E., Augustine, A., & Blomgren, E. (1982). Teaching profoundly retarded adults to ascend stairs safely. *Education and Training of the Mentally Retarded, 17,* 51–54.

Geralis, E. (Ed.). (1991). *Children with cerebral palsy—A parents' guide.* Bethesda, MD: Woodbine House.

Gruber, B., Reeser, B., & Reid, D. H. (1979). Providing a less restrictive environment for profoundly retarded persons by teaching independent walking skills. *Journal of Applied Behavior Analysis, 12,* 285–297.

Kriegsman, K. H., Zaslow, E. L., & D'Zmura-Rechsteiner, J. (1992). *Taking charge—Teenagers talk about life and physical disabilities.* Bethesda, MD: Woodbine House.

Presland, J. (1982). *Paths to mobility in "special care": A guide to teaching gross motor skills to very handicapped children.* Kidderminster, Worcestershire, England: BIMH Publications.

Angney, A., & Hanley, E. M. (1979). A parent-implemented shaping procedure to develop independent walking of a Down's syndrome child: A case study. *Education and Treatment of Children, 2,* 311–315.

Bergen, A. (1974). *Selected equipment for pediatric rehabilitation.* Valhalla, NY: Blythedale Children's Hospital.

Bergman, T. (1989). *On our own terms, children living with physical disabilities.* Milwaukee, WI: Gareth Stevens.

Beter, T. R., Cragin, W. E., & Drury, F. D. (1972). *The mentally retarded child and his motor behavior.* Springfield, IL: Thomas.

Block, M. E. (1992). What is appropriate physical education for students with profound disabilities? *Adapted Physical Activity Quarterly, 9,* 197–213.

Bobath, B., & Bobath, K. (1975). *Motor development in the different types of cerebral palsy.* London: Heineman Medical.

Cipani, E., Augustine, A., & Blomgren, E. (1980). Teaching the severely and profoundly retarded to open doors: Assessment and training. *Journal of Special Education Technology, 3,* 42–46.

Colvin, N. R., & Finholt, J. M. (1981). *Guidelines for physical educators of mentally handicapped youth: Curriculum, assessment, IEP's.* Springfield, IL: Thomas.

Cratty, B. J. (1975). *Remedial motor activity for children.* Philadelphia: Lea & Febiger.

Finnie, N. R. (1975). *Handling the young cerebral palsied child at home.* New York: Dutton.

Fraser, B. A., Galka, G., & Hensinger, R. N. (1980). *Gross motor management of severely multiply impaired students. Vol. I: Evaluation guide.* Austin, TX: PRO-ED.

Galka, G., Fraser, B. A., & Hensinger, R. N. (1980). *Gross motor management of severely multiply impaired students. Vol. II: Curriculum model.* Austin, TX: PRO-ED.

Geddes, D. (1974). *Physical activities for individuals with handicapping conditions.* St. Louis, MO: Mosby.

Hallahan, D., & Kauffman, J. (1991). *Exceptional children: Introduction to special education.* Englewood Cliffs, NJ: Prentice-Hall.

Hughes, J., & Riley, A. (1981). Basic gross motor assessment: Tools for use with children having minor motor dysfunction. *Physical Therapy, 61,* 502–511.

Jenkins, J. R., Fewell, R., & Harris, S. R. (1983). Comparison of sensory integrative therapy and motor programming. *American Journal of Mental Deficiency, 88,* 221–224.

Millen, H. M. (1974). *Body mechanics and safe transfer techniques.* Detroit: Aronsson.

Mullins, J. (1979). *A teacher's guide to management of physically handicapped students.* Springfield, IL: Thomas.

Ottenbacher, K., Short, M. A., & Watson, P. J. (1981). The effects of a clinically applied program of vestibular stimulation on the neuromotor performance of children with severe developmental disability. *Physical and Occupational Therapy in Pediatrics, 1*, 1–11.

Pearson, P., & Williams, C. (Eds.). (1972). *Physical therapy services in the developmental disabilities.* Springfield, IL: Thomas.

Rarick, G. L., & Dobbins, D. A. (1972). *Basic components in the motor performance of educable mentally retarded children: Implications for curriculum development.* Berkeley: University of California Press.

Riani, R. M., & McNeny, R. (1981). Wheelchair clinic: A better way to prescribe. *Clinical Management in Physical Therapy, 1*, 18–19.

Robinault, L. P. (1973). *Functional aid for the multiply handicapped.* New York: Harper-Collins.

Schmidt, R. A. (1975). *Motor skills.* New York: HarperCollins.

Sellick, K. J., & Over, R. (1980). Effects of vestibular stimulation on motor development of cerebral palsied children. *Developmental Medicine and Child Neurology, 22*, 476–483.

Sherrill, C. (1980). Posture training as a means of normalization. *Mental Retardation, 18*, 135–138.

Stainback, S., Stainback, W., Wehman, P., & Spangiers, L. (1983). Acquisition and generalization of physical fitness exercises in three profoundly retarded adults. *Journal of The Association of the Severely Handicapped, 8*, 47–55.

Stein, J. U. (1977). Physical education, recreation and sports for special populations. *Education and Training of the Mentally Retarded, 12*, 4–13.

Stephens, B., Baumgartner, B. B., Smeets, P. M., & Wolfinger, W. (1976). Promoting motor development in young retarded children. In R. Anderson & J. Greer (Eds.), *Educating the severely and profoundly retarded.* Baltimore: University Park Press.

Stewart, B., & Vargas, J. (1990). *Teaching behavior to infants and toddlers: A manual for caregivers and parents.* Springfield, IL: Thomas.

Vannier, M. (1977). *Physical activities for the handicapped.* Englewood Cliffs, NJ: Prentice-Hall.

Wehman, P., & Marchant, J. (1977). Development of gross motor recreation skills in children with severe behavioral handicaps. *Therapeutic Recreation Journal, 11*, 48–54.

Wheeler, R. H., & Hooley, A. M. (1976). *Physical education for the handicapped.* Philadelphia: Lea & Febiger.

Selected Materials/Resources

KITS/CURRICULAR MATERIALS

- *Goal Oriented Gross and Fine Motor Lesson Plans*
  VORT Corporation
  PO Box 60880
  Palo Alto, California 94306
  (415) 322-8282

- *Tips from Tots: Developmental Activity Pamphlets*
  VORT Corporation
  PO Box 60880
  Palo Alto, California 94306
  (415) 322-8282

- *Young Children in Action* (English and Spanish)
  Kaplan School Supply Corporation
  1310 Lewisville-Clemmons Road
  PO Box 609
  Lewisville, North Carolina 27023-0609
  (800) 334-2014

VIDEOS

- *Armchair Fitness*
  Hammatt Senior Products
  PO Box 727
  Mount Vernon, Washington 98273
  (206) 428-5850

- *Children with Motor Impairments* (two videocassettes)
  HOPE, Inc.
  809 North 800 East
  Logan, Utah 84321
  (801) 752-9533

- *I Can Fundamental Skills* (two videotapes and guide)
  PRO-ED, Inc.
  8700 Shoal Creek Boulevard
  Austin, Texas 78758-9965
  (512) 451-3246

- *Living with Spinal Cord Injury* (three videocassettes)
  Fanlight Productions
  47 Halifax Street
  Boston, Massachusetts 02130
  (800) 937-4113

- *Pediatric Developmental Diagnosis Videotape Set*
  (Birth–6 years)
  DDM, Inc.
  PO Box 6919
  Denver, Colorado 80206-0919
  (303) 355-4729

- *Promoting Motor Development*
  Learner Managed Designs, Inc.
  2201-K West 25th Street
  Lawrence, Kansas 66047
  (913) 842-9088

- *Rolling Along: Children in Wheelchairs at School*
  (Skill videotape)
  Learner Managed Designs, Inc.
  2201-K West 25th Street
  Lawrence, Kansas 66047
  (913) 842-9088

ASSISTIVE DEVICES

- *Maddacrawler:* Crawler for play and therapeutic activities
  Jesana Ltd.
  PO Box 17
  Irvington, New York 10533
  (800) 443-4728

- *Scooter Lift/Carrier: Load Without Lifting*
  R-D Butler & Co., Inc.
  65 Ryan Drive F-1
  Raynham, Massachusetts 02767
  (508) 823-7799

- *Touch Turner-Page Turning Devices*
  Touch Turner Company
  443 View Ridge Drive
  Everett, Washington 98203
  (206) 252-1541

Fine Motor Skills

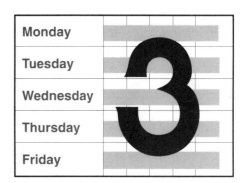

| Monday |
| Tuesday |
| Wednesday |
| Thursday |
| Friday |

Proficiency in the use of the hands, arms, and upper torso is vital to progress in most activities of daily living. Foremost among these skills are those involved in activities that enable individuals to care for themselves in their environment. Self-care development, including eating and dressing, manipulation of toys and other playthings, as well as the use of utensils and other tools, is largely dependent upon growth in fine motor skills (Edgar, Maser, & Haring, 1977; Sternlicht & Hurwitz, 1981; Clark & Humphrey, 1985; Stinson, 1990). The intent of this unit is to provide the reader with goals, specific objectives, and suggested activities that highlight the acquisition of *functionally relevant* fine motor skills.

In past editions of this curriculum, the unit on fine motor skills has included goals, objectives, and activities in the prevocational area. Prevocational skills were included to stress their great dependence upon facilitation of proficiency in the area of fine motor skills, while still recognizing the critical role of cognitive and effective skills in vocational adjustment. After consultations and reviews from specialists in the employment, career, and technology areas, these goals, objectives, and activities, due to their increased importance, have expanded as a curricular area, and will be included in Volume IV, *Interpersonal Skills, Competitive Job-Finding, and Leisure Time Skills* (Bender, Valletutti, & Baglin, in press), of this curriculum series.

The objectives for initial, and therefore fundamental, manipulative skills, including grasping, releasing, touching, and passing objects, were developed from a review of professional literature (Banus, Kent, Norton, Sukiennicki, & Becker, 1979; Erhardt, 1994; Lombardi, 1992). In addition, we consulted with occupational therapists and developmental pediatricians and nurses; Part H coordinators of infants' and toddlers' programs; parents; and other professionals who work in early intervention programs serving populations of children with a range of disabilities.

The fine motor skills involved in dressing and undressing are included in both the Self-Care Skills and Fine Motor Skills units of this curriculum because these skills have been designated as priority needs of individuals with disabilities by occupational therapists, special educators, and parents. The emphasis in the self-care experiences is on achieving the task. The goal of the fine motor area activities is to use the task as a means of enhancing fine motor skills (Kramer & Whitehurst, 1981; Redleaf, 1994).

The fine motor areas involving goals, objectives, and activities associated with leisure-time activities have been extracted from this unit and expanded and will be more fully developed as a total curriculum area in Volume IV (Bender, Valletutti, & Baglin, in press). The decision to separate curricular content in this area and place it in its own volume was a natural evolution resulting from the increased emphasis on leisure, or nonwork activities, in the lives of individuals with disabilities. Additionally, leisure-time activities should be employed as a means of encouraging fine motor development because almost all toys and games require some use of the hands and arms, especially the toys and games of young children.

Although the use of the upper extremities in operating simple appliances, objects, conveniences, and home accessories also involves the development of fine motor skills, the discussion of these skills is more appropriately presented in Unit 4 ("Household Management and Living Skills"), which contains the functional settings and suggested instructional activities for these skills.

The Suggested Readings and Selected Materials/Resources at the end of this unit provide information on the fine motor skill areas discussed in the unit. The reader should decide which materials and information are applicable to a specific student or students being taught. Toys or games mentioned in the unit can be found in local toy stores or can be ordered through educational catalogs. Recent publications, such as the *Toy Guide for Differently-Abled* by Toys R Us (1994), have started to address the area of toys being developed or adapted for use by children with ranges of abilities. Organizations such as the National Parent Network on Disabilities can be consulted for additional information in these areas.

General Goals of This Unit

I. The student will acquire those initial manipulative skills that will facilitate the development of more advanced fine motor skills and the functional use of the upper extremities.

II. The student will undress and dress using those fine motor skills that will allow him or her to function as optimally as possible.

III. The student will engage in leisure-time activities involving the use of the upper extremities and will do so using those fine motor skills that will allow him or her to function optimally.

IV. The student will acquire those fine motor skills that will enable him or her to use his or her upper extremities optimally in vocational/work activities.

V. The student will acquire those fine motor skills that will allow him or her to use his or her upper extremities optimally in operating simple appliances, objects, conveniences, and home accessories.

GOAL I.

The student will acquire those initial manipulative skills that will facilitate the development of more advanced fine motor skills and the functional use of the upper extremities.

SPECIFIC OBJECTIVES

The student:

- ❐ A. Touches and holds objects, toys, and playthings.
- ❐ B. Reaches for and grasps objects.
- ❐ C. Releases small objects, toys, and playthings.
- ❐ D. Picks up objects, materials, and playthings.
- ❐ E. Passes objects, materials, and playthings.
- ❐ F. Places objects, materials, and playthings into appropriate forms.

SUGGESTED ACTIVITIES

 ### Specific Objective A

The student touches and holds objects, toys, and playthings.

Teacher Interventions

Infant and Toddler/Preschool Level. Place a board covered with various materials in front of the student. Include sandpaper, felt, silk, leather, and wood. Tell the student to touch different parts of the board, or touch one yourself and urge the student to imitate your behavior. Emphasize the characteristics or properties of the materials as they are being touched.

Primary Level. If there is a juice or snack time or time when materials are to be passed out to other students in the room, give the student the material or containers of juice to hold for you. Point out to the student that he or she is holding the juice or other materials, and thank him or her for being a good helper. Practice this activity daily.

Identify objects or things that should never be touched. Examples are functioning hot plates, stove burners that are on, exposed wires, and objects with razor-type edges. Also identify objects or things that can be touched, but only under certain conditions. Examples include a light bulb that has been off for a period of time, and appliances such as fans and irons.

Family Interventions

Infant and Toddler/Preschool Level. Ask the parents to demonstrate touching and feeling different common objects. Tell them to have their child touch soft items such as pillows or felt and hard objects such as appliances and furniture.

Ask the parents to visit a neighborhood playground during play time. Have them give their child several pieces of play equipment to hold. When other children need the equipment, have them tell their child to give it to them. Have parents provide opportunities for other children to hold equipment and point this out to their child.

Specific Objective B

The student reaches for and grasps objects.

Teacher Interventions

Primary Level. Take the student out to the playground or into the gym where there is a chinning bar. Lift the student up (make sure all safety precautions are observed) and tell him or her to reach and grasp the bar. Reinforce the student with verbal praise if he or she does it appropriately.

Present small objects for the student to grasp that he or she would come in contact with on a regular basis. These could include salt and pepper shakers, articles of clothing, toys, and writing instruments. Monitor how well he or she grasps these articles and reinforce him or her when he or she does it correctly.

Family Interventions

Infant and Toddler/Preschool Level. Ask the parents to place a small object in front of their child. Ask them to demonstrate reaching for the object and bringing it close to them. Ask them to tell the child to imitate their actions by reaching for the objects in front of him or her. They should reinforce this activity by saying, "Good job," if the child reaches for the object. If the child reaches for the object, he or she should be allowed to play with it.

Primary Level. Ask the parents, when they have a letter to mail, to take their child to a mailbox on the street. Select a mailbox that requires the pulling down and holding of a handle to reveal the mail slot. Ask them to tell their child to mail the letter after demonstrating how the handle of the mailbox has to be grasped, held, and pulled down. Have them ask their child to imitate their actions and insert the letter in the mailbox slot.

 ## Specific Objective C

The student releases small objects, toys, and playthings.

Teacher Interventions

Primary Level. As part of a leisure activity, play the game Blockhead, in which the student has to pile, balance, and release blocks. Emphasize the words "Let go" to the student as he or she withdraws his or her hand from a block that has just been balanced.

Ask the student to pass out small paper plates and paper cups during a party. Praise him or her if he or she releases the plates and cups correctly.

Family Interventions

Infant and Toddler/Preschool Levels. Ask the parents to bring their child to a playground where there is a sandbox. Have them bring some plastic containers with them and ask their child to place some sand in his or her hand and fill the containers by releasing the sand into them.

Ask the parents to play with their child when he or she is playing with his or her toys. Ask them to tell the child to pass toys to them and praise him or her if he or she releases the toys at the appropriate time. Ask them to practice this activity with their child.

 ### Specific Objective D

The student picks up objects, materials, and playthings.

Teacher Interventions

Infant and Toddler/Preschool and Primary Levels. Play a matching game in which you place a set of objects in front of you and a duplicate set in front of the student. You pick up and hold up an object, and the child must pick his or her duplicate object and hold it up. The child then goes first, and you continue taking turns. Vary the types of objects and include ones that may be difficult to pick up.

During a leisure activity, play games that involve picking up playing objects (e.g., dominoes, bingo space markers, checkers, and marbles).

Family Interventions

Infant and Toddler/Preschool and Primary Levels. Ask the parents to play leisure-time games with their child such as pick-up sticks. Ask them to reinforce their child for efforts in trying to pick up the sticks.

Ask the parents to take their child to a field that has flowers that may be picked. (Avoid fields with poison ivy, obstacles, or vines that may lead to accidents.) Have them ask the child to pick as many flowers as he or she can and bring them back a bouquet. Reward the child for doing a good job by tying a bow around the bouquet and asking him or her to whom he or she would like to give the flowers.

Specific Objective E

The student passes objects, materials, and playthings.

Teacher Interventions

Primary Level. At the end of the day, tell the student to help you pass out papers or materials to the other students. Give the student a pile of papers that are to be sent home, and tell him or her to pass one paper to each student.

Play recreational games that require the passing of an object. For example, place the students in a circle and give one student a beanbag. Tell the students to pass the beanbag as long as they hear music playing in the background. When the music stops, the one holding the beanbag has to sit down. The student who is left is the winner. Similar games such as Time Bomb can be played.

Family Interventions

Primary Level. Ask the parents to request certain condiments to be passed during a meal. Ask them to praise their child if he or she passes these items appropriately. The parents should use judgment regarding objects that are too heavy or fragile or that have contents that are easily spilled.

Have the parents ask their child to pass them some sporting equipment while on the playground or at a recreational center. Tell them to praise the child if he or she does it correctly and tell him or her to play or participate in games as a reward. Caution the parents to observe appropriate safety procedures for passing different types of objects.

Specific Objective F

The student places objects, materials, and playthings into appropriate forms.

Teacher Interventions

Primary Level. During leisure time, present the student with many toys that require the placing of one part on or into another. Present games to the student such as Lego, Rig-a-Jig, Lincoln Logs, Tinkertoys, and erector sets.

    If the student uses a lunch box or container, see if he or she puts away his or her thermos after eating. If the student needs help, assist him or her in correctly putting away his or her thermos in its lunch box holder.

Family Interventions

Primary Level. Ask the parents to demonstrate the placing of puzzle parts into their corresponding forms. Ask them to tell their child to imitate what they have done, and have them give their child a simple four- or five-piece wooden puzzle.

    At the time of a birthday or when candles are part of holiday celebrations or decorations, ask the parents as part of a home leisure activity to place candle holders in front of their child and tell him or her to place candles in them. If the child does it correctly, they should tell him or her that he or she may put the birthday candle holders on the cake or help with the holiday decorations.

GOAL II.

The student will undress and dress using those fine motor skills that allow him or her to function as optimally as possible.

SPECIFIC OBJECTIVES

The student:

❏ A. Opens and closes zippers.

❏ B. Opens and closes Velcro.

❏ C. Buttons and unbuttons clothing.

❏ D. Opens and closes snaps.

❏ E. Hooks and unhooks hooks and eyes.

❏ F. Laces and ties a bowknot.

SUGGESTED ACTIVITIES

Specific Objective A

The student opens and closes zippers.

Teacher Interventions

Primary Level. Show the student how to zip and unzip boots and shoes with zippers. Assist him or her in doing so during actual dressing and undressing times. Avoid zippers that are poorly made or extremely small. Also emphasize safety precautions while teaching any process involving zipping and unzipping.

When both opening and closing zippers have been mastered, show the student how to dress in clothes such as jackets or car coats with zippers that need to be started on their track by the wearer. Demonstrate how to line up the two sides of the zipper and then insert the right prong into the zipper track casing. Once the student masters this operation and has practiced sufficiently, show him or her how to complete the zipping and unzipping processes.

Family Interventions

Primary Level. Ask the parents to show their child how to open and close non-clothing items such as carrying cases, pillowcases, and shaving kits. Tell them to show their child how to use his or her thumb and index finger in opposition to hold the zipper tag. Tell them to use an oversize tag if necessary, especially during the beginning stages.

Ask the parents to then proceed to opening and closing zippers on clothing items (pants, dresses, and skirts). Encourage the parents to select clothing with zippers that are well made and that work easily.

Specific Objective B

The student opens and closes Velcro.

Teacher Interventions

Toddler/Preschool and Primary Levels. When appropriate, plan a Halloween party where the student dresses up. Provide costumes that use Velcro fasteners. Praise the student if he or she puts on and uses the Velcro fasteners correctly.

Plan an exhibit or demonstration of the different ways clothing can be fastened (i.e., buttons, zippers, snaps, and Velcro). Point out the Velcro fasteners and encourage the student to use them. Also include articles such as shoes and sporting equipment/accessories that use Velcro as fasteners.

Family Interventions

Toddler/Preschool and Primary Levels. When appropriate, ask the parents to sew Velcro on clothing that their child has difficulty in opening or closing. Ask them to practice the making of these fasteners with their child.

Ask the parents to include clothing with Velcro fasteners as part of their child's wardrobe at appropriate times (going shopping, going to school, or running an errand). Ask them to tell their child to select clothing with these fasteners and praise the child if he or she uses the fasteners correctly.

 ## Specific Objective C

The student buttons and unbuttons clothing.

Teacher Interventions

Primary Level. When appropriate, play dress-up in a parent's clothes, costumes, or oversize clothes. Tell the student to select garments that have buttons.

Once the student has shown some skill in buttoning, show him or her how to unbutton. Demonstrate how to use the thumb and index finger of one hand to pull the cloth over the button while pushing it through the hole with the other hand. It may be necessary to use large buttons and oversize clothing in the beginning.

Family Interventions

Toddler/Preschool and Primary Levels. Ask the parents to assist their child in buttoning his or her clothing during actual dressing times. Tell the parents to establish a buttoning pattern (e.g., top to bottom) and to select a variety of buttons used as fasteners. The parents may wish to use buttoning aids, when necessary.

Ask the parents to engage in unbuttoning activities with their child during actual undressing times such as toileting, before showers and baths, before changing clothes for recreational and work activities, and before bedtime.

 ## Specific Objective D

The student opens and closes snaps.

Teacher Interventions

Primary Level.   During leisure time, demonstrate to the student how to snap (age-appropriate) wooden toys together by inserting the snap into its holding receptacle. Assist the student in connecting these toys together. Once the student succeeds in snapping these toys together, show him or her how to slip his or her thumb tip under the snap and pull it open with the index fingertip and thumb tip acting in opposition.

For the student who appears to be having difficulty with snapping, demonstrate these movements on a snapping frame. Assist the student in doing so. Use a selection of different snaps as fasteners and avoid those snaps that are poorly made, too small, and/or just decorative.

Family Interventions

Infant and Toddler/Preschool Level.   When appropriate, ask the parents to use aids in helping to teach their child how to open and close snaps. For example, the parents can use a Dapper Dan and/or Dressie Bessie doll to demonstrate the snapping or unsnapping procedure.

Ask the parents to then proceed to snapping and unsnapping clothing during dressing and undressing situations. Suggest that they use oversize clothing with oversize snaps in the beginning and gradually reduce the size of the clothing and snaps.

 ## Specific Objective E

The student hooks and unhooks hooks and eyes.

Teacher Interventions

Primary Level.   Show the student how to use the thumb and index finger of one hand to hold the eye in place and the other hand's thumb and index finger to guide the hook into the eye. Begin by using an appropriate hook-and-eye board. Assist the student in modeling and practicing your actions.

During dressing activities, practice with the student putting on a skirt, dress, or pants with hooks and eyes. (Note: For this activity, male teachers should ask a female aide, class mother, or female teacher to assist a female student and vice versa.)

Family Interventions

Primary and Secondary Levels.   Ask the mother to encourage her daughter to practice hooking and unhooking a dress or bra with a hook and eye or similar closure in the back or front. Tell her to remind her daughter to use a mirror to help her find the hook and eye. Also remind her to tell her daughter to feel with her fingers to find the hook and eye. The daughter should also close her eyes and practice relying on touch alone.

It may be necessary for the father to assist his son in using the modified hook and eye often found at the top of a pair of pants. This hook and eye is a sort of sliding hook that slips into a channel. Tell the father that he should assist his son in hooking and unhooking this modified hook and eye whenever he is dressing and undressing until he does it independently. Suggest the avoidance of hooks and eyes that are poorly made, are too small, or serve only a decorative function.

 Specific Objective F

The student laces and ties a bowknot.

Teacher Interventions

Primary Level.   Show the student how to tie and knot shoelaces used during recreational activities (on sneakers, running and sports shoes, bowling shoes, roller and ice skates, and tennis shoes). Assist the student in doing so during recreational pursuits. Lacing shoes in order to participate in an athletic event or to be part of a team may provide the motivation that will assist the student in simple shoelace tying.

During leisure time, show the student how to lace a lacing card. Assist him or her in lacing. Most lacing cards come with patterns; therefore, help the student follow the pattern. Begin with simple patterns and work up to those that are increasingly more difficult.

Family Interventions

Primary Level. Ask the parents to show their child how to tie a shoelace in a bowknot. (Note: It may be more practical to buy only loafers or shoes with Velcro fasteners for the child if there is inordinate difficulty in learning to tie a shoelace.)

 Tell the parents to show their daughter how to tie a bowknot on the top of nightgowns, some blouses, and capes. Tell them to assist her in doing so and reward her for dressing neatly.

GOAL III.

The student will engage in leisure-time activities involving the use of the upper extremities and will do so using those fine motor skills that will allow him or her to function optimally.

SPECIFIC OBJECTIVES

The student:

☐ A. Holds, picks up, and plays with small toys and playthings such as noisemakers, clothespins, pot covers, and boxes.

☐ B. Passes small toys and playthings to a peer or significant adult.

☐ C. Builds with blocks and other playthings.

☐ D. Sifts, shapes, pours, and builds with sand.

☐ E. Fills containers, pours, and otherwise engages in play with water.

☐ F. Strings beads, spools, and other playthings.

☐ G. Finger paints.

☐ H. Fits pieces of puzzles, pegs, and other playthings into their corresponding forms.

☐ I. Pastes paper and objects onto paper.

☐ J. Colors with crayons on paper or in a coloring book.

☐ K. Molds and shapes clay, Play Doh, and plasticene and makes objects with these materials.

☐ L. Bends and shapes pipe cleaners.

☐ M. Weaves using simple forms.

☐ N. Folds and constructs out of paper and cardboard.

☐ O. Spins wheels and dials and also throws dice in table games.

☐ P. Cuts with scissors.

☐ Q. Shuffles, deals, and performs other tasks involved in playing simple card games.

☐ R. Sketches and draws simple objects with crayons, colored pencils, charcoal, and/or colored chalk.

☐ S. Draws and paints with a brush and paints.

☐ T. Sews and makes simple clothing out of fabric.

☐ U. Constructs using one medium, such as wood or other natural materials.

☐ V. Constructs using several media, including paper, wood, fabric, leather, cord, yarn, and natural materials (shells, grass, rice, beans, and macaroni).

☐ W. Embroiders, crochets, knits, and does needlepoint and macrame.

SUGGESTED ACTIVITIES

 ## Specific Objective A

The student holds, picks up, and plays with small toys and playthings such as noisemakers, clothespins, pot covers, and boxes.

Teacher Interventions

Toddler/Preschool and Primary Levels. During play time, give the student clay or Play Doh balls that he or she can hold and squeeze. Show him or her how to play with them. Use a Nerf ball for variety.

Place in front of the student a colorful stuffed animal, doll, or other soft toy such as a squeeze toy with a noisemaker. Demonstrate how to pick up the object by using the thumb in opposition to all of the fingers. Encourage the student to model your behavior and assist if necessary. A squeeze toy with a noisemaker is often reinforcing. Select toys that are age appropriate and avoid toys with small parts, sharp edges, or parts that can be easily swallowed.

Family Interventions

Toddler/Preschool and Primary Levels.   Ask the parents to observe young children at play as they explore their world with their hands. Ask them to make an inventory of objects that fascinate their child. Remind them that nontoys are often more intriguing to children than commercial products, and they should provide opportunities for their child to play with both. Emphasize that the parents should select objects and toys that are well constructed and have a minimum of parts.

Ask the parents to play games that include picking up small objects, such as checkers, dominoes, bingo, and pick-up sticks.

 ## Specific Objective B

The student passes small toys and playthings to a peer or significant adult.

Teacher Interventions

Toddler/Preschool and Primary Levels.   Play the "Hidden Object" game. Hide a favored toy in your hand. Encourage the student to find the hand in which it is hidden. When the student does so, pass the object to him or her. Then reverse roles; encourage the student to hide the object and to pass it to you when you guess the hand in which it is hidden.

Arrange the students in a circle and play a game of passing objects. Use a beanbag, ball, or stuffed toy. For variation, play music and tell the student to stop passing the object when the music stops and to start passing it again when the music starts. When needed, modify the objects so they can be easily held.

Family Interventions

Infant and Toddler/Preschool and Primary Levels.   Ask the parents to play games with their child that involve passing small toys to each other (e.g., miniature furniture to be placed in a dollhouse). Use safe, age-appropriate toys that are well constructed and have a minimum number of parts.

Ask the parents to carry out an assembly task while the child passes them needed objects (e.g., a large toy nut to be attached to a large toy bolt). Ask them to avoid objects with sharp points or sharp edges and objects that can be easily swallowed.

Specific Objective C

The student builds with blocks and other playthings.

Teacher Interventions

Toddler/Preschool and Primary Levels.   Give the student, during play time, two 3-by-3-inch blocks, and take two for yourself. With your pair of blocks, stack one on top of the other. Indicate to the student in some way that he or she is to construct a building just like yours. Assist the student if necessary. If the student is successful, give him or her three, then four, then five blocks, and indicate in some way that he or she is to build a taller building each time. For variety, use paper cups, poker chips, books, and boxes. Encourage the student to construct tall houses and buildings. Assist when necessary.

Give the student a collection of cartons of varying sizes, and encourage him or her to build various structures. Assist when necessary.

Family Interventions

Infant and Toddler/Preschool and Primary Levels.   Ask the parents to use large wooden blocks constructed by makers of educational toys and games to build roads, platforms, and tunnels. Tell them to encourage their child to build similar structures. Tell them to start with large blocks and then build small towns and cities with standard-size blocks. Toys should be age appropriate and safe.

Ask the parents to give their child a collection of nontoys (e.g., pudding boxes and cans) and encourage their child to build various structures. Ask them to avoid objects with sharp edges or points, small objects that can be easily swallowed, and objects that cannot be held easily.

Specific Objective D

The student sifts, shapes, pours, and builds with sand.

Teacher Interventions

Primary Level. Supply the student with a sand pail and shovel and bring him or her to a sand table or sandbox. Show him or her how to fill the pail and to pour sand from a pail back into the sandbox or sand table. Use other containers to repeat this activity. Assist him or her in doing so.

Show the student how to dig holes in sand for tunnels and valleys and how to mold and pack slightly wet sand to make mountains, buildings, and castles. Assist him or her in creating his or her own castles in the sand. Reward the student for a job well done.

Family Interventions

Infant and Toddler/Preschool Level. Ask the parents to take their child to a playground where there is a sandbox. Tell them to join him or her in playing with the sand. Caution should be exercised so the sand being used is not contaminated with glass, debris, or other foreign substances.

If possible, ask the parents to take their child to the beach where they can join him or her in building sand castles and other structures. Emphasize the safety factors involved in playing with sand (i.e., avoiding getting it in one's eyes or in open cuts).

Specific Objective E

The student fills containers, pours, and otherwise engages in play with water.

Teacher Interventions

Primary Level. Show the student how to fill various containers with water at a water table, including pouring water from one container to another. Assist him or her in doing so and give him or her containers of various sizes.

Show the student how to pour water through a sieve and to feel the water as it comes out. Also show the student how to fill plastic detergent bottles with water, and how to squirt water out into the water table. Finally, show the student how to float plastic containers such as margarine tubs and then sink them by putting in weights. When necessary, assist the student in doing the above activities.

Family Interventions

Primary Level. Ask the parents to give their child plastic toy dishes, toy pots and pans, a dishrag, and soap. Ask them to show their child how to scrape, wash, and rinse the dishes and pots, and assist him or her in doing so.

If age appropriate, ask the parents to give their child a Busy Bath Toy and place their child in a tub of water. Have them demonstrate how to play with the toy. Emphasize to them the safety factors to consider when their child is engaging in water play (e.g., spilling water on the floor, changing water temperature, forgetting to shut off the sink or tub, and using toys or playthings that are easily broken).

Specific Objective F

The student strings beads, spools, and other playthings.

Teacher Interventions

Primary Level. Tie knots at the ends of two pieces of shoelace or heavy string. Give the student one of the strings or laces and several spools. Take your own lace and string several spools on it. While doing this, explain your actions. Then ask the student to make a chain like yours. Assist him or her if necessary. When the chain is completed, tie the two ends together and make a bracelet or necklace to put on a doll, stuffed toy, the student, or yourself. Repeat the activity, this time using wooden beads of different sizes and shapes and string in any pattern.

Use macaroni that has been safely dyed with various colors of food dye. Collect pasta of various shapes. Show the student how to create single-strand bracelets, necklaces, belts, and headbands. Show the student how to create simple designs by alternating various macaroni shapes and colors. For variety, add beads and/or spools. Give the student the finished product and ask him or her to make one just like yours. Assist if necessary. If the student is successful, encourage him or her to make these items as gifts for special occasions.

Show the student how to string buttons using a needle and thread. Begin by using large buttons. Encourage him or her to copy your design.

If necessary, thread the needle and knot the thread for the student. Challenge him or her to create his or her own designs. Reward the student for creating interesting designs and jewelry. String other objects such as cranberries and popcorn to make party or holiday decorations.

Family Interventions

Primary Level. Ask the parents to show their child how to string wooden beads in different color patterns and shapes. They may wish to purchase inexpensive stringing kits found in toy stores, which contain a variety of beads in different sizes and shapes.

Ask the parents to show their child how to string buttons into different patterns. Tell them to avoid buttons that are too small and can be swallowed or put in eyes, ears, or other body openings.

Specific Objective G

The student finger paints.

Teacher Interventions

Primary Level. Show the student how to use all parts of his or her hands, such as the fingertips, fingernails, knuckles, palms, sides, and heels, to create linear shapes and patterns with finger paints. At first, use only one color, and then gradually add one or two more. Encourage the student to make designs of his or her own. (It is important to establish procedures for working to minimize problems with keeping clothes and the learning area as clean as possible.)

Make a finger paint picture, and cover the finished painting with a clean sheet of paper and rub evenly. Lift the print off by pulling evenly from one side to the other. Hang the print up to dry. Show the student how to make his or her own print. Remind the student to wash his or her hands completely before making the print. Display the print on the classroom bulletin board or in a building display case or on a building bulletin board.

Family Interventions

Primary Level. Ask the parents to join their child in finger painting as a leisure activity. Have them use finger paints that are nontoxic. Also have them stress to their child the need to clean up after finger painting.

Ask the parents to display their child's finger paintings in a suitable place in the house.

Specific Objective H

The student fits pieces of puzzles, pegs, and other playthings into their corresponding forms.

Teacher Interventions

Primary Level.   Show the student a form board with simple geometric shapes. Show the student how to match the shape of the wooden insert with its embedded form. Show the student how to line it up with the background. Encourage him or her to model your actions and to work the form board him- or herself.

Give the student a form board with differently sized cutouts of the same basic geometric shape. Show the student how to match the individual pieces to their corresponding backgrounds. Assist him or her in completing the form board.

Family Interventions

Primary Level.   Ask the parents to obtain simple wooden puzzles of two or three pieces. Advise them that they need to verify that the paint on brightly colored puzzles is nontoxic. Tell them to show their child how to study the puzzle, remove the pieces (one at a time or by turning the board over), and pick up the puzzle pieces and put them back into the form board.

(Note: Children who have difficulty picking up puzzle pieces should be given Simplex puzzles with knobs on each piece, or should be taught to slide pieces of puzzles off the table into their hands.)

Ask the parents to show their child how to form shapes and simple constructions by putting together pieces of Lego, Rig-a-Jig, Lincoln Logs, Tinker Toys, and erector sets. (Note: Parents should encourage the child to copy the designs provided with the instructions as well as creating his or her own patterns.)

Specific Objective I

The student pastes paper and objects onto paper.

Teacher Interventions

Primary Level.   Show the student how to create a collage by pasting and overlapping pictures taken from picture magazines. Assist the student in making his or her collage. Repeat the collage activity using various colored papers, including tissue paper, crepe paper, cellophane, construction paper, wrapping paper, and foil.

Show the student how to make an assemblage by gluing objects on a piece of cardboard or foam board. Use natural objects such as tree bark, leaves, small twigs, stones, pebbles, weeds, flowers, pine cones, acorns, berries, or sea shells that have been collected on trips. Encourage the student to touch and examine the objects before making his or her own collage. Do not select objects that contain sharp edges or are in any way toxic.

Make mosaic designs by pasting seeds, beans, berries, rice, and pasta on tag board, foam board, cardboard, or wood. Encourage the student to create his or her own mosaics. Use paste or glue that is nontoxic and washable.

Family Interventions

Primary Level.   Ask the parents to cut interesting pictures out of picture magazines. Tell them to assist their child in pasting pictures on colored construction paper. Tell them to make a scrapbook of pictures and use the scrapbook to develop communication skills.

Ask the parents to collect yarn, sticks, stones, leaves, gravel, and twigs. Tell them to make a bas-relief by pasting the materials on cardboard. Tell them to show their child how to develop items to create interesting shapes. They should assist their child in collecting materials and in creating his or her own bas-relief.

 ### Specific Objective J

The student colors with crayons on paper or in a coloring book.

Teacher Interventions

Toddler/Preschool and Primary Levels.   Give the student a large crayon and a piece of paper. Show him or her how to hold the crayon so that he or she can easily make marks on the paper. Place the crayon in his or her hand so that it rests on the third finger. Assist the student in holding the crayon in place with the thumb held in opposition to the index finger. After the crayon is positioned properly, hold it in the student's hand and encourage him or her to scribble on his or her own. Reward the student for any attempts as well as for successes. Crayons may need to be modified by wrapping tape or clay around them for children who have difficulty holding a crayon.

Using a Magic Marker, outline bold shapes on a piece of paper and encourage the student to scribble or color within the lines. Play music and encourage the student to color with a crayon as he or she listens to the music.

Family Interventions

Toddler/Preschool and Primary Levels. Ask the parents to find pages in a coloring book of animals, people, and scenes that interest their child. Tell them to help the child select different colors for different parts of the picture. They should remind him or her to stay within the boundaries while coloring.

Ask the parents to take walks around the community with their child and point out the colors in the environment. Tell them to take a box of crayons with them and ask the child to match the correct color of crayon with the real color.

 ## Specific Objective K

The student molds and shapes clay, Play Doh, and plasticene and makes objects with these materials.

Teacher Interventions

Primary Level. Show the student how to roll clay, Play Doh, and plasticene between his or her fingers to make long, snakelike coils of clay. Assist the student in making his or her own lengths of clay.

Give the student a large ball of clay, Play Doh, or plasticene. Show him or her how to pinch, pull, pound, and dig with his fingertips, and to squeeze this ball into a variety of shapes. Assist him or her in creating new shapes.

Family Interventions

Primary Level. Ask the parents to engage their child in leisure experiences using clay to create simple objects (e.g., fruit and foods). Emphasize the importance of using nontoxic materials, of protecting furniture and floors before beginning, and of reminding the child that he or she must participate in clean-up after playing with clay.

Ask the parents to join their child in making clay figures and animals. Have them use the figures and animals to act out a familiar scene or story the child knows.

 ## Specific Objective L

The student bends and shapes pipe cleaners.

Teacher Interventions

Primary Level.   Bend and shape pipe cleaners into interesting shapes. Give the student a pipe cleaner and show him or her how to bend and shape it. Use colored pipe cleaners for variety. Emphasize the safety factors involved in using pipe cleaners and avoid using pipe cleaners with sharp edges or points, or pipe cleaners that are poorly made.

Show the student how to bend and shape pipe cleaners into simple figures by using more than one pipe cleaner. For example, a simple human figure can be made with three pipe cleaners.

Family Interventions

Primary Level.   Ask the parents to join their child in creating interesting shapes with pipe cleaners. Stress the safety factors involved with these types of activities.

Ask the parents to purchase differently colored pipe cleaners and to encourage their child to use them during supervised free play or quiet activities.

 ## Specific Objective M

The student weaves using simple forms.

Teacher Interventions

Primary Level. Show the student how to weave sticks through slits in oilcloth. Assist him or her in doing so. Repeat the activity with colored sticks to form a pattern.

Using a small weaving frame and colored yarn, demonstrate how to weave squares. The squares may then be sewn together.

Family Interventions

Primary Level. Ask the parents to show their child how to weave colored paper strips into slits in paper. The parents should have the child use the process to make a placemat on which to serve snacks.

Ask the parents, when looking for birthday gifts or gifts for their child on a special occasion, to look at the weaving kits available at craft or hobby stores. Ask the parents to select one that is age appropriate and that uses a variety of materials for weaving.

Specific Objective N

The student folds and constructs out of paper and cardboard.

Teacher Interventions

Primary Level. Show the student how to fold paper to make an old-fashioned fan with pleats. Use heavy and colorful wrapping paper. Fold the paper in folds of about $\frac{1}{2}$ inch. To form the handle, glue together a section of the fan. Assist the student in making his or her own fan.

Show the student how to make snowflakes and other decorations by folding and cutting paper. Make a circle of 6 to 8 inches by drawing around an edge of an overturned dish or saucer. Cut the circle out of the paper, fold it in half, in half again, and in half two more times. Cut pieces out of the sides and the base of the paper. Assist the student in making colorful chains. Suggest different color patterns.

Show the student how to make a single decorative paper chain by cutting strips of colored paper, pasting the first strip in a circle, slipping the next strip through the circle, pasting the ends of that strip together, and so on. Assist the student in making colorful chains, suggesting different color patterns.

Family Interventions

Primary Level. Ask the parents to show their child how to fold paper into different shapes. Tell them there are books in the library or in craft stores that provide clear instructions on how to fold paper and other materials.

Ask the parents to show their child how to fold paper napkins for setting a table. Tell them to show how to fold napkins in half and in a triangular pattern. Have them use the napkins during meals.

Specific Objective O

The student spins wheels and dials and also throws dice in table games.

Teacher Interventions

Primary Level. Collect table games such as Fat Cat that require the spinning of a wheel by snapping the index finger against the thumb and into the wheel before moving a marker on the game board. Show the student how to start the wheel moving. Encourage the student to spin the wheel him- or herself. Assist the student if necessary; play the game.

Collect games (age appropriate) such as Monopoly, Scooby Doo, and Which Witch that require the rolling of dice before moving a marker on the game board. Show the student how to pick up the dice, enclose them in his or her hand, shake them, and roll them on a surface. Ask the student to imitate you and assist him or her if necessary. Play the games.

Family Interventions

Primary Level. Ask the parents to engage their child in playing various table games involving the rolling of dice (e.g., Yahtzee and Candy Land).

Ask the parents to join the child in playing games involving spinning a wheel (e.g., roulette). Stress that they should select age-appropriate games that require different cognitive strategies.

Specific Objective P

The student cuts with scissors.

Teacher Interventions

Primary Level.   When appropriate, using teaching (double-handed) scissors, show the student how to cut paper. Point out the caution required during scissor use.

Once the student has developed the skill of picking up scissors and moving them in the cutting movement, show him or her how to use the scissors to cut paper into strips. These strips may be used for a meaningful follow-up project such as weaving. It will probably be necessary in the beginning to make cutting lines with a black crayon or a felt pen. Show the student how to guide the tips of the scissors and the blades along the marked lines.

Show the student how to cut out a picture with straight-line borders from an old magazine. Give the student the picture when you have cut three of the four sides and ask the student to complete the job. Then give the student his or her own picture to cut out of a magazine. Ask the student to cut this picture out and use it later in a scrapbook or mount it for display on the bulletin board.

Family Interventions

Primary Level.   Ask the parents to show their child how to cut pictures out of magazines as part of making collages or a picture scrapbook.

Ask the parents to find library books that describe craft projects requiring cutting. For example, age-appropriate books on paper weaving or paper design would include many projects of interest.

   ## Specific Objective Q

The student shuffles, deals, and performs other tasks involved in playing simple card games.

Teacher Interventions

Primary Level.   Show the student how to shuffle a deck of cards by slipping parts of the deck in and out of the pack. While you are shuffling one deck in this manner, give the student a pack to shuffle at the same time. Assist him or her if necessary in shuffling his or her own deck.

Show the student how to deal cards for simple two-handed games. Give the student a deck of cards and ask him or her to deal out a set number of cards. Assist if necessary.

Family Interventions

Primary Level. Ask the parents to purchase some simple card games (e.g., "Fish"). Tell them to play these games with their child after explaining the rules.

Tell the parents to include a deck of cards when they pack for a trip with their child. Tell them to suggest playing card games during leisure time on the trip. Ask them to select age-appropriate games that involve a variety of strategies and skills.

Specific Objective R

The student sketches and draws simple objects with crayons, colored pencils, charcoal, and/or colored chalk.

Teacher Interventions

Primary Level. Place a common, everyday object on a table. Use objects with simple shapes, such as an apple, block, can, bottle, banana, or book. Use a crayon to sketch and then color the object drawn. Encourage the student to make a drawing also. Show him or her how to select appropriate colors. Assist if necessary. After the student has demonstrated competency with crayons, introduce him or her to the use of colored pencils, charcoal, and colored chalk.

Once the student has mastered drawing some simple objects, ask him or her to draw and color more complex everyday objects such as a flower, clock, radio, chair, lamp, telephone, sink, or refrigerator. Assist if necessary.

Family Interventions

Primary Level. Tell the parents to include a sketch pad, colored pencils, and colored chalk as part of any gifts they purchase for their child at holidays or birthdays. Tell them to engage their child in using these materials.

If the child shows skill in drawing common objects, encourage him or her to draw scenes (without people) of the school, the hospital, the community, and the playground. Assist if necessary. Display his or her work prominently.

Specific Objective S

The student draws and paints with a brush and paints.

Teacher Interventions

Primary Level. Set up a paint area with paint pans, brushes, and water containers. Put a file of pictures in this learning area to encourage ideas and pictures of what to draw and paint. Encourage the student to use this paint area when he or she has free time and feels like painting.

Show the student how to make a leaf painting. Show him or her how to paint the veined surface of various sizes and shapes of leaves and then place the leaf, paint side down, on paper and gently press it. Assist the student in collecting his or her own leaves and in making his or her own leaf print.

Family Interventions

Primary Level. If appropriate, ask the parents to purchase a paint set for their child. Tell them to model its use as a leisure activity. Use a variety of sizes of brushes and a variety of colors of nontoxic paints.

Ask the parents to introduce their child to different colors by painting natural objects in their natural colors.

 Specific Objective T

The student sews and makes simple clothing out of fabric.

Teacher Interventions

Primary Level. Show the student how to cut fabric to make a scarf or handkerchief. Show the student how to thread the needle and to make a knot at the end of the thread. If the student is unable to thread the needle, do it for him or her. Demonstrate how to fold back the material along the edges to make a narrow hem. Sew the hem. Emphasize the safety precautions required for using needles or pins.

Show the student how to attach simple appliqué designs out of felt, denim, or other heavy fabric. Show the student how to sketch the design, cut it out, and sew it on a garment.

Family Interventions

Primary Level. Ask the parents to show their child how to replace a missing button. Emphasize the safety required to perform this activity.

Ask the parents to show their child how to sew a simple hem on a variety of materials and cloth.

Specific Objective U

The student constructs using one medium, such as wood or other natural materials.

Teacher Interventions

Primary Level.   Show the student how to make a clay figure by using the pinch and pull method. Make a solid base so that the figure can stand alone. Again with clay, show the student how to make clay pottery by using the coil method (i.e., roll out clay and then wind it in coils around a jar or bottle). Attach this to a flat base of clay that you have shaped with your hands. Remove the jar or bottle and complete the top of the piece. Allow the clay to dry, then fire it in a kiln.

Show the student how to make a Popsicle stick sculpture or functional pieces such as a mat to go under a flowerpot. Create a design and then glue the sticks together. Assist the student in creating his or her own sculpture. Sand. Use felt pens or poster paints to add details.

Family Interventions

Primary Level.   Ask the parents to show their child how to build a city or town with building blocks. Have them show their finished work to other people.

Ask the parents to show their child how to use empty boxes to build a city or town or to make rhythm instruments. Suggest that they review craft and construction books in the library for additional ideas.

Specific Objective V

The student constructs using several media, including paper, wood, fabric, leather, cord, yarn, and natural materials (shells, grass, rice, beans, and macaroni).

Teacher Interventions

Primary Level. Construct a sculpture out of discarded materials. Arrange the pieces and attach the parts together to form the whole unit. Assist the student in finding suitable discarded objects and in creating his or her own sculptured piece.

Show the student how to create a multimedia picture using such things as colored chalk, colored paper, scraps of material, sandpaper, foil, feathers, wax, and tempera nontoxic paints. Use a variety of tools, including brushes, felt pens, tooth- and nailbrushes, sponges, and wire screens. Assist the student in creating his or her own picture.

Show the student how to make people and animals from plastic bottles. Attach facial features cut from tag board to the bottle using masking tape. Wrap the bottle with newspaper strips and use kitchen paper toweling for the last layer. Use tissue paper, yarn, beads, and fabric to decorate.

Family Interventions

Primary Level. Ask the parents to purchase magazines that have instructions for creating craft objects out of scrap and junk material. Tell them to select appropriate activities and join their child in their execution.

Ask the parents to use natural materials found in the home or in the neighborhood to create collages, dioramas, or table displays.

  Specific Objective W

The student embroiders, crochets, knits, and does needlepoint and macramé.

Teacher Interventions

Primary and Secondary Levels. Buy a needlepoint kit with a simple pattern. Show the student how to thread the needle with the yarn. Read the directions in the kit. Teach the basic horizontal continental stitch and assist the student in completing the design.

Purchase or borrow books from the library on beginning crocheting or knitting. Crochet and/or knit a variety of simple articles.

Go to the library and take out a book on macramé. Select a simple article to make such as a belt or wall hanging. Use heavy string or cord and teach the student how to macrame.

Family Interventions

Primary and Secondary Levels. Ask the parents to determine which thread or yarn skill would be appropriate for their child in terms of skills and interests.

Ask the parents to teach the simplest needlework skills to their child and to gradually increase the complexity of the task until the child is able to produce something of functional value. Some children will be able to advance in needlework from simple patterns to projects such as quilts.

GOAL IV.

The student will acquire those fine motor skills that will enable him or her to use his or her upper extremities optimally in vocational/work activities.

SPECIFIC OBJECTIVES

The student:

- ❏ A. Picks up and holds simple tools.
- ❏ B. Assembles parts of an object to make the whole object.
- ❏ C. Assembles parts of an object to make a section of the object.
- ❏ D. Disassembles small units of two or more parts.
- ❏ E. Separates continuous rolls of paper, plastic sheeting, cloth, and bagging material into measured parts.
- ❏ F. Sorts by type of object.
- ❏ G. Sorts by size of object.
- ❏ H. Sorts by shape of object.
- ❏ I. Sorts by color of object.
- ❏ J. Inserts literature into envelopes for mailing.
- ❏ K. Inserts objects into corresponding forms.
- ❏ L. Inserts objects into envelopes.
- ❏ M. Inserts objects into boxes.

☐ N.   Inserts and packs assorted objects into a package.

☐ O.   Wraps objects in paper and inserts them into containers.

☐ P.   Seals clasp-type envelopes.

☐ Q.   Seals packages and cartons using tape.

☐ R.   Wraps and ties packages of various shapes and sizes.

☐ S.   Pastes and sticks labels on containers.

☐ T.   Sorts small objects using tweezers.

☐ U.   Uses a stapler.

☐ V.   Uses scissors.

☐ W.   Uses stencils.

☐ X.   Uses a hammer.

☐ Y.   Uses a screwdriver.

☐ Z.   Uses pliers.

☐ AA. Uses a standard and an adjustable wrench.

☐ BB. Uses hand and electric drills.

☐ CC. Uses a soldering iron, pencil, or gun.

☐ DD. Uses sandpaper.

☐ EE. Paints and stains wood.

☐ FF. Inspects objects by manipulating and using them.

☐ GG. Maintains grounds.

SUGGESTED ACTIVITIES

  ## Specific Objective A

The student picks up and holds simple tools.

Teacher Interventions

Primary Level. Place several different screwdrivers on a table near the student. Obtain a board 1 inch thick, 3 inches wide, and 8 inches long. Drill four holes at equal intervals in the board. Place four different screws in the holes and tell the student that each one requires a different-sized screwdriver. Tell the student to hold the different screwdrivers and give them to you when you ask for them. Emphasize that these are common tools that are easily handled.

Place different-weight hammers (8, 12, and 16 ounces) on a table. Tell the student to pick up each hammer, hold it, and then put it down.

Family Interventions

Primary Level. If there is a home workshop or tools are available, ask the parents to place a screwdriver, hammer, and pair of pliers on a table. Tell them to ask their child to safely pick up the hammer by its handle and, after a few seconds, tell him or her to put the hammer down. Tell them to repeat this activity with screwdrivers and pliers. Ask them to emphasize putting tools down gently so that they will not mark surfaces. Also, have them avoid using tools that are poorly made and/or easily broken.

Tell the parents to demonstrate hammering a nail into a piece of wood while their child is watching. Tell them to give their child the hammer and to tell him or her to hold it for them while they are lining up another nail to hammer. Repeat this activity with a screw and screwdriver, and then a nut and bolt and a pair of pliers. Tell them to emphasize a variety of simple tools and judgment regarding when to use a specific tool for a specific task.

Specific Objective B

The student assembles parts of an object to make the whole object.

Teacher Interventions

Toddler/Preschool and Primary Levels. Tell the student to bring in a jigsaw puzzle from home or provide one. Set up the puzzle on a table in the corner of the room. At certain times of the day, ask the student to go to the table and work on the jigsaw puzzle. When necessary, demonstrate how the pieces of the puzzle fit together to form a whole part or section of the puzzle.

Place on a table a large ball (4 to 6 inches) of Play Doh or clay. Tell the student to flatten the ball with his or her hands until it is the shape of a flat circle. Cut the flat shape into four parts with a butter knife. Separate the pieces and rearrange them so the pointed ends and corners are not in the correct position. Tell the student to put the pieces back together so they form the flat circle.

Family Interventions

Toddler/Preschool and Primary Levels.   Ask the parents to give their child a three-dimensional, three- to four-piece puzzle commensurate with the child's cognitive ability. Tell them to separate the three or four pieces that make up the puzzle and place them on a desk or tabletop and tell the child to put the pieces of the puzzle together to form a picture.

Tell the parents to place several empty jars of different sizes and shapes on a table in front of their child while placing the lids of these jars in a separate pile. Ask them to tell the child to put each jar lid on the appropriate jar. Tell them to emphasize how parts fit together to form a whole object.

Specific Objective C

The student assembles parts of an object to make a section of the object.

Teacher Interventions

Primary Level.   Draw an 8-foot square with chalk (or use masking tape) on the floor or outside on the playground. Give the student enough 12-by-12-inch floor tiles to cover half of the 8-foot area. Tell the student to fill in half of that particular area.

Place parts of a large model airplane or car kit in front of the student. Tell the student to put together pieces of a specified section, such as the tail assembly or part of the frame. After that is completed, tell the student to prepare another section and put it to one side. Use plans, pictorials, schematics, and drawings to aid in assembling parts of an object.

Family Interventions

Toddler/Preschool and Primary Levels.   Tell the parents to set up a table with strings and large beads on it. Tell them to place at the front of the table, as a model, a string with two beads strung on it. (Remind them to make sure that there is a knot in the end of the string.) Tell them to give the child a pile of beads and several strings and ask him or her to string two beads on each string just as in the model.

Tell the parents to give their child a four- to eight-piece puzzle. Ask them to tell the child to complete half of the puzzle and pass it to them. For the child who might not understand the concept of halves, the pieces can be color-coded and the child requested to complete all the blue pieces or all the red ones. Emphasize that the puzzles should be well made.

Specific Objective D

The student disassembles small units of two or more parts.

Teacher Interventions

Primary Level.   Obtain large toy plastic nuts, washers, and bolts that come in various colors. Place several nuts and washers on the large bolts, and tell the student to take them apart. Provide the student with a box full of such parts and instruct the student to take them apart. Emphasize to the student that many creative toys require disassembly in order to make a different toy out of the same parts.

Provide the student with a variety of age-appropriate toys that require disassembly in order to build new projects. Examples include large Tinkertoys, Lincoln Logs, and primary-level erector sets.

Family Interventions

Infant and Toddler/Preschool Level.   Ask the parents to show their child a toy stacking ring (a dowel rod with rings on it). Tell them to require the child to remove just two of the rings. They can then vary the activity by increasing or reducing the number of rings they want the child to remove.

Tell the parents to give their child a take-apart toy airplane already put together (Fisher-Price toy airplane). Tell them to point out to the child that the airplane comes apart in sections. Ask them to tell the child to take apart the entire airplane (four to six pieces) when it is ready to be put away.

Specific Objective E

The student separates continuous rolls of paper, plastic sheeting, cloth, and bagging material into measured parts.

Teacher Interventions

Primary Level. Place a roll of aluminum foil in its box on a table with a piece of foil partially rolled out. Place a piece of masking tape on the desk marking out a specified interval, such as 8 inches. Tell the student to hold the box, pull out the aluminum foil until it reaches the masking tape mark, and then tear off the foil. Tell the student to practice this activity until he or she provides the required amount. Emphasize the safety involved in tearing off the foil.

Place a large box of trash bags (20-gallon or more capacity) on a table. Give the student dry garbage or a pile of raked leaves. Assist him or her in tearing off the plastic bags and filling them with the garbage or leaves.

Family Interventions

Primary Level. Ask the parents to take their child to the bathroom. Tell them to point out the toilet paper on the toilet paper holder and demonstrate removing five or six sections. Ask them to demonstrate how toilet paper comes in sections that can easily be separated and tell the child to either count or use a measuring aid (a stick that measures out pieces of paper) to tear off the required amount.

Ask the parents to take their child into the kitchen. Tell them to point out the paper towel holder and the paper towels on it. Ask them to give the child one paper towel torn off the roll and, using that piece as a model, tell him or her to tear off a specific number of towels needed for a project. Tell them to avoid packaging that involves sharp-edged cutoffs.

 ## Specific Objective F

The student sorts by type of object.

Teacher Interventions

Primary Level. Lay out on a table a plastic box with six or more compartments (these boxes are usually used for holding objects such as fishing gear). In a large cardboard box, mix a variety of paper clips, buttons, rubber bands, and beads. Seat the student in front of the cardboard box and the plastic compartmentalized container, and instruct him or her to sort the objects by placing a different object in each compartment of the plastic container. Continually check to make sure the student is sorting the objects correctly.

Obtain a grab bag of electrical parts such as resistors, capacitors, and diodes. Discontinued models of such parts can be purchased cheaply from electronics firms, through mail order, or from stores such as Radio Shack. Lay out on the table five 12-inch squares of masking tape. Put one type of electronic component in each square and tell the student to sort through the box and place the objects he or she finds in the appropriate square. Use the parts for a class project.

Family Interventions

Primary Level. Tell the parents to give their child a box with different types of beads during play time. Tell them to place in front of him or her five different strings, each one with a different type of bead on it. Ask them to tell the child to look through the box and place in front of him or her the beads that he or she finds that match the beads on the strings. Remind them to tell the child to place the matching beads next to the correct string.

Ask the parents to obtain a box full of plastic silverware (knives, forks, and spoons). Tell them to place three large plastic glasses or other containers in front of the box. Tell them to ask the child to place all the forks in one glass, all the spoons in another glass, and all the knives in the third glass.

Specific Objective G

The student sorts by size of object.

Teacher Interventions

Primary Level. Obtain from the hardware store 1 pound each of 6-penny, 8-penny, 10-penny and 12-penny nails. Mix them together and place them in the middle of the table. Tell the student to sort the nails and put them back into their original boxes. Tell him or her to sort this way whenever he or she has nails that are mixed together. Caution the student on handling nails cautiously, especially those that may have sharp points.

Give the student a bowl full of paper clips of various sizes. Place the appropriate number of empty envelopes in front of the student and tell him or her to put a different size of clip into each envelope and then continue sorting the clips this way until the bowl is empty. Use the clips when appropriate.

Family Interventions

Primary Level. Ask the parents to obtain a bushel basket of fruit or vegetables appropriate to the season. Tell them to make sure that there are various sizes in the basket. Ask them to tell the child to sort the fruit or vegetables from the biggest to the smallest size.

Tell the parents to place a bowl containing a single type of nut in front of their child. They should make sure the nuts are in various sizes ranging from jumbo to small. Tell them to ask the child to place the nuts into plastic bags according to size. The plastic bags can be sandwich bags or bags obtained from candy companies. Eat the nuts for snacks.

 ### Specific Objective H

The student sorts by shape of object.

Teacher Interventions

Primary Level. Place in front of the student a toy that requires angles, circles, or squares to be pushed through holes of the same shape. Mix up the shapes that go into the box and place them in a stack in front of the student. Tell the student to push the shapes through the appropriate holes into the box.

During play time, give the student a mailbox (Play Skool) with openings for various sizes and shapes. Mix up the shapes that come with the mailbox and tell the student to sort and place each one into appropriate openings in the mailbox.

Family Interventions

Primary Level. Tell the parents to have their child sort his or her toys by shape and put them in different containers or compartments of his or her toy chest. Tell them to urge the child to practice this activity when he or she has to clean up his or her toys.

Ask the parents to obtain a box of various shapes of wood scraps. Tell them to show their child the different shapes of wood that are in the scrap box and ask him or her to sort them according to their shapes as part of a play activity. When possible, parents should build a project with their child.

Specific Objective I

The student sorts by color of object.

Teacher Interventions

Primary Level. Place a small box of assorted poker chips in front of the student. Place three plastic boxes, one for each color, in front of the student. Tell the student that you want him or her to place a different color into each of the containers.

Construct a spool holder by gluing $\frac{1}{4}$-by-8-inch dowels onto a piece of wood. Make sure the dowels are evenly spaced and can accommodate spools of various sizes of thread. Give the student a large box containing spools of assorted colors of thread. Tell the student to put all the spools of one color on a single dowel until the dowel is filled. Stress that the spools will be going into a package marked to be a specific color, so they should not be mixed up.

Family Interventions

Primary Level. If age appropriate, tell the parents to give their child three large packages of assorted colored construction paper, and to tell the child that they want him or her to pick out all the papers of certain colors so they can be used for holiday decorations (e.g., orange and black for Halloween). Ask the parents to tell their child to place the papers into separate piles according to color.

Ask the parents to give their child a large box of mixed crayons that have been accumulated during the year. The child is to sort the crayons by color and place them in empty crayon boxes or plastic bags labeled by color.

Specific Objective J

The student inserts literature into envelopes for mailing.

Teacher Interventions

Primary Level. Contact a paper warehouse or discount card store for free or inexpensive calendars. Select an appropriately sized envelope for these calendars and tell the student to put one calendar into each envelope. Emphasize to the student that he or she should avoid wrinkling or bending calendars while inserting them into the envelopes. Have the student send the calendars to friends as gifts.

Plan a party by writing invitations on index cards of different sizes. Obtain the appropriately sized envelopes for them. Set up two or three piles of different-sized cards with their appropriate envelopes in front of the student. Seat the student close to the work and point out the different types of cards and their envelopes. Tell the student to insert the cards into the envelopes until all the cards or envelopes are used up.

Family Interventions

Primary Level. Tell the parents to arrange for their child to complete a mailing project (e.g., party invitations). Tell them to assist him or her in completing the mailing, and reward him or her for a job well done.

As part of a charity event or community service, have the parent enlist the child's help in sending out brochures and literature. The Heart Fund and similar organizations are often looking for people to perform this activity.

 ## Specific Objective K

The student inserts objects into corresponding forms.

Teacher Interventions

Primary Level. In preparation for a potential job, obtain from a food market or grocery store the foam, cardboard, or plastic forms used to ship apples, pears, plums, and eggs. Take the student to the grocery store to show him or her how the produce is packed, pointing out the particular types of containers and their forms. Set up a production line where the student is required to take, for example, an apple and put it in the form. Repeat this activity until the form is filled. Then tell the student to pass the completed form down to the end of the table.

Purchase thumbtacks in bulk quantity. Construct cards of old parts of corrugated cardboard cut to the desired size to hold the thumbtacks. Place pencil dots at equal intervals on the card to indicate where you want the thumbtacks placed. Show the student a completed card and tell him or her to fill in the pile of cards that are placed in front of him or her in exactly the same way. Be sure to tell the student that he or she must exercise caution because thumbtacks are sharp and can be dangerous.

Use the thumbtacks when needed. This activity should be supervised closely.

Family Interventions

Primary Level. Ask the parents to purchase an age-appropriate toy that comes with parts that are in forms—a stencil toy with many pieces, for example. Ask the parents to show their child how to put the pieces away in their forms after playing with the toy.

Ask the parents to visit a craft and hobby store to view the wide array of craft items that have components in forms. Have them select an age-appropriate one that their child likes and assist the child in inserting objects into their corresponding forms when he or she is finished working.

 ## Specific Objective L

The student inserts objects into envelopes.

Teacher Interventions

Primary Level. Simulate the mailing out of samples. Stack 20 bars of soap into several piles. Tell the student to put one bar of soap into each of the mailing envelopes provided next to the pile. Tell him or her to do so as quickly as he or she can. Caution the student not to damage the soap by dropping it or forcing it into the envelope. Repeat this activity by varying the time to complete the task. Initially, provide encouragement and warning as to how much time is left.

When possible, obtain craft items such as pipe cleaners in bulk quantities (many distributors will sell them to you by the thousands). Purchase envelopes that can accept the pipe cleaners. Set up piles of pipe cleaners according to how many will fit into an envelope, such as 25, 50, or 100. Tell the student to put the pipe cleaners into appropriately sized envelopes. Caution the student that he or she should not bend the cleaners or stretch them out of shape. Inspect the quality of the student's job. Use the pipe cleaners during a craft activity.

Family Interventions

Primary Level. Tell the parents to monitor how their child cleans up small parts from toys like Legos or erector sets. If the child is having difficulty, tell them to provide envelopes so he or she can insert the small parts in them and keep them all together.

Tell the parents to demonstrate to their child as part of a hobby activity how to keep stamps, coins, or similar items together by inserting them into envelopes. Tell the parents to participate with their child in this activity and provide encouragement and guidance. Ask them to use a variety of envelopes and objects that require insertion into envelopes (e.g., coins or stamps).

 ## Specific Objective M

The student inserts objects into boxes.

Teacher Interventions

Primary Level. Place a large pile of paper clips (these can be bought in bulk) in the middle of a table. Obtain appropriately sized boxes into which these clips can be placed. These boxes can usually be purchased in a discount card or craft store. Show the student how to fill as many boxes as possible within a predetermined amount of time, then place the boxes in a third pile.

Repeat the above activity using different types of boxes, objects, and materials that can be later used in class.

Family Interventions

Primary and Secondary Levels. Tell the parents to demonstrate to their child how to put away fragile items such as jewelry into their respective boxes. Tell them to praise their child when he or she does it appropriately.

Tell the parents to ask their child for help when they are storing objects that will not be used for a long time (e.g., holiday decorations). Tell the parents to demonstrate how to safely insert the objects into their boxes.

 ## Specific Objective N

The student inserts and packs assorted objects into a package.

Teacher Interventions

Primary Level. When appropriate, ask the student to bring his or her lunch box (or cloth lunch bag) to school. Remove the sandwiches, desserts, and so forth from the lunch box and place them in front of the student. Tell the student to repack his or her lunch box in a way that will allow everything to fit and not be crushed. As part of a follow-up activity, arrange for the student to make and pack his or her own lunch on the following day.

Make first aid kits. Obtain quantities of Band-Aids, Mercurochrome, burn ointment, gauze, and adhesive tape from a discount drugstore or a drug supply company. Set up piles of the various items. Obtain the appropriately sized cardboard or plastic containers into which these materials will be inserted. Tell the student to insert the various components of a first aid kit into the plastic containers and then pack them into a carton that has been placed on the floor next to the student.

Family Interventions

Primary Level. Tell the parents, as part of a leisure activity, to purchase in bulk form assorted fishing material such as lures, hooks, and flies. Tell them to obtain plastic compartmentalized containers and place the containers in a pile next to the fishing materials. Ask them to place one of each object into each of the compartments and to tell their child to complete the package by inserting a specific number of objects into each of its appropriate compartments and then closing the lid. When possible, the parent should take the child fishing and use the packaged materials.

Tell the parent to obtain empty trading card boxes that children use to store their trading cards. Ask the parents to work with their child by demonstrating how to insert the cards into the boxes without damaging the corners. Tell them to remind their child to insert and pack the cards after playing with them.

 ## Specific Objective O

The student wraps objects in paper and inserts them into containers.

Teacher Interventions

Primary Level. Purchase a large number of small bars of soap such as those found in motel or hotel rooms. The soap should be unwrapped. Have the student select a wrapper for the soap that has been cut to size. Another pile should include a rectangular or square box to hold the wrapped soap. First demonstrate and then tell the student to wrap each individual bar of soap in its paper and insert it into the box.

Collect articles and canned goods as part of a charity drive. When the student comes across a fragile item, tell him or her to wrap it in paper and then insert it in a package, box, or container that is available. Tell him or her that this will protect the item from breaking or being damaged.

Family Interventions

Primary Level. Tell the parents to place a pile of plastic plates, a pile of heavy packaging paper, and a pile of large cartons into which the packaged plates are to be vertically inserted and packed in front of the child. Tell them to demonstrate wrapping a plate and inserting it into the carton. Tell them to ask their child to wrap each plate individually and then place it in the carton. The child who is successful in wrapping plastic plates may proceed to the wrapping of china and glass plates. Suggest that the parents use this activity to help someone move.

Tell the parents to place a pile of jewelry, such as small tie clasps and rings, on a table. Ask them to obtain an appropriate quantity of small plastic boxes into which these materials can be placed and to obtain some tissue paper that is used to wrap jewelry. Tell them to demonstrate to their child how to wrap a piece of jewelry and place it into a container. Ask them to tell the child to imitate their actions and wrap the remaining jewelry. Tell them to avoid objects that are so fragile that wrapping them requires special procedures or handling.

Specific Objective P

The student seals clasp-type envelopes.

Teacher Interventions

Primary Level. Obtain a large supply of calendars and envelopes and place them in two piles in front of the student. Tell the student to place each of these calendars in its appropriately sized envelope, make sure it fits securely, and then seal it. Point out that some types of calendars have spiral bindings, and it is important that these do not stick out or rip any part of the envelope before sealing. It is important to emphasize to the student that he or she must seal these envelopes carefully and that he or she should not bang the flap or clasp down in the envelope. Send the calendars to friends as gifts.

As part of a class project, ask the student to collect proof-of-purchase seals from grocery store products. After an adequate supply has been collected, encourage the student to place them in a mailing envelope with the appropriate information required by the company. Tell the student to seal the envelope using the gummed flap and the clasp. Inspect the finished project and point out, when appropriate, what a good job he or she has done.

Family Interventions

Primary Level. Tell the parents to allow their child to seal clasp-type envelopes whenever they have to mail one. Practice when necessary.

Ask the parents to purchase a large greeting card that requires a clasp-type envelope at holidays or birthdays. Ask them to tell their child to seal it and mail it to a special person.

 ## Specific Objective Q

The student seals packages and cartons using tape.

Teacher Interventions

Primary Level. Tell the student to bring an empty box into school. Tell the student he or she is going to make a grab box. Place an object or a toy in the student's grab box. Assist the student in wrapping the box and then tell him or her to seal the package using tape provided in a dispenser.

Give the student shoe boxes of several sizes and ask him or her to place some favored objects that he or she would like to have mailed home in a box. These objects could be class projects or items that the student was planning to give to his or her family. Simulate or carry out the activity.

Family Interventions

Primary Level. Tell the parents to obtain a package that needs to be sealed. Tell them to demonstrate how to measure a length of self-sealing packaging or masking tape approximately 6 to 8 inches longer than the flap to be sealed and tear it off. Ask them to tell their child to watch as they place the tape on the two flaps that meet, securing them in place. Then the parents should instruct their child to rub his or her hands over the tape gently, forming a tight seal.

When a birthday gift needs to be wrapped, ask the parents to assist their child in using cellophane tape to wrap the gift. The parents should monitor this activity to ensure that the child conserves tape and does a neat job.

Specific Objective R

The student wraps and ties packages of various shapes and sizes.

Teacher Interventions

Primary Level. Supply the student with two shoe boxes, one placed on top of the other. Demonstrate to the student how to wrap the shoe boxes in brown or decorative paper. Make sure they are securely wrapped. Take a length of string and tell the student to wrap it around the boxes horizontally two or three times.

Next, tell the student to wrap the boxes vertically two or three times. Demonstrate slowly so that the student can see how you change the direction of the string without losing its tension. Tell the student to watch you as you make a knot with the ends of the string and encourage the student to imitate your actions. Capitalize on times when packages need to be tied for mailing or gift giving by asking the student to help you with the activity. It is advisable to call the post office in advance to find out the type of tying material acceptable for mailing.

Repeat the previous activity with other articles, such as books, presents, and flat items.

Family Interventions

Primary Level. Ask the parents to plan with their child to send clothes to a charity such as Goodwill, Am Vets, or the Salvation Army. Tell them to place a large pile of clothes that are to be donated on a piece of brown wrapping paper in the middle of the floor. Ask them to tell the child to wrap the clothes as well as he or she can and then tie them into a bundle. Tell the parents to closely monitor this activity.

Repeat the previous activity using plastic bags that require the use of a variety of ties for closing.

Specific Objective S

The student pastes and sticks labels on containers.

Teacher Interventions

Primary Level. Demonstrate placing the student's name label on a mailbox, his or her locker or storage area, and other belongings located in the classroom. Tell him or her to label other appropriate articles.

Demonstrate how to use a plastic label maker or similar label-making machine. Print out names or words that need to be adhered to objects or areas in the classroom. Demonstrate how to print the labels and how to remove the backing from the label. Ask the student to imitate your actions and print and place labels in appropriate places.

Family Interventions

Primary Level. Ask the parents to obtain Mr. Yuk or similar labels from the poison control center of their state. Ask them to give their child some of the labels and a supply of cans or bottles that need such a label pasted on them. Ask them to tell him to paste one label on each bottle and to return the bottles to their appropriate storage place. Have them supervise this activity closely.

Ask the parents to obtain cloth labels that can be applied by pressing on clothing. Ask them to put their child's name, assigned color cue when appropriate, or rebus clue on the label and place a pile of these in front of the child. Tell them to demonstrate cautiously to the child how to paste or stick these labels on parts of clothing where they will not be seen when the clothes are worn. They should also point out the labels that are already there. Ask them to encourage the child, with adult supervision, to apply the labels to his or her clothes.

Specific Objective T

The student sorts small objects using tweezers.

Teacher Interventions

Primary and Secondary Levels. Demonstrate the use of tweezers to the student. Assist him or her in holding a pair of large tweezers, gently pressing the points together, and then releasing them. Place a small object such as a pin on the table in front of the student and assist him or her in picking it up. Place several pins in front of the student and tell him or her to pick them up and place them in a small container that has been placed next to him or her.

Obtain from an electronics supply house or a store such as Radio Shack an assortment of small electronics parts needed make several class projects. Place these small objects in a pile in front of the student and give him or her a pair of tweezers. Tell the student to use the tweezers to sort the parts that are in front of him or her into piles. Provide tweezers of various sizes for the student, and tell him or her to try each type of tweezers to find out which one is best for a given job.

Family Interventions

Primary and Secondary Levels. Ask the parents to obtain a boxful of stamps as part of a leisure activity. Tell them to give their child a pile of stamps and ask him or her to use tweezers to sort the stamps by color, the number written on them, or size. Tell the parents to point out that stamps are easily ripped or damaged unless they are handled carefully.

Tell the parents to ask their child to sort seashells, beads, buttons, or similar items using tweezers during free time or hobby time. Ask the parents to tell their child to sort these materials and to place them in appropriate containers so they will be ready for use in other activities.

 ## Specific Objective U

The student uses a stapler.

Teacher Interventions

Primary and Secondary Levels. Demonstrate how to safely use a stapler. Next, assist the student in stapling. Tell him or her to place pieces of folded paper in the stapler and then to press down with a quick thrust on top of the stapler, completing the stapling action. Caution the student to make sure his or her fingers do not go near the stapler's opening. Tell him or her to practice this activity as you supervise.

Tell the student you would like him or her to help you construct a bulletin board by stapling the background material. Give the student a package of colored construction paper (all the same color) and show him or her how to staple each piece onto the bulletin board. Closely monitor this activity until the complete background of the bulletin board has been stapled. Check to see that the entire board is covered.

Family Interventions

Primary and Secondary Levels. Tell the parents to ask their child to help them staple bills, receipts, or papers they are planning to file. This can be an activity done at the end of each month. Have the parents monitor that the stapler is used safely. Tell them to caution their child not to play with or try to remove with fingers staples that have not gone in properly (a staple remover can be introduced at this time).

As a leisure activity, have the parents encourage their child to draw and color five or six pictures of something they like on separate pieces of paper. When the pictures are complete, have them staple them together in a book.

 Specific Objective V

The student uses scissors.

Teacher Interventions

Primary Level. Plan a papier-mâché project. Draw lines on pieces of newspaper and ask the student to cut out long strips of the newspaper to use in making papier-mâché. Encourage him or her to continue this activity until the desired amount of paper has been cut. Use the paper in a papier-mâché project.

Provide various sizes of scissors for the student to use. Demonstrate the use of fine instrument scissors, which are used for very fine work such as cutting thread, and very large scissors, such as those used in cutting wallpaper. Tell the student to practice using different types of scissors on various kinds of materials.

Family Interventions

Primary Level. The above activities, as well as similar ones, can also be done in the home. It is important to stress to the parents knowledge of safety factors involved in using scissors and selecting the most appropriate size of scissors for the job.

 Specific Objective W

The student uses stencils.

Teacher Interventions

Primary Level. Obtain a large stencil that forms a letter or shape that you wish to reproduce. Demonstrate to the student how the stencil is placed on the appropriate surface, then line it up according to the guide holes or place it within the area to be stenciled. Point out to the student that the stencil should be straight and held or taped firmly in place. Using paint, watercolor, or other media, paint over the stencil. Take the stencil off and point out to the student how the paint has come through to create the shape desired. Tell the student to make his or her own shape and give him or her a stencil.

Cut a stencil or purchase one corresponding to the student's first name. Point out to the student that his or her name will appear on an object after he or she places the stencil on the object and paints over it. Tell the student to bring in shoe boxes or other cardboard boxes, or obtain some. Tell the student to stencil his or her name on the boxes, which can then be used to hold supplies such as toothpaste and a toothbrush.

Family Interventions

Primary Level. Ask the parents to give their child a stencil toy during play time that utilizes plastic stencils. Tell them to help their child make various forms by following the plastic stencil edges and to try the different types of stencils in the toy kit.

Ask the parents to obtain a package of holiday decoration stencils. Tell them to ask their child to stencil a different design on several holiday packages that are wrapped in different colors. Ask the parents to demonstrate how to use crayons, watercolor, and other available media.

 ## Specific Objective X

The student uses a hammer.

Teacher Interventions

Primary Level. Demonstrate to the student how to hold a real hammer by placing your hand at the end of the hammer handle and grasping it tightly. Place several sizes of hammers (8, 12, and 16 ounces) on a table in front of the student. Tell him or her to pick up each of the hammers and then to put each one down. Give the student a hammer with which he or she feels comfortable. Gently move the hammer up and down over a board in imitation of the hammering motion.

For the student who has difficulty in controlling the hammer, tell him or her to grasp the hammer at its handle with one hand. Tell the student to push with his or her other hand from the top of the hammerhead down until his or her hand slides somewhere on the handle where it is more comfortable so that he or she can control it better. Tell him or her to gently tap nails into soft pine wood. Make sure that he or she has control of the hammer.

Family Interventions

Primary Level. The activities listed above may also be done at home, provided there is adequate instruction and supervision.

When appropriate, ask the parents to show how to use a hammering bench (Fisher-Price) to hammer nails through one side, turn it over, and then hammer them back again through the other side.

Tell the parents to select a place in the house where it would be appropriate to hang a picture once the child has mastered hammering. Ask them to start the nail into the wall and then give the hammer to their child and tell him or her to hammer it gently, most of the way. They should be careful to check that the child does not hammer the nail in completely. When this activity is completed, the parents should give their child a picture to hang on that nail.

  Specific Objective Y

The student uses a screwdriver.

Teacher Interventions

Primary Level. Demonstrate the use of a screwdriver (regular head and Phillips head) by placing its blade in a screw that has been partially started and then turning it. Tell the student to imitate your actions and hand him or her the screwdriver. For those students who have difficulty keeping the screwdriver blade in the slot of the screw, use screwdrivers with screw holders or grips on the side.

Decrease the screw size and have the student use a screwdriver to turn screws into various types of material. First give the student a piece of balsa wood with a screw started in it, and tell him or her to turn the screw completely in. The student should have little trouble because balsa wood is an extremely soft and light wood and accepts screws easily. Repeat this activity with woods such as pine, whitewood, mahogany, and oak. Make sure that the student uses caution and does not hurt his or her hands, because some woods, such as oak, are quite hard.

Family Interventions

Primary Level. The activities listed under Teacher Interventions may also be done at home provided there is adequate instruction and supervision.

 Specific Objective Z

The student uses pliers.

Teacher Interventions

Primary Level. Show the student a pair of slip joint pliers. Point out that the pliers are adjustable according to the way you hold them and show the student the way the slip joint opens. Demonstrate how to tighten a nut on a bolt with a pair of pliers. Hand the student the pliers and tell him or her to imitate your actions.

Find articles around the school (or home) that need tightening. Tighten them using an appropriate pair of pliers. Emphasize that the items being tightened should not be marred or damaged.

Show the student various types of electrical or jeweler's pliers, such as needle-nose and side cutters. Construct a bolt board that requires the use of these particular types of pliers and tell the student to tighten the nuts on the corresponding bolts. When working with pliers such as those used in micro and fine electrical work, be sure to tell the student to be careful not to mar the surface of the bolt or damage the pliers.

Family Interventions

Primary Level. The activities listed above may also be done at home provided there is adequate instruction and supervision.

 Specific Objective AA

The student uses a standard and an adjustable wrench.

Teacher Interventions

Primary Level. Show the student a standard wrench and point out that each wrench has a specific opening that fits a specific nut. Demonstrate how the wrench fits around the nut by placing it over the corresponding nut and tightening it. Give the student a standard wrench and encourage him or her to imitate your actions. Practice.

Show the student an adjustable wrench and point out the adjusting knob on its side. Take the student's finger and assist him or her in turning the knob. Point out to the student that the jaw is either opening or closing as he or she performs this action. Tell the student to practice opening and closing the adjustable wrench. Make sure the wrench is of high quality.

Construct a board or select a piece of furniture that requires the tightening of nuts. Select the equipment or construct the board in such a way that there are various shapes of nuts, such as hexagonal, square, machine-fine thread, or coarse thread. Tell the student to tighten all of the nuts with one adjustable wrench and point out to him or her that the wrench will have to be readjusted for each type of nut to be tightened. Practice.

Family Interventions

Primary Level. Tell the parents to bring their child to a hardware store. While there, they should point out to their child the different types of wrenches.

Tell the parents to select several toys that require repairing by tightening with a wrench, such as wheels on a toy bicycle or toy truck. Tell them to place the toys in a pile. Ask them to tell the child to take one and, from several wrenches, select the correct one to tighten any bolts that need tightening. Tell the parents to reinforce when appropriate, but also to point out when the child is not doing the activity correctly or safely.

 Specific Objective BB

The student uses hand and electric drills.

Teacher Interventions

Primary and Secondary Levels. Demonstrate the use of the hand drill. Be certain to point out how you hold the handle of the drill with one hand and that you turn the drill by the knob on its side with the other hand. Give the student the drill and encourage him or her to imitate your actions.

Show the student an electric drill (a battery-powered one is preferred initially because safety hazards are somewhat reduced). Show the student how to press the trigger of the drill and point out how fast it is going. Point out the drill chuck and the key; open and close the drill jaws. Give the drill to the student and encourage him or her to imitate your actions. Practice opening and closing the jaws of the drill and starting and stopping it. For the more advanced student, you may want to point out the little button next to the trigger on most drills, which keeps the drill running continuously. Supervise closely whenever the student is using electric tools.

Show the student a drill press. Point out the drill press wheel and turn it to adjust the height of the drill. Point out the on–off switch or treadle mechanism. Woodworking books are recommended for suggested reading if a drill press is to be incorporated into daily activities. Wear safety glasses whenever working on the drill press.

Family Interventions

Primary and Secondary Levels. The activities above may also be done at home provided there are adequate instruction and supervision and available tools and equipment.

Specific Objective CC

The student uses a soldering iron, pencil, or gun.

Teacher Interventions

Primary and Secondary Levels. Show the student a soldering iron with a long, thin tip (this is usually called a soldering pencil). Emphasize safety precautions in using a tool such as this and, at all times, provide close supervision. Demonstrate how to plug the soldering iron into the wall and explain to the student that he or she should wait several moments until the tip warms up. Remind the student that the tip is very hot, so he or she should not touch it. Repeat this activity with a soldering iron and a soldering gun. When using the soldering gun, demonstrate how the pressing of the trigger almost instantly turns the tip hot.

Show the student some solder in a coil. (Make sure the solder you use is rosin core if you are doing electrical work.) Demonstrate how you place a tiny bit of the end of the coil of solder at the tip of the soldering iron and how it melts. Again, stress that the solder is extremely hot and will burn the student if he or she is not careful. Give the soldering iron and a piece of the soldering coil to the student and ask him or her to imitate your actions. (Note: This type of activity should be done on a table that is protected by a board or on a surface that is able to withstand heat. Wear safety glasses at all times and monitor the process carefully. If the student melts too much solder, tell him or her so. A good soldering job will leave the finished wires bright and shiny.)

Family Interventions

Primary and Secondary Levels. The activities listed above may also be done at home provided there are adequate instruction and supervision and available tools or equipment.

 Specific Objective DD

The student uses sandpaper.

Teacher Interventions

Primary Level. Show the student an $8\frac{1}{2}$-by-11-inch piece of medium sandpaper. Tell him or her to touch the sandpaper and feel how rough it is. Rub the sandpaper in a back-and-forth motion over a piece of wood. Show the student the sawdust that has been created and ask him or her to feel the wood where you have just sanded. Ask him or her if it is smooth.

Wrap a piece of fine sandpaper around a board that is 1 inch wide by 4 inches long. Place a large board in front of the student and demonstrate the back-and-forth motion of sanding. Point out that the board inside the sandpaper makes sanding easier. Tell the student to imitate your actions and sand the board. Construct a project with the board.

Family Interventions

Primary Level. Ask the parents to find objects or furniture around the home that need to be sanded (e.g., objects that do not close well or are uneven because the wood has warped). Tell them to demonstrate to their child how to sand the objects or furniture. Ask them to encourage their child to inspect their sanding and then ask him or her to sand.

Ask the parents to plan a simple project with their child that involves sanding. The project could be making a trivet or coasters. Tell them to monitor the child as he or she sands.

Specific Objective EE

The student paints and stains wood.

Teacher Interventions

Primary Level.   Show the student a half-pint can of water stain. Stains are usually used on new wood and can be either brushed or wiped on and then off. First, dip a $\frac{1}{2}$-inch brush into the stain and spread it on the wood. Wipe it off with a cheesecloth or a soft, clean rag. Show the student the difference between the stained wood and the clean, new wood.

Give the student a wide paintbrush (1 to $1\frac{1}{2}$ inches) and a pint or quart can of paint. Place a board that needs painting in front of the student and tell him or her to paint the entire board using the wide brush. Carefully check the student's painting skills and point out drips or areas on the board that have either too much or too little paint. If the board is not painted in an acceptable fashion, ask the student to repeat the activity.

Family Interventions

Primary Level.   Tell the parents to show their child a pint can of paint and an article that needs painting. Tell them to dip a $\frac{1}{2}$-inch-wide brush into the can and slowly spread the paint on a piece of wood. They should tell the child that he or she must not touch the paint with his or her hands and that he or she should use only the brush to spread the paint. It is suggested that latex or water-based paints be used before oil-based paint and enamels due to their easier clean-up (with water instead of turpentine or thinner).

Tell the parents to select a project or piece of wood that needs to be painted and to spread newspaper on the table where painting is to be done. Tell them to place all the materials (paint, brush, and rag) within easy reach of their child and assist him or her in dipping his or her brush into the paint or stain and spreading it on the wood. (Note: It is important that the child wear appropriate clothing for painting activities, with sleeves rolled up, and that the parents provide supervision.)

Specific Objective FF

The student inspects objects by manipulating and using them.

Teacher Interventions

Primary Level. Give the student a finished project such as a wall plaque that has been painted and is dry. Tell the student to look at the plaque and see if the paint has covered the wood in the appropriate places. Tell the student to look for places that have been missed by the painter. Encourage the student to turn the board or plaque all around and to check the sides, back, and front. If the plaque requires additional painting, it can be placed in a box near other plaques the student is inspecting.

Give the student a box of small wooden toys, such as cars and planes, that have been constructed as part of wood projects. These toys should have movable parts such as wheels and propellers. Instruct the student to place those toys with parts that do not move into a carton.

Family Interventions

Primary Level. Tell the parents to encourage their child to inspect a project after completing it and tell what, if anything, could be improved. Tell them to praise their child if he or she correctly points out flaws or poor construction.

For a birthday or special occasion, ask the parents to buy a gift for their child that needs to be put together (e.g., a model, Legos, an erector set, or Capsula).

 ## Specific Objective GG

The student maintains grounds.

(Note: These are just a few examples of the many activities that might be included under this objective.)

Teacher Interventions

Primary Level. Show the student how to use hand and power lawn mowers. (A training program based upon safety issues and job expectations is recommended before use of the lawn mower is taught.) Once the student knows how to use a lawn mower safely, assign him or her an area to mow. Tell the student to inspect the area for rocks before mowing. After the student has completed the job, tell him or her to inspect the lawn and mow any missed areas.

Take the student to an area or garden where dirt needs to be shoveled. Demonstrate how to hold the shovel by grasping its handle, putting it into the dirt, and stepping on the shoulder of its blade. Ask the student to dig a hole in the ground where you will be planting a small shrub or tree.

Family Interventions

Primary Level. Ask the parents to connect a hose to an outside faucet and demonstrate how to turn the hose on and off by adjusting the water nozzle. Ask them to tell their child to imitate their actions and to water the flowers or grass in the immediate area.

Ask the parents to demonstrate to their child how to rake leaves.

In climates where there is snow, tell the parents to have their child help shovel the walk when appropriate.

GOAL V.

The student will acquire those fine motor skills that will allow him or her to use his or her upper extremities optimally in operating simple appliances, objects, conveniences, and home accessories.

SPECIFIC OBJECTIVES

See Unit 4, "Household Management and Living Skills," for specific objectives and suggested activities in this area.

Sample Lesson Plan 1

Topic Area: Fine Motor Skills

Designed by: Sally Hewitt

Time Recommended: 30 Minutes

Student Involved: Tommy (Infant/Toddler Special Class)

Background Information:

The student has limited oral receptive language. He does appear to comprehend some spoken words; for example, when asked, he looks at objects with which he is familiar if they are located in the room and he can select objects from a group in front of him. He can follow simple, one-step directions and is compliant with routine requests. The student does not respond to instructional situations without oral praise or token/food rewards. The student has no known food allergies and has good oral motor ability. The student can sit up and engage in purposeful arm and hand movements, although muscle control can vary and strength may be weak, depending on the size of the object.

General Goal *(Fine Motor Skills I):*

The student will acquire those initial manipulative skills that will facilitate the development of more advanced fine motor skills and the functional use of the upper extremities.

Specific Objective *(Fine Motor Skills I-B):*

The student reaches for and grasps objects.

Lesson Objective:

When the student is presented with varying sizes of objects, the student will track the object, reach for it, and grasp the object with control.

Materials and Equipment:

- Red rings
- Nerf balls
- Plush animals
- Whiffle balls
- Small, brightly colored blocks
- Bell with a handle

Motivating Activity:

Have the student select several objects to play with by naming them and holding them up one at a time, asking the student if he wants to play with the object. After you have at least three different types of toys, arrange the student in front of you with the objects just out of reach of the student. Hold them up one at a time, naming them as you do.

Instructional Procedures:

Initiation—Tell the student that each object is worth a certain reward. You can select such things as cereal, gummy bears, pieces of fruit, or other appropriate food stimuli that the student likes.

Guided Practice—Select the red rings and dangle them just out of reach of the student. Tell the student to reach for the rings, swinging them gently into the student's grasp. Repeat this activity until the student reaches independently. Reward the student with food. Repeat this with the plush toy and a bell, for example.

Independent Practice—Move the objects closer to the student and have him reach for an object and hand it to you as you reach your hand out next to the object. Use abundant verbal praise as the student reaches to grasp the object.

Closure—Provide the student with additional objects within range and have the student select additional objects of similar shapes.

Assessment Strategy:

Observe the student to determine whether he grasps the objects and is able to hold them independently, varying the shape and size.

Follow-Up Activity or Objective:

If the student achieves the lesson objective, proceed to a lesson involving transferring the objects into a container.

Sample Lesson Plan 2

Topic Area: Fine Motor Skills

Designed by: Serena Blake

Time Recommended: 30 Minutes

Student Involved: Sammy (Secondary Class)

Background Information:

The student has well-developed oral receptive language. He comprehends a variety of spoken words and phrases but is not expressive verbally. He responds poorly to changes in routine and conflicting directions. He also has a limited sight-reading vocabulary. He prefers to work independently and, once a task is mastered, does not respond well to additional instruction on the same task.

General Goal *(Fine Motor Skills IV):*

The student will acquire those fine motor skills that will enable him to use his upper extremities optimally in vocational/work activities.

Specific Objective *(Fine Motor Skills IV-Y):*

The student uses a screwdriver.

Lesson Objective:

When the student is asked to select a screwdriver from a toolbox to tighten a screw, the student will select the correct tool.

Materials and Equipment:

- Toolbox

- Basic set of tools, including hammer, screwdriver, pliers, and file
- Flashcards for names of tools

Motivating Activity:

Identify furniture in the classroom that may have loose screws. Involve the student in checking for screws in each chair that may require tightening.

Instructional Procedures:

Initiation—Tell the student that, when he finishes his current activity, he will help you select a tool to tighten a screw on the desk. Explain that you will be pointing to the objects in the tool box and then naming them. At this point, show the student the tool box and explain that you will be picking up each tool and naming it so that he may learn the names of the tools to help you. Demonstrate with the screwdriver.

Guided Practice—Pick up each tool and name it. Show the student the flashcard with the name of each tool as you name the tool. Hand the student each tool, naming it as you do, and have him place it in the tool box. Continue to do this until the student is able to hand you the screwdriver and name it.

Independent Practice—Ask the student to help a classmate select the screwdriver from the tool box.

Closure—Ask the student to help you by getting the screwdriver from the tool box to assist you as you tighten the desk screws.

Assessment Strategy:

Observe the student to determine whether he correctly and quickly responded to "Give me the screwdriver."

Follow-Up Activity or Objective:

If the student achieves the lesson objective, proceed to a lesson involving the use of the screwdriver.

References

Banus, B. S., Kent, C. A., Norton, Y., Sukiennicki, D. R., & Becker, M. L. (1979). *The developmental therapist.* Thorofare, NJ: Charles B. Slack.

Bender, M., Valletutti, P. J., & Baglin, C. A. (in press). *A functional curriculum for teaching students with disabilities: Vol. IV. Interpersonal Skills, Competitive Job-Finding, and Leisure Time Skills.* Austin, TX: PRO-ED.

Clark, J. E., & Humphrey, J. H. (Eds.). (1985). *Motor development: Current selected research.* Princeton, NJ: Princeton Book Co.

Edgar, E., Maser, J. T., & Haring, N. G. (1977). Button up! A systematic approach for teaching children to fasten. *Teaching Exceptional Children, 9,*104–105.

Erhardt, R. P. (1994). *Developmental hand dysfunction* (rev. ed.). Tucson, AZ: Therapy Skill Builders.

Kramer, L., & Whitehurst, C. (1981). Effects of button features on self-dressing in young retarded children. *Education and Training of the Mentally Retarded, 16,* 277–283.

Lombardi, T. P. (1992). *Learning strategies for problem learners.* Bloomington, IN: Phi Delta Kappa Educational Foundation.

Redleaf, R. (1994). *Busy fingers, growing minds.* Mt. Rainier, MD: Redleaf Press.

Sternlicht, M., & Hurwitz, R. (1981). *Games children play: Instructive and creative play activities for the mentally retarded and developmentally disabled child.* New York: Van Nostrand Reinhold.

Stinson, W. J. (1990). *Moving and learning for the young child.* Reston, VA: American Alliance for Health, Physical Education, Recreation and Dance.

Toys R Us. (1994). *Toy guide for differently-abled.* Nevada, IA: Author.

Adelson, N., & Sandow, L. (1978). Teaching buttoning to severely/profoundly multihandi-capped children. *Education and Training of the Mentally Retarded, 13,* 178–183.

Bayley, N. (1969). *Manual for the Bayley scales of infant development.* New York: Psycholog-ical Corp.

Bender, M., & Baglin, C. A. (Eds.). (1992). *Infants and toddlers—A resource guide for practi-tioners.* San Diego: Singular Publishing.

Bower, T.G.R. (1977). *A primer of infant development.* San Francisco: Freeman.

Brown, F. R., & Elksnin, N. (1994). *Introduction to developmental disabilities—A develop-mental perspective.* San Diego: Singular Publishing.

Church, G., & Glennen, S. (Eds.). (1991). *The handbook of assistive technology.* San Diego: Singular Publishing.

Cipani, E., Augustine, A., & Blomgren, E. (1980). Teaching the severely and profoundly retarded to open doors: Assessment and training. *Journal of Special Education Technology, 3,* 42–46.

Copeland, M., Ford, L., & Solon, N. (1976). *Occupational therapy for mentally retarded chil-dren.* Baltimore: University Park Press.

Crnic, K. A., & Pym, H. A. (1979). Training mentally retarded adults in independent living skills. *Mental Retardation, 17,* 13–16.

Dunn, M. L. (1979). *Pre-scissor skills: Skill-starters for motor development.* Tucson, AZ: Com-munication Skill Builders.

Ford, L. J. (1975) Teaching dressing skills to a severely retarded child. *American Journal of Occupational Therapy, 29,* 87–92.

Fulkerson, S. C., & Treeman, W. M. (1980). Perceptual–motor deficiency in autistic children. *Perceptual and Motor Skills, 50,* 331–336.

Healy, H., & Stainback, S. B. (1980). *The severely motorically impaired student: A handbook for the classroom teacher.* Springfield, IL: Thomas.

Kissinger, E. M. (1981). *A sequential curriculum for the severely and profoundly mentally retarded/multihandicapped.* Springfield, IL: Thomas.

Leff, R. B. (1975). Teaching mentally retarded children and adults to dial the telephone. *Mental Retardation, 13,* 9–11.

Masters, L. F., Mori, B. A., & Mori, A. A. (1993). *Teaching secondary students with mild learning and behavior problems* (2nd ed.). Austin, TX: PRO-ED.

Maynard, M. (1976). The value of creative arts for the developmentally disabled child: Impli-cations for recreation therapists in community day service programs. *Therapeutic Recreation Journal, 10,* 10–13.

McCormick, J. E. (1977). *Motor development: Manual of alternative procedures.* Medford: Massachusetts Center for Program Development and Evaluation.

Minneapolis Public Schools. (1978). *Task analyses and objectives for trainable mentally retarded: Communication skills, daily living skills, motor skills, and quantitative skills.* Minneapolis: Author.

Montgomery, P., & Richter, E. (1977). Effect of sensory integrative therapy on the neuromotor development of retarded children. *Physical Therapy, 57,* 799–806.

Mori, A. A., & Masters, L. F. (1980). *Teaching the severely mentally retarded: Adaptive skills training.* Germantown, MD: Aspen Systems.

Mullins, J. (1979). *A teacher's guide to management of physically handicapped students.* Springfield, IL: Thomas.

Penso, D. (1993). *Perceptuo-motor difficulties—Theory and strategies to help children, adolescents, and adults.* San Diego: Singular Publishing.

Robinson, C. C., & Robinson, J. H. (1978). Sensorimotor functions and cognitive development. In M. E. Snell (Ed.), *Systematic instruction of the moderately and severely handicapped.* Columbus, OH: Merrill.

Roman, B. (1978). *Infant stimulation training skills from infancy to 36 months.* Johnston, PA: Mafex Association.

Snell, M. E. (Ed.). (1978). *Systematic instruction of the moderately and severely handicapped.* Columbus, OH: Merrill.

Stainback, S., & Stainback, W. (1988). Educating students with severe disabilities in regular classes. *Teaching Exceptional Children, 21,* 16–19.

Walls, R. T., Crist, K., Sienicki, D. A., & Grant, L. (1981). Prompting sequences in teaching independent living skills. *Mental Retardation, 19,* 243–246.

Whitney, P. L. (1978). Measurement for curriculum building for multiply handicapped children. *Physical Therapy, 58,* 15–20.

Selected Materials/Resources

KITS/CURRICULAR MATERIALS

- *AEPS Curriculum for Birth to Three Years*
  Paul H. Brookes Publishing Co.
  PO Box 10624
  Baltimore, Maryland 21285-0624
  (800) 638-3775

- *Readiness: Strategies and Practice*
  The Brigance System
  Curriculum Associates, Inc.
  5 Esquire Road
  North Billerica, Massachusetts 01862-2589
  (800) 225-0248

- *Self-Help Skills Kit*
  EBSCO Curriculum Materials
  Division of EBSCO Industries, Inc.
  Box 11521
  Birmingham, Alabama 35202-1521
  (800) 633-8623

VIDEOS

- *Normal Infant Reflexes and Development*
  Therapy Skill Builders
  3830 East Bellevue
  PO Box 42050-TS4
  Tucson, Arizona 85733
  (602) 323-7500

- *Positioning for Infants and Young Children with Motor Problems*
  Learner Managed Designs, Inc.
  2201-K West 25th Street
  Lawrence, Kansas 66047
  (913) 842-9088

- *Teaching People with Developmental Disabilities* (4 videocassettes)
  Research Press
  Department N
  PO Box 9177
  Champaign, Illinois 61826
  (217) 352-3273

ASSISTIVE DEVICES

- *Assistive Technology Sourcebook*
  Special Needs Project
  1482 East Valley Road A-121
  Santa Barbara, California 93108
  (800) 333-6867

- *Customized Activity Boxes*
  Jesana, Ltd.
  PO Box 17
  Irvington, New York 10533
  (800) 443-4728

- *IntelliTools, Inc.*
  5221 Central Avenue
  Suite 205
  Richmond, California 94804
  (800) 899-6687

- *Meeting Street Center*
  Assistive Technology Center
  667 Waterman Avenue
  East Providence, Rhode Island 02914
  (401) 438-9500

- *Right-Line Paper: The Paper with Raised Lines*
  PRO-ED, Inc.
  8700 Shoal Creek Boulevard
  Austin, Texas 78757-6897
  (512) 451-3246

- *Utilizing Switch Interfaces with Children Who Are Severely Physically Challenged*
  (by Carol Goossens & Sharon Sapp Crain)
  PRO-ED, Inc.
  8700 Shoal Creek Boulevard
  Austin, Texas 78757-6897
  (512) 451-3246

Household Management and Living Skills

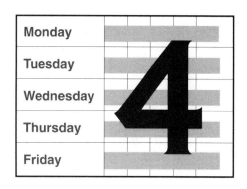

Monday	
Tuesday	
Wednesday	**4**
Thursday	
Friday	

Functioning successfully in a home environment is a basic skill required of all people. The skills associated with acquiring and maintaining a suitable and appropriate household must therefore be included in curricular experiences as early as possible in the school career and then must be continually stressed into adulthood.

When home-oriented school experiences are provided in the schools, they traditionally are scheduled in the secondary years. Unfortunately, many such experiences are last-minute attempts to bridge the gap between the artificiality of typical curricula and the reality of the world the soon-to-graduate student will face. It therefore becomes imperative that preparation for successful functioning as a member of a household should start with the beginning school years and not just before upper school commencement. School and home experiences must be coordinated in cooperative attempts by teachers, related staff, and parents to provide consistency, reinforcement, and practice (Schloss, Smith, & Schloss, 1990). The home, as the natural environment, provides a special laboratory where newly acquired skills can be practiced in vivo, thus increasing the likelihood that the skills will be maintained and will be expressed independently at a future time.

This unit illuminates the critical need for modification and adaptations in school design and equipment. To successfully program for these instructional experiences, it would be valuable to have a model living unit and to have present the furniture and appliances normally found in a home (Patton, Cronin, Polloway, Hutchinson, & Robinson, 1989). A broom, dustpan, and vacuum cleaner thus become important educational equipment equal to or surpassing the functional value of a piece of equipment more usually identified as important, such as a tape recorder.

The home not only provides the natural setting in which students may acquire the variety of skills pertinent to that setting, but also provides a place where parents or their counterparts may work with their children on a variety of other skills that transcend settings, for example, communication and interpersonal skills. Because of the critical role parents must play in the education of children with disabilities, and because education for this population cannot be restricted to a school schedule, school programs must include a strong parental training program (VanBuren, 1989).

205

The myriad tasks inherent in becoming and being an integral part of a cohesive and successful household must receive the attention of curriculum planners and must be assiduously taught. These tasks include those activities of daily life that arise from planning, purchasing, storing, and preparing food (Amary, 1979; Johnson & Cuvo, 1981), as well as purchasing and maintaining clothes (Bender & Valletutti, 1982; Cuvo, Jacobi, & Sipko, 1981). They also extend to the many activities required to satisfactorily maintain the household and its various functional and decorative equipment, appliances, and accessories (Brolin, 1991). Further, they encompass those competencies that make any home a satisfying and pleasurable place to live, to carry out countless household duties and responsibilities, to engage in various interpersonal exchanges, and to spend time in leisure activities (Bender, 1994; Stacy-Sherrer, 1981).

Designing a curriculum that proposes to prepare individuals with disabilities for competent participation in the life of a household demands the identification of the broad range of skills that effective, efficient, and safe household membership requires. This challenge to instructional planners at first glance seems a simple one because to appreciate the scope of the functional requirements of membership in a household, one merely must analyze the skills necessary to function in one's own household. However, to those who have already acquired the skills, the automatic nature of these behaviors masks their subtle presence, interfering with the process of defining their scope and sequence.

As with the other units, the Suggested Readings and Selected Materials/Resources at the end of the unit provide additional information for the reader. In this case, the information is specific to skills involving household management and living. The reader should decide which materials and information are applicable to a specific student or students being taught.

I. The student will be functionally independent in planning meals and in purchasing, storing, and preparing food in a manner that allows him or her to perform optimally.

II. The student will be functionally independent in purchasing and maintaining his or her clothes in a manner that allows him or her to perform optimally.

III. The student will be functionally independent in caring for his or her living quarters, appliances, and furnishings in a manner that allows him or her to perform optimally.

IV. The student will operate simple appliances, objects, conveniences, and home accessories.

GOAL I.

The student will be functionally independent in planning meals and in purchasing, storing, and preparing food in a manner that allows him or her to perform optimally.

Independent living skills are an essential component of a comprehensive education program for children with disabilities. Skills related to the preparation of meals enhance the abilities of young children to contribute in their home environment and is a significant measure in assessing the readiness of young adults for independent community living.

A basic understanding of nutrition is crucial for increasing the likelihood of long-term success for any young person in independent living. Understanding that proper nutrition not only is a component of good health but also must be incorporated in the selection and storage of food enriches the curriculum beyond the more traditional scope of basic cooking skills.

SPECIFIC OBJECTIVES

The student:

❑ A. Plans nutritious meals and snacks.

❑ B. Purchases the food needed for nutritious meals and snacks.

❑ C. After shopping, stores food in appropriate places before eating or cooking.

❑ D. Opens and closes food packages without the use of tools.

❑ E. Opens food packages using various can and bottle openers.

❑ F. Throws out food that is spoiled or contaminated.

❑ G. Effectively and safely uses kitchen utensils.

❑ H. Prepares simple, nutritious snacks or parts of meals that require no heating or cooking.

❑ I. Effectively and safely operates major appliances, including a stove, microwave oven, and dishwasher.

❑ J. Effectively and safely operates simple appliances used in cooking.

❑ K. Prepares simple, nutritious snacks or parts of meals requiring heating or minimal cooking.

❑ L. Prepares simple, nutritious meals using cooking utensils and appliances.

❑ M. Sets the table for serving informal meals.

❑ N. Washes, dries, and stores kitchen equipment, dishes, glasses, and silverware.

❑ O. Stores unused and/or leftover food in appropriate wrappings, containers, and places.

SUGGESTED ACTIVITIES

 ### Specific Objective A

The student plans nutritious meals and snacks.

Teacher Interventions

Primary Level.   Draw a balanced menu chart (see Figure 4.1) for each meal as a reference guide for the student.

Place pictures of nutritious foods on the chart from which the student can select his or her meals. Color-code those items that represent the same nutritional category; for example, a red circle underneath the picture of two eggs and a red circle underneath the picture of a small bowl of cereal will show that they may be substituted for each other.

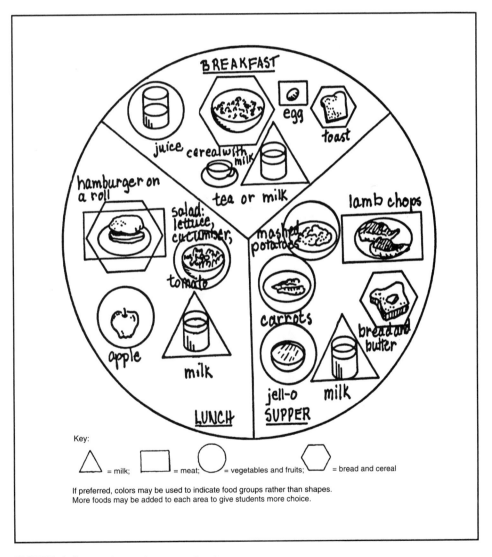

FIGURE 4.1.   Balanced menu chart.

Indicate to the student that he or she should have one red-marked food, one blue-marked food, one yellow-marked food, and so forth. (Geometric shapes, rebuses, or other symbols may be used as substitutes for color cues. Use pictures of nutritious foods that the student likes.)

Help the student to select his or her own daily menu from this chart. Prepare a meal. While the student is eating the meal, remind him or her that he or she has selected a balanced meal.

Conduct a nutritious food tasting party for the student and his or her guests.

Family Interventions

Primary Level. Ask the parents to help their child plan a small breakfast, luncheon, or dinner party for friends or classmates. After the meal planning has been completed, tell the parents to prepare and serve the meal to the child and his or her guests.

Ask the parents to offer nutritious snacks at established times during the day (midmorning and/or midafternoon). Snacks such as nuts, raisins, fruit, sliced carrots, and other raw vegetables may be used. Tell them to indicate that these are good foods to snack on between meals if they get hungry.

At all times, parents should consider the individual medical record as it relates to body weight, skin blemishes, allergies, and metabolic problems.

Secondary Level. Suggest to the parents that they find a local restaurant that has nutritious meals and nutritious hints on their menu. Ask them to obtain a copy of the menu and review it with their child. Have them follow up this activity by taking their child to the restaurant for a nutritious meal.

 ## Specific Objective B

The student purchases the food needed for nutritious meals and snacks.

Teacher Interventions

Primary Level. (Note: The activities listed below can also be done at home as part of Family Interventions. The parents should be urged to allow their child as much freedom as possible in implementing these critical survival activities.)

Encourage the student to fill out a shopping list form similar to the one in Figure 4.2. The form, when needed, should include pictures or sketches of the items to be purchased. Amounts may be penciled in next to each article (e.g., 1 dozen, 5 pounds). Encourage students to check off each article as it is purchased.

Once the student has developed his or her own individualized meal chart, take him or her on a trip to a supermarket or grocery store. Walk around the store with the student and match each of the foods on the chart with its actual counterpart.

Begin making purchases by concentrating first on buying the foods needed for breakfast. As you place each item in the shopping basket,

FIGURE 4.2. Shopping list form.

comment on the fact that it is a good breakfast food. Show the student the quantity to buy.

Make a chart for breakfast shopping; for example, a dozen eggs, a container of milk, a loaf of bread, cereal, and juice. Indicate on the chart the next shopping day and the quantity needed to take the student to that date. Add the exact number or amount of each article by showing pictures that indicate the exact quantity. For example, a picture of two cans of orange juice could be used to indicate the exact purchase needed. Repeat this activity for lunch foods and then for dinner.

Gradually reduce the amount of assistance given to the student until he or she has reached the point when he or she can "solo" in the supermarket or grocery. Reward the student for his or her independent performance. (Note: Whenever the student purchases an item that can be used for several meals, this should be indicated.)

Secondary Level. Ask the student to plan a nutritious "snack" party. Provide the student with a budget and the daily food section of the newspapers or a food store flyer. After the student selects the foods, check to see if they are indeed within the range of being considered nutritious.

Point out foods that may not be considered appropriate and tell the student why. After the activity, purchase the foods and have a nutritious snack party with some of the student's friends.

 ## Specific Objective C

The student, after shopping, stores food in appropriate places before eating or cooking.

Teacher Interventions

Primary Level. In the case of fresh fruits and vegetables, indicate that they go in the refrigerator so they will last longer. Conduct a demonstration by refrigerating part of a purchase of fruit or vegetables while not refrigerating the other part of the same purchase. Show the student the spoilage that occurs, including the discoloration, shriveling, and odor of the unrefrigerated fruits and vegetables. Praise the student for putting fresh fruits and vegetables in the refrigerator. (Note: Teach handling of bananas separately.)

Indicate that most jars or bottles that have been opened should be refrigerated. (Note: Although there are some items in opened jars and bottles that do not need to be refrigerated, it is best to teach the general practice because it is extremely unhealthy not to refrigerate mayonnaise, for example, whereas it is not unhealthy to refrigerate an item like honey, which does not need refrigeration.)

Family Interventions

Primary Level. Ask the parents to demonstrate to their child how to unpack the groceries after grocery shopping. Tell them to assist their child in unpacking the bags and in separating the food items into three groups: those to be refrigerated, those to be put in the freezer, and those to be stored in cabinets. Use a food storage chart (see Figure 4.3) to which the child may refer when necessary. The family should establish a routine to assist their child (for example, canned goods are always put in the same cabinet) and encourage their child to unpack and store food as soon as he or she returns from shopping.

Tell the parents to label the cabinets, refrigerator, and freezer, if necessary, by attaching small pictures of the appropriate items to them. Actual labels from products purchased may also be used.

Parents should show their child how the storing of the items at home relates to the way they are arranged in the store. When removing an item from a store shelf, the parents should say to their child, "This can go on a shelf at home." They should remind him or her to notice that the item is not cold and say, "It isn't kept cold at the store, so we don't have to keep it cold at home before using it." (Note: This general rule does not hold in the case of fresh fruits and vegetables, which must be taught as an exception.)

Similarly, when a refrigerated item is purchased, the parents should indicate to their child that it is cold because it is being kept in the store's refrigerator, so it must be refrigerated at home, too. They should also point out the differences in the hardness of the frozen items in the frozen food storage bins as compared to the display cases, and indicate that items kept in the store's freezer are to be put in the home freezer.

Secondary Level. Ask the parents to have their child, as part of routine chores, be responsible for putting away the groceries after shopping. Suggest that the parents purchase several new products each time they go shopping.

Ask the parents to monitor where their child places these new products, as well as providing help in case the child does not know where to store them.

Specific Objective D

The student opens and closes food packages without the use of tools.

FIGURE 4.3. Food storage chart.

Teacher Interventions

Primary Level. (Note: The activities listed below can also be done at home. The parents should be encouraged to teach the opening of a variety of types of packages that are normally found in the child's home and immediate environment. Also, many of these activities can be used at both the primary and secondary levels.)

For each of the food items included in the student's food charts, demonstrate to the student how to open the package before using it. Begin by opening packages that require only the use of the hands.

Demonstrate opening and closing boxes that simply require lifting the top flap out. Assist the student in identifying the top of the package. Point out pictures on the package as a guide to the top and bottom of each box. If a package has no pictures, try showing the student the difference between upside-down and right-side-up letters.

If this is not possible, furnish the student with a reference chart of familiar packages (see Figure 4.4) to which he or she can match his or her package. Pictures may be drawn to size, or actual box fronts may be pasted on to aid in recognition. Remind the student to close the box and put it away.

Demonstrate opening and closing boxes that require the pulling of tear strips on cellophane wrappers, such as a box of tea bags. Assist the student. Practice opening the top of the box. Give the student a taste of the food or beverage when appropriate. Remind the student to close the box and put it away, assisting when necessary.

Demonstrate opening and closing boxes that require the pulling of cardboard tear strips, such as a package of Jell-O. Point out the pull tab and assist the student in opening the package and removing the contents. Prepare the food and give the student his or her share. If there is unused material, remind the student to close the box and put it away.

Demonstrate opening and closing boxes that require moving a cellophane strip placed over a pour spout, such as a box of salt. Point out the cellophane or adhesive strip and assist the student in removing it and opening the pour spout. Assist the student in closing the pour spout. Remind the student to put the box back where he or she found it.

Demonstrate opening and closing boxes with attached cap tops or snap tops, such as spice and bread crumb containers. Assist the student in opening the container and in shaking out or removing the contents. Remind him or her to close the container and put it away.

Demonstrate opening and closing containers with a pull-up cylindrical spout such as a mustard container. Assist the student in squeezing out just enough of the food and moving the spout back into its closed position. Remind the student to wipe the spout and to clean and return the jar to its storage place.

Demonstrate opening and closing containers with a tab zip-top such as a can of soda. Assist the student in doing so. Point out the danger of cuts. (Note: Tell students not to stick their tongues into the opening.) Remind the student to throw away the empty can or place it in a recycling bin. Remind him or her to place the unused portion in the refrigerator. Caution the student to dispose of the tab before drinking the beverage.

Demonstrate opening and closing boxes that require pressing in a tab and pulling a strip or section of the box open. Assist the student in

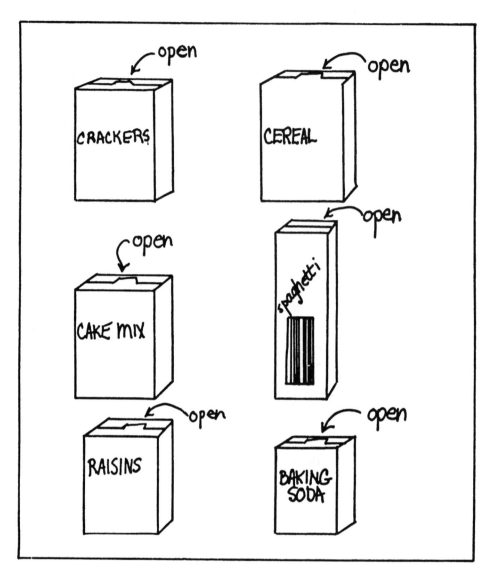

FIGURE 4.4.   Familiar packages chart.

removing the contents and closing the package. Remind him or her to return the package to its storage place.

Demonstrate opening and closing a container of milk, juice, or lemonade. Assist the student in doing so. Remind him or her to return the container to its storage place. Use different-sized containers of milk.

Demonstrate opening and closing a carton of eggs. Assist the student in doing so. Remind him or her to return the container to its storage place.

Demonstrate opening and closing a wrapped loaf of bread. Demonstrate the use of a twist tie in closing the package. Assist the student in doing so. Remind him or her to return the bread to its storage place.

Demonstrate opening and closing packages (often contained in boxes) that require tearing off the top, such as dry soup mixes. Assist the student in locating the top strip and tearing it open. Remind him or her to close the package and store it.

Demonstrate opening and closing containers with wheel tops, such as spice containers. Assist the student in opening the container, shaking out the contents, closing the container, and putting it back.

Demonstrate opening and closing tops of bottles and jars that require no tools. Assist the student in opening and closing jars or bottles. Reward the student with a taste of the food or beverage. Remind him or her to store the remainder in the refrigerator.

Demonstrate opening and closing a lidded can, such as powdered cocoa or baking powder. Assist the student in using the handle of a spoon to do so. Observe safety precautions. Assist the student in closing the container and remind the student to return it to its storage place.

 ## Specific Objective E

The student opens food packages using various can and bottle openers.

Teacher Interventions

Primary Level. (Note: The activities listed below can also be done at home. Exposure to opening as many types of food packages as possible is recommended.)

Demonstrate opening a can with ridged edges on the top and the bottom using a manually operated can opener. Help the student to identify cans with ridged edges. Assist him or her in opening a can. Follow safety precautions. When available, use an electric can opener.

Do not rely solely on the electric can opener, however, because the student must not be so reliant on an electric can opener that he or she would not be able to open a can if the electric opener should break or malfunction.

Demonstrate opening a can without ridges by using a "church key" or a juice opener. Assist the student in opening a juice can and pouring him- or herself and others glasses of juice. Help the student open a can of evaporated milk. Use the evaporated milk in a cooking activity.

Demonstrate opening a bottle with a twist top or cap by using a bottle opener. Assist the student in opening a bottle of carbonated beverage and pouring drinks for him- or herself and a friend.

Demonstrate opening a can with a key that is attached to the top or bottom of the can (e.g., a can of sardines). Help the student remove the key and wrap the metal on the key. Observe safety precautions.

Family Interventions

Secondary Level. After attending a community event, if their child is thirsty, the parents should purchase a beverage for their child from a vending machine. Ask them to monitor how the child opens the beverage in terms of safety and procedure. Suggest they emphasize where to discard any used cans or bottles. Have them praise the child if he or she does this appropriately.

 ## Specific Objective F

The student throws out food that is spoiled or contaminated.

Teacher Interventions

Primary Level. Indicate to the student that if something he or she normally eats looks bad, tastes bitter, or smells unpleasant, he or she should not eat it. Encourage him or her to use taste and smell as monitoring devices for rejecting food that might be spoiled.

Demonstrate how to check a can for swelling. Show the student samples of swollen cans. Assist him or her in throwing these cans out. When discarding these cans, indicate verbally and/or through gestures that the contents are not good to eat. Also use this checking activity in purchasing foods. Tell the student not to purchase dented cans.

Secondary Level. Just before a holiday when the school will be closed for an extended time, suggest that the student help you clean out a refrigerator. Many times, a small refrigerator can be found in a teacher's lounge, a home economics department, or the cafeteria.

After seeking permission to clean out the refrigerator, jointly go through different items for potential spoilage or contamination and discard them. After a while, have the student make his or her own decisions concerning which items need to be discarded.

Family Interventions

Primary Level. Ask the parents to point out food that is decayed. Tell them to show their child "before" and "after" samples and point out the visual signs of decay, including molds, wilting, and curdling. Tell them to indicate unpleasant odors as a sign of decay. (It is the contrast in appearance and smell between the good and bad samples that is the key.)

Tell the parents to join the child in eating the good sample and in rejecting the spoiled sample. Tell them to smile with satisfaction when eating the good sample, and to look upon the spoiled sample with disgust and push it aside, perhaps with an "ugh!" or gesture of disgust.

Ask the parents to encourage their child to check stored food for signs of spoilage (looks or odor). Tell them to reward their child for checking foods for spoilage.

Ask the parents to help their child to check uncooked eggs for cracked shells. Tell them to encourage the child to throw out cracked eggs or to return them to the store.

 ## Specific Objective G

The student effectively and safely uses kitchen utensils.

Teacher Interventions

(Note: The activities listed below can also be done at home. Using kitchen utensils appropriately is an especially critical area in terms of eating, cooking, and socialization skills and should be taught carefully and practiced often. Also, many of these activities can be used for both primary- and secondary-level interventions.)

Primary Level. Use a knives, forks, and spoons chart to identify different kinds of silverware (see Figure 4.5). Pictures may be sketched or cut from magazines, or real tableware may be attached to heavy cardboard for identification purposes. Begin by talking with the student about various kinds of knives, including butter knives, potato peelers, paring knives, steak knives, and electric knives. Demonstrate how to use various knives in preparing, cutting, and eating foods. Explain the safety rules to follow and demonstrate the precautions.

Use a chart (see Figure 4.5) and/or pictures to help the student identify different kinds of forks (regular, salad or cake, and long fork). Demonstrate how to use various forks. Assist the student in using each of these forks in preparing and eating foods.

FIGURE 4.5. Knives, forks, and spoons chart.

Demonstrate how to use a knife and fork together in cutting meat. Assist the student in doing so; cut, and, if appropriate, eat some slices of meat.

Use a chart (see Figure 4.5) and/or pictures to identify different types of spoons, such as a wooden spoon for mixing, a basting spoon, a soup spoon, and a teaspoon. Demonstrate the use of the various types of spoons. Assist the student in actually using spoons in preparing and eating foods.

Use a chart and/or pictures to identify various kinds of measuring spoons and cups (see Figure 4.6). Demonstrate how to use measuring spoons and cups for measuring. Assist the student in using them to prepare simple snacks or parts of a meal.

Use a chart and/or pictures to identify various pots and pans used for boiling, frying, broiling, roasting, and baking (see Figure 4.7). Color-code pots and pans according to their use (e.g., red = oven, blue = top of stove). For more advanced use, color-code for boiling, baking, and frying. Demonstrate how to use various pots and pans for cooking. Assist the student in using each of these in preparing a snack or part of a meal.

 ## Specific Objective H

The student prepares simple, nutritious snacks or parts of meals that require no heating or cooking.

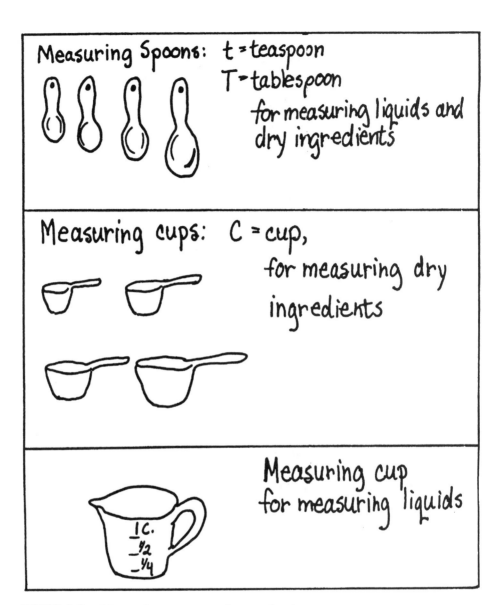

FIGURE 4.6. Measuring spoons and cups chart.

Teacher Interventions

(Note: The activities listed below can also be done at home. Use of nutritious snacks instead of "junk food" needs to be stressed to both parents and child. Also, many of these activities can be used for both primary- and secondary-level interventions.)

Primary Level. Demonstrate to the student how to prepare foods that require peeling before eating (e.g., tangerines, bananas, and hard-boiled eggs). Help

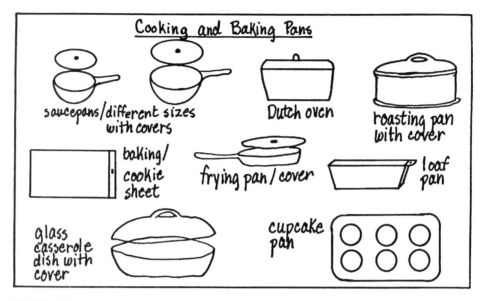

FIGURE 4.7.   Cooking and baking pans chart.

the student peel each of these foods. Praise and encourage the student throughout the task. When the food is peeled, allow him or her to eat it at appropriate times.

Demonstrate to the student how to prepare foods that require washing before eating (e.g., apples, peaches, pears, plums, grapes, leafy vegetables, carrots, and celery). Tell the student to wash each of these foods, indicating that each of them may be eaten immediately after being washed clean, with no further preparation needed.

Demonstrate to the student how to prepare foods that merely require pouring from a container (e.g., fruit juices and milk). Assist the student in opening and pouring these liquids and let the student enjoy the snack at an appropriate time.

Demonstrate to the student how to prepare foods that can be eaten directly from the container: finger foods such as peanuts, raisins, dry cereals, dried fruits, and pickles; and foods that require utensils, such as cottage cheese, yogurt, applesauce, canned fruits, pickled beets, sauerkraut, three-bean salad, pig's feet, gefilte fish, and sardines.

Assist the student in preparing these foods and eating them. (Note: In selecting foods, pay attention to the student's individual tastes, special dietary needs, and cultural and religious background.)

Demonstrate how to prepare foods that require cutting (e.g., tomatoes, cucumbers, peppers, celery, and carrots) before eating. Assist the student in preparing each of these foods and follow through by letting the student eat them at appropriate times.

Demonstrate the preparation of foods that require spreading, such as mayonnaise, butter, margarine, mustard, ketchup, jellies, jams, spreadable cheese, and peanut butter. Assist the student in spreading each of these on bread, crackers, or celery, and then have the student eat the prepared snacks at appropriate times.

Demonstrate how to make sandwiches. Identify foods that can be used as sandwich filler (e.g., meats, cheese, spreadables, and salads). Assist the student in preparing sandwiches with the above foods either singly or in combination (e.g., peanut butter and jelly or ham and cheese). Assist the student in adding condiments such as mustard or mayonnaise when appropriate.

Demonstrate how to prepare foods that may be mixed, such as vegetable, tuna, chicken, ham, cottage cheese, and fruit salads; fruit; cereal; milk (also instant powders such as skim milk); frozen concentrates; peanuts; and raisins. Assist the student in preparing each of these snacks, and let the student eat the prepared meals at appropriate times.

 ## Specific Objective I

The student effectively and safely operates major appliances, including a stove, microwave oven, and dishwasher.

Teacher Interventions

(Note: The activities listed below require the use of a school stove. If one is available, practice the following activities. *In all cases,* emphasize the use of safety precautions and predetermine if the following activities are appropriate for the student's present skills and abilities. All activities in this section require adult supervision.)

Primary and Secondary Levels. Demonstrate regulating flames underneath pots and pans. Encourage the use of a low flame (flames should never extend out beyond the sides of the pan). Assist the student and praise him or her for effectively and safely carrying out the cooking task.

Demonstrate the checking of water levels, cooking status of food, and boiling levels to prevent boiling over or burning of foods. Demonstrate turning the burner off.

Demonstrate the use of a pot holder to remove lids and to remove pots and pans from the stove. Caution the student that he or she should be careful to avoid escaping steam. Assist the student in these processes and reward him or her for effectively and safely doing them. Hang up or put away the pot holder after using it.

Demonstrate turning an oven first on and then off. Indicate that an oven is helpful for heating foods; for baking cakes, bread, and cookies; and for broiling and roasting foods. Warn that an oven can be dangerous.

Demonstrate turning the oven dial to various levels. Use an enlarged teacher-made dial or gauge for practice purposes. Assist the student in doing so safely and effectively.

Help the student to identify temperatures on packages to be heated in an oven. Tell the student to match the numbers to corresponding ones on an oven dial.

Prepare foods that require the use of an oven. Encourage the student to become familiar with the oven, especially with how long it takes for the oven to go on (automatic pilot).

Assist the student in removing foods from the oven safely, including sliding of trays, use of pot holders, and waiting for some cooling to occur.

Practice the above activities for a variety of social occasions.

Family Interventions

Primary and Secondary Levels. Ask the parents to take their child into the kitchen and point out the stove. Tell them to indicate to the child in some way that the stove is needed to help cook food. Tell them to stress that a stove can be dangerous if it is not used correctly and point out hazards such as gas escaping because the burner has failed to light, has gone out, or is partially turned on.

Tell them to warn the child of the heat of the flames or coils (electric), the heat occurring during cooking, and the heat remaining in pots, pot lids, and pot handles recently used for cooking. The child should be reminded never to leave metal cooking utensils in pots because they retain heat and could burn his or her hand if grasped.

Ask the parents to demonstrate turning each burner on and off. Tell them to make continual references to safety hazards and safety checks. Remind them to indicate that, if a gas burner fails to light, it should be turned off immediately.

Ask the parents to demonstrate putting pots and pans on the stove. Tell them to indicate that the child should make sure handles are on tight and that, when the pot or pan is placed on the stove, the handle should not be over another burner or hanging over the front of the stove. Tell them to help the child to do this and praise him or her for doing it effectively and safely.

 ## Specific Objective J

The student effectively and safely operates simple appliances used in cooking.

Teacher Interventions

(Note: Some activities listed below can also be done at home using the same or similar appliances.)

Primary and Secondary Levels. Plan a party that requires the student to open cans (e.g., making lemonade or orange juice). Observe whether the student uses the can opener appropriately and safely. Praise the student if he or she does it correctly.

Demonstrate the use of a toaster. Show the student how to plug the toaster in and show him or her that the dial is color- or number-coded. Warn the student of the following points: (a) always keep the dial or arrow in the middle, (b) never butter bread before you toast it, and (c) never insert anything but food in the toaster or in any electrical appliance.

Tell the student that, if toast does not pop up in time or if it starts burning or smoking, he or she can push the button up to make it pop up. Demonstrate how to push the button up and remove the toast from the toaster.

Show the student how to unplug the toaster. Urge the student never to wrap cords around appliances or cover appliances while they are still warm and never to immerse electrical appliances or cords in water.

Demonstrate the use of a can opener to the student by following these steps. First, put the plug in the outlet. Second, demonstrate how to lift the lever, and explain to the student that the blade and magnet are on the lever. Holding the can by the bottom, put the can directly against the can opener and push the lever down using force. The blade should cut the can on the edge and the can will begin to rotate. After the can is completely opened, hold the can by the bottom and lift or release the lever. Remove the can and empty the contents from it. Carefully remove the lid from the magnet and discard it in a safe manner.

 ### Specific Objective K

The student prepares simple, nutritious snacks or parts of meals requiring heating or minimal cooking.

Teacher Interventions

Primary Level. Demonstrate the use of a toaster for waffles, Pop Tarts, bread, English muffins, and bagels. Assist the student in doing so safely and effectively. Eat the prepared food as part of a regular meal.

Secondary Level. Demonstrate the use of frying for cooking eggs, bacon, sausage, meats, and fish. Show the student how to put oil in the pan first. Practice. Assist the student in safely and effectively preparing these fried foods. Eat the prepared foods as part of a regular meal.

Family Interventions

Primary and Secondary Levels. Ask the parents to demonstrate to their child the use of boiling water for cooking vegetables, rice, macaroni, noodles, potatoes, prepared packages, soups, eggs, frankfurters, bouillon, tea, and hot chocolate. Tell them to assist their child in doing so safely and effectively. The prepared food should be served as part of a regular meal.

Ask the parents to demonstrate to their child the use of the oven for heating frozen dinners, frozen pies, cakes, cookies, and bread, and for baking, roasting, and broiling. Tell them to assist their child in doing so safely and effectively. The prepared food should be served as part of a regular meal. Ask the parents to emphasize the identification of cooking directions and/or pictures found on food and food products.

 ## Specific Objective L

The student prepares simple, nutritious meals using cooking utensils and appliances.

Teacher Interventions

Primary and Secondary Levels. With the students, visit the school cafeteria or other location where food is prepared in the school to observe the utensils that are used for cooking. Return to the class and discuss what was observed, and ask the student to explain why certain utensils are used for certain foods.

Family Interventions

Primary Level. Ask the parents to assist their child in preparing breakfast or one of the other daily meals. Tell them to provide an opportunity for him or her to use appliances and cooking utensils. The prepared meal should be served.

Secondary Level. Ask the parents to plan a party with their child. Tell them to suggest that the child invite a few friends or family members. Tell the parents to assist their child in preparing for the party by planning a menu and cooking food (e.g., spaghetti, fruit drink, and pudding).

 ## Specific Objective M

The student sets the table for serving informal meals.

Teacher Interventions

Primary Level. Assist the student in setting the table. Show the student where and how to place items. Demonstrate and then assist the student in folding napkins. Guide him or her in placing the napkins at the place settings on the table.

Secondary Level. Plan a surprise party for one of the students or staff. As part of giving assignments, ask the student to be responsible for setting the entire table. Suggest that he or she ask others to help, but tell him or her he or she is responsible for how it looks when the job is completed. If it is done correctly, praise the student at the appropriate time.

Family Interventions

Primary and Secondary Levels. Ask the parents to practice the above activities at home with their child.

Ask the parents to point out to their child how the tables are set when the family is dining out in a restaurant.

 ## Specific Objective N

The student washes, dries, and stores kitchen equipment, dishes, glasses, and silverware.

Teacher Interventions

Primary and Secondary Levels. After a party or meal, ask the student to help in washing and drying the dishes. Praise him or her for doing a good job.

Bring the student to the school cafeteria and point out the various equipment, dishes, and silverware. Point out how the dishes are washed (both by hand and by machine).

Family Interventions

Primary Level. Ask the parents to identify the dishwashing detergent to be used and distinguish it from other cleaning agents. Tell them to demonstrate the cleaning of dishes to their child.

Tell the parents to demonstrate different water temperatures to their child. Tell them to first help their child fill three dishpans with water of different temperatures, and then to ask him or her to feel the water in each pan (be sure none is too hot). They should select the water temperature that is most suitable for dishwashing and tell him or her why they selected it (e.g., hot water cuts grease, kills germs).

Ask the parents to display a dishcloth, dish towel, dishpan, scouring pad, dish rack, and draining board for their child to identify.

Ask the parents to stack the dishes on the counter in preparation for washing. Tell them to place the glasses in soapy water before storing table leftovers, and to use a wet dishcloth or sponge to wash off the table.

Ask the parents to demonstrate to their child washing first the glasses, then the china, then the silverware, and then the pots and pans. Remind them to show the proper use of scouring pads and the placement of dishes on the drain board. Tell them to encourage the child to imitate their actions and practice washing the dishes.

Secondary Level. Once the parents feel their child is proficient at washing and drying dishes, have them suggest that the child volunteer to do this as his or her contribution for having a small family party where he or she can invite several friends. Have the party and monitor how well the child does this activity.

 ## Specific Objective O

The student stores unused and/or leftover food in appropriate wrappings, containers, and places.

Teacher Interventions

(Note: The Teacher Interventions activities, when appropriate, can be taught in the same manner as the Family Interventions listed below.)

Family Interventions

Primary and Secondary Levels. Ask the parents to demonstrate to their child wrapping an unused portion of meat or meat leftovers in aluminum foil or clear plastic wrap. The child is to imitate their actions and to wrap left-overs. Remind the parents to indicate that all leftover meats or unused portions of meat are to be put in the refrigerator.

Tell them to assist their child in refrigerating the meat and to warn him or her in some way that defrosted meats and other things go into the refrigerator and never back into the freezer.

Ask the parents to demonstrate to their child placing nonmeat left-overs and unused portions of food into covered bowls, Pyrex containers, Tupperware, and cleaned used jars. Tell them to assist their child in doing so. They should indicate that all leftovers and all unused portions of foods that were not originally in paper or cardboard packages are to be stored in the refrigerator. Tell them to assist their child in doing this and reward him or her for doing it appropriately.

GOAL II.

The student will be functionally independent in purchasing and maintaining his or her clothes in a manner that allows him or her to perform optimally.

SPECIFIC OBJECTIVES

The student:

- ❏ A. Purchases needed clothes.

- ❏ B. Cleans his or her clothes, linens, and towels.

- ❏ C. Sews and mends his or her clothes.

- ❏ D. Sends his or her clothes to an appropriate person or place for cleaning, major repairs, and/or alterations.

- ❏ E. Stores clothes after purchasing or cleaning.

- ❏ F. Packs clothes for trips and outings.

SUGGESTED ACTIVITIES

 ## Specific Objective A

The student purchases needed clothes.

Teacher Interventions

Primary Level.   Make a list of clothes the student should have on hand, including shoes, socks or stockings, undergarments, and outer garments. The list should include the quantity of each article required to meet the student's individual needs. Help the student determine the colors, fabrics, and style that best suit his or her needs, age, body type, and coloring.

Make a clothing chart (see Figure 4.8) to which the student may refer to determine whether his or her clothing stock is complete. This chart should include his or her size for each article of clothing and the quan-

Student's Name			
Article	Number Needed	Size	Approximate Price
Shorts	10	34	3/8.00
T-Shirts	10	34	3/8.00
Socks	10	9½	1.19 each
Work Shirts	5	Medium	12.00 each
Work Pants	3	34 Regular	18.00 each
Pajamas	2	Medium	12.00 each
School Shirts	5	Medium	14.00 each
School Pants	3	34 Regular	18.00 each
Sport Jacket	1	34	56.00 each
Winter Coat	1	34	85.00 each
Misc.			

FIGURE 4.8.   Clothing chart: sizes, numbers, and prices.

tity needed. Also indicate the price range for each item appropriate to the student's economic status. Update the chart periodically as the student's economic situation changes and as his or her sizes change. For non-readers, use pictures of clothing rather than written words.

Family Interventions

Primary Level. Ask the parents to demonstrate checking their child's articles of clothing for excessive wear and tear. Tell them to show their child samples of clothing that are no longer serviceable and contrast these with samples of clothing of varying conditions and age that are still wearable. Tell them to assist their child in making comparisons and in separating the wearable from the unwearable.

The parents should assist the child in making a wallet-size card on which has been written or typed his or her sizes for various items of apparel (update when necessary). The parents should indicate that their child should use the card for reference and/or for communicating information to a salesperson. On this card, the parents should also include the price range for each article of clothing. Then they should go on a shopping trip, at first checking their child's purchases each time, then spot-checking after he or she shows some success.

Seconday Level. Ask the parents to review with their child newspaper ads for clothing sales. Have them assist their child in making a list of clothes he or she needs to purchase and their approximate cost. Have them go with him or her to these stores to assess the quality of the items, and, if suitable, suggest that he or she purchase the items.

 ## Specific Objective B

The student cleans his or her clothes, linens, and towels.

Teacher Interventions

Primary Level. Demonstrate the use of an automatic washing machine, including the use of coins, detergents, and powdered bleaches. Separate clothing to be machine washed into two categories: colored fabrics and white fabrics. Assist the student in using the washing machine.

Demonstrate the use of the automatic dryer. Assist the student in using the dryer.

Family Interventions

Primary Level.   Ask the parents to assist their child in separating his or her clothes that are dirty and need washing from clothes that are still clean enough to wear. Tell them to show their child how to examine clothes for dirt marks, grease, and other stains.

   Ask the parents to establish a routine schedule for washing their child's clothes—for example, undershorts and undershirts are to be washed after one day's wear, bed linens and towels after one week's use. Tell the parents to make a clothing wear and washing chart indicating the day of the week for washing clothes as well as the number of days each article of clothing is to be worn.

   Ask the parents to assist their child in separating dirty clothes, linens, and towels into cleaning categories. Suggest that they use rebus labels sewn into garments to indicate how each article is to be cleaned (e.g., a sketch of a washing machine for washable clothes, a sink for hand washing, and a storefront for dry cleaning). Tell them that color labels may be substituted for rebuses when appropriate.

   Ask the parents to demonstrate to their child how to hand wash items in the sink. Tell them to assist him or her in washing and in hanging up clothes for drying in a suitable place. Suggest that they use Woolite or a similar product to protect garments from shrinking and fading.

Secondary Level.   Ask the parents to take their child to a laundromat and assist him or her in using the washing and drying machines. Ask them to point out special washing instructions (e.g., knowledge of how to measure exact amounts of detergent, bleach, or fabric softeners) and supervise their child as he or she does the laundry.

   Ask the parents to assist their child in preparing clothes to be dry-cleaned and go with the child to the dry cleaner.

 ## Specific Objective C

The student sews and mends his or her clothes.

Teacher Interventions

Primary and Secondary Levels.   Demonstrate how to replace a missing button. Assist the student in selecting a suitable button from a container of buttons.

   Plan a project that requires sewing using appropriate needles and materials. Ask the student to bring in a garment that needs mending and use this for his or her sewing project.

Family Interventions

Primary and Secondary Levels. Ask the parents to demonstrate to their child how to sew a seam that has come apart. Tell them to assist him or her in threading a needle, knotting one end of the thread, and closing the seam. Tell them to practice with the child and reward him or her for accomplishing the task.

Tell the parents to demonstrate to their child how to sew a patch on jeans, pants, and shirts when appropriate. Tell them to review threading a needle and knotting the thread. Tell them to assist their child in placing the patch over a hole. Suggest that they help him or her to pin the patch in place, sticking pins around the inner edge of the patch, and remind him or her to remove and replace pins as necessary. Ask them to emphasize the safety precautions needed for working with needles, pins, and scissors.

 ## Specific Objective D

The student sends his or her clothes to an appropriate person or place for cleaning, major repairs, and/or alterations.

Teacher Interventions

Primary and Secondary Levels. Explain to the student that we sometimes need help from other people in sewing. Indicate in some way that there are people called "tailors" who perform special sewing tasks for money.

Show the student the kinds of repairs and alterations that require the services of a tailor (these should be determined on the basis of the individual skills of the student). Such services might include shortening sleeves, taking in or letting out seams, or putting on cuffs.

Family Interventions

Primary and Secondary Levels. Ask the parents to gather their child's clothes that need cleaning. Tell them to point out where the clothing is soiled or dirty. Tell them to take their child to a dry cleaner and indicate that this is where his or her clothes can be professionally cleaned.

Tell the parents to take a trip through the community with their child. Tell them to point out businesses (in areas they know and that appear safe) that do cleaning, tailoring, and/or alterations.

When the child has the need for tailoring services, the parents should take him or her to a tailor for this purpose. When the garment is ready, the parents should praise their child's appearance, when appropriate, when the child is wearing the altered garment.

 ## Specific Objective E

The student stores clothes after purchasing or cleaning.

(Note: When putting clothes in storage for a long period of time, some cleaners and/or parents often use strong-smelling chemicals as well as moth flakes or mothballs to help preserve the clothing. Make sure the student or child is not allergic to these chemicals before any of the following activities are undertaken, and always avoid handling chemicals, mothballs, cleansers, and so forth, without protection.)

Teacher Interventions

Primary and Secondary Levels.   Take the student on a trip to a department store. Once there, visit the area of the store that sells garment bags. Point out how garment bags are used and which ones are appropriate for certain clothes.

At the end of a season, visit a dry cleaning store that provides clothes storage. Bring in some clothes (e.g., winter coats) that you would like to have professionally stored. Explain to the student that, although this is an excellent way of protecting clothes, it can be expensive.

Family Interventions

Primary and Secondary Levels.   Tell the parents to bring their child with them when they have to pick up dry cleaning. Tell them to show the child where they put the clean clothes (e.g., in a closet, garment bag, or chest) when they arrive home.

Tell the parents to point out to their child where certain clothes are stored (e.g., coats, rainwear, and seasonal outfits). Tell them to check at certain times to see if their child is putting his or her clothes away appropriately.

 ## Specific Objective F

The student packs clothes for trips and outings.

Teacher Interventions

Primary Level.   (Note: Some of the activities listed below can be modified and used in the school program, provided that appropriate parental permissions have been granted.)

Family Interventions

Primary and Secondary Levels.   Tell the parents to show their child how to pack his or her clothes in a suitcase and, when appropriate, a garment bag when planning a trip. Tell them to start the packing and then urge him or her to finish.

Tell the parents to plan an outing with their child as part of a leisure experience. Tell them to prepare for the outing by having the child pack sports clothes in a duffel bag or knapsack. Tell them to monitor how well the child packs his or her clothes and provide praise when appropriate.

Plan to have the child stay overnight with a friend. Once these arrangements have been made, tell him or her to pack the right amount of clothes for the trip. Emphasize the need for toiletries, sleepware, and any special medications.

GOAL III.

The student will be functionally independent in caring for his or her living quarters, appliances, and furnishings in a manner that allows him or her to perform optimally.

SPECIFIC OBJECTIVES

The student:

- ❐ A. Purchases appropriate equipment and materials necessary for the maintenance of his or her living quarters.

- ❐ B. Appropriately uses the appliances needed to keep his or her living quarters clean.

- ❐ C. Uses cleaning materials appropriately.

- ❐ D. Stores small appliances and cleaning materials in appropriate places.

☐ E. Follows a schedule for general housecleaning.

☐ F. Appropriately uses furniture and household accessories.

☐ G. Makes his or her own bed.

☐ H. Makes minor household repairs.

☐ I. Seeks appropriate help for repairs to household appliances and accessories when necessary.

SUGGESTED ACTIVITIES

 ## Specific Objective A

The student purchases appropriate equipment and materials necessary for the maintenance of his or her living quarters.

Teacher Interventions

Primary and Secondary Levels. Look through catalogs from major hardware, chain stores, and discount stores and newspaper ads and circulars with the student. Find the equipment needed for maintenance of the student's living quarters. Put markers in the catalogs to note where the materials are.

Cut out ads from newspapers and circulars for needed cleaning equipment, such as mops, brooms, vacuum cleaners, or electric brooms.

Point out the prices for a variety of cleaning equipment. Make a language experience chart and list the equipment needed and the prices from each catalog or circular.

Family Interventions

Primary Level. Ask the parents to show their child different cleaning equipment and materials. Tell them to explain and demonstrate the use of mops, brooms, dustpans, a vacuum cleaner, dust cloths, sponges, furniture polish, cleanser, and window cleaner when they are cleaning the house.

Secondary Level. Ask the parents to take their child on a shopping trip to different stores to buy cleaning equipment and materials.

Specific Objective B

The student appropriately uses the appliances needed to keep his or her living quarters clean.

Teacher Interventions

Primary and Secondary Levels. If appropriate, invite a member of the school maintenance department to come to the classroom as a guest lecturer to discuss the importance of a clean building, stressing health, safety, and appearance factors.

If the student lives in a residential setting, make him or her responsible for cleaning his or her own living area. Perhaps visit each student's room to see how well he or she maintains it. This should encourage the student to keep his or her quarters neat.

Family Interventions

Primary and Secondary Levels. Ask the parents to demonstrate equipment they use during house cleaning (e.g., broom, mop, dustpan, vacuum cleaner, and electric broom).

Ask the parents to make a housekeeping chart. As the child completes his or her work for the week with a particular piece of equipment, the parents should evaluate it. If the child has mastered the use of the equipment, they should place a small picture of that piece of equipment beside the child's name on the chart and assign him or her another job.

If the child has not mastered the use of the equipment, the parents should praise him or her for trying hard and assign him or her the same job for the next week. Tell them to explain to the child why he or she did not get a picture on his or her chart.

Specific Objective C

The student uses cleaning materials appropriately.

Teacher Interventions

Primary Level. (Note: Although some of the activities associated with this objective can be done as part of Teacher Interventions, the majority of activities will be done at hom.

Family Interventions

Primary and Secondary Levels. Ask the parents to demonstrate the use of window cleaners, cleansers, sponges, dust cloths, household cleaners, and furniture polish. (Note: Because many furniture polishes are poisonous, it is best to use a spray can or pump spray rather than a bottle that requires pouring.)

Ask the parents to present various cleaning situations to their child and ask their child what materials would be needed for each. Encourage them to ask their child to point to the objects and carry out the operation (e.g., cleanser and sponge for sink stains, furniture polish and dust cloth for dusty furniture, and household cleanser and sponge for fingerprints on doors or woodwork).

 ## Specific Objective D

The student stores small appliances and cleaning materials in appropriate places.

Teacher Interventions

Primary and Secondary Levels. Arrange with the maintenance department of the school to have someone available who can show the student where cleaning materials are stored. Stress that it is necessary to store cleaning materials in appropriate places and that it is safer for children and pets if materials are stored in high or locked places.

Upon returning to the classroom, instruct the student to assemble the cleaning equipment and materials. Help him or her to choose an appropriate storage place for the materials—perhaps a part of the clothing closet that is not in use or that has separate shelves. Put the name or a picture of the item in or on the storage area.

Family Interventions

Primary and Secondary Levels. Ask the parents to take their child around the home and point out all the small appliances. Tell them to point out places where these appliances are kept when not in use. Also tell them to show the child where appliances used daily are kept (e.g., toaster or electric can opener).

Ask the parents to emphasize that, when stored, all the appliances should always be clean so they will not attract insects or create unsanitary conditions.

Tell the parents to discuss the storage of cleaning materials and appliances with their child. Tell them to explain that appliances should be stored carefully in a closet or kitchen. They should stress that cleaning materials often contain dangerous chemicals and are flammable and should never be stored with food or in hot places; a separate box, bag, or bucket is the safest place for the storage of cleaning materials.

Specific Objective E

The student follows a schedule for general housecleaning.

Teacher Interventions

Primary Level.   During the class day, encourage the student to do specific cleaning jobs at specific times of the day. For example, the student can wash off the tables after eating, empty wastebaskets at the end of the school day, and wipe the sink after grooming times.

Make a schedule chart (see Figure 4.9) for the student's classroom duties. Instruct the student to check daily to find his or her job assignment and the time to do it.

Family Interventions

Primary and Secondary Levels.   Ask the parents to discuss schedules with their child. Ask them to talk about doing certain things at the same time each day (e.g., getting up, eating, and going to bed). Tell them to help their child make up a daily schedule.

Tell the parents to provide their child a place to hang his or her schedule. Tell them to talk about the daily cleaning jobs their child does and when he or she can do them (e.g., making the bed after getting up, washing up after making the bed, getting dressed after washing up).

Specific Objective F

The student appropriately uses furniture and household accessories.

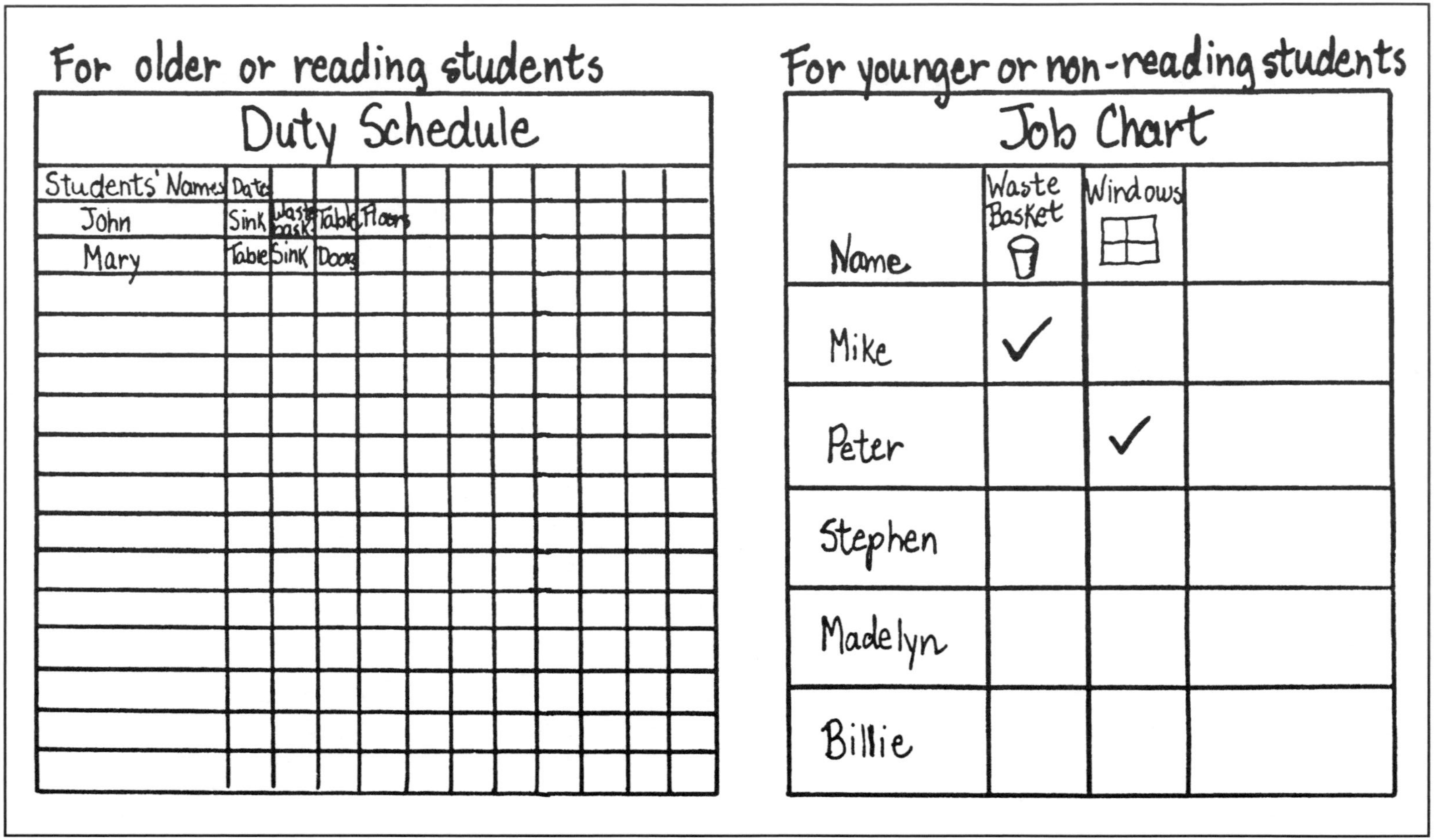

FIGURE 4.9. Class duty schedule and job chart.

Teacher Interventions

Primary Level. Use scale model furniture or pictures of furniture and ask the student to name each piece of furniture and its use.

Help the student to make posters or pictures illustrating the do's and don'ts for using household things and add these items to a safety bulletin board.

Family Interventions

Primary Level. Ask the parents to discuss household accidents with their child, making the key point that accidents are often the result of careless and inappropriate use of household furniture.

Secondary Level. Ask the parents to tell their child to choose a household article or piece of furniture (chair, table, lamp, toaster) in the home. Tell them to ask their child to name its proper use and discuss the danger of misuse. Tell them to do this with each piece of furniture and appliance the child can think of or with those items he or she comes in contact with. Select furniture and accessories that are well made, safe, and have warranties.

 ## Specific Objective G

The student makes his or her own bed.

Teacher Interventions

Primary Level. Find a place in the school that has a bed, such as the nurse's office or a home living suite. If these are not available, see if someone on the teaching staff can bring in a small bed. Show the student the linen (avoid materials that are not permanent press) needed to make a bed. For making the bed, the student will need two sheets, a pillowcase, one or two blankets, and a bedspread. (Initially, flat sheets should be used as both top and bottom sheets because fitted sheets are often difficult to get on.) Ask the student to name or identify each item and to demonstrate its use.

On a housekeeping chart, place a picture or sketch of a bed next to the student's name once he or she independently makes his or her bed.

Family Interventions

Primary Level. Ask the parents to demonstrate making a bed to their child.

Ask the parents to engage their child in making a bed after he or she has had the opportunity to observe the activity several times. Tell the parents to make the bed themselves until the last step (i.e., tucking the spread under the pillow) and then have their child do the last step.

Once he or she has mastered this last step, the parents should make the bed for him or her until the next to the last step, and then have him or her do the last two steps. They should proceed in this way until the child can make a bed independently.

 ## Specific Objective H

The student makes minor household repairs.

Teacher Interventions

Primary and Secondary Levels. Discuss with the student those occasions when screws and a screwdriver would be needed for home repairs (e.g., to tighten handles of cooking pots and to tighten screws on doorknobs or switch plates).

Ask one or two of the students to bring in a small object that requires a minor repair (e.g., a plug on a lamp). Be sure to get the parents' permission. Demonstrate how to repair the object.

Family Interventions

Primary and Secondary Levels. Ask the parents to show their child a lamp with a burned-out light bulb. Tell them to explain that the lamp will not work until the light bulb has been changed. Tell them to demonstrate changing a light bulb.

Ask the parents to discuss with their child those occasions when hammering would be done in the home: hanging pictures, fastening down loose floor molding when nails are protruding, and securing parts of objects. Have the parents stress to their child the use of appropriate sizes and types of tools.

Specific Objective I

The student seeks appropriate help for repairs to household appliances and accessories when necessary.

Teacher Interventions

(Note: Many of the activities listed below can also be done at home. Parents should be consulted if they are to be part of Teacher Interventions.)

Primary and Secondary Levels. With the less able student, it is best to tell him or her to go to an adult for assistance (e.g., parents, a resident manager, a familiar neighbor). Show him or her how to explain the problem or take the adult to the problem.

Make a pictorial list (pictures from catalogs or circulars) of household appliances and accessories. Discuss with the student the possibility that they may break. Ask the student what he or she would do if his or her toaster, TV, toilet, or sink broke. During the discussion, mention that there are people called "repair persons" who can help. Stress that these people are especially trained to fix things.

Play a question-and-answer game while referring to the list made in the above activity. Ask the student, "If your ____ broke, who would repair it?" For example, ask about a broken television (TV repair person), toaster (small appliance repair shop), or iron (small appliance repair shop), or a clogged sink or toilet drain that runs over (plumber or apartment maintenance person/landlord).

GOAL IV.

The student will operate simple appliances, objects, conveniences, and home accessories.

SPECIFIC OBJECTIVES

The student:

❒ A. Plugs in and unplugs appliances.

☐ B. Uses light switches and switches that turn appliances and conveniences on and off.

☐ C. Locks and unlocks catches, locks, and chains on doors.

☐ D. Picks up and dials a regular and a push-button phone and engages in a telephone conversation.

☐ E. Raises, lowers, and adjusts venetian blinds and window shades.

☐ F. Opens and closes cabinets, cupboards, drawers, and doors.

☐ G. Uses cooking utensils, including pots, pans, and kettles.

☐ H. Operates small and large electrical appliances.

☐ I. Uses bathroom facilities and accessories.

☐ J. Uses grooming accessories and appliances.

☐ K. Winds and sets clocks.

☐ L. Operates recreational appliances for entertainment and information, including video games, televisions, radios, stereos, CD players, and VCR recorders and tapes/disks.

☐ M. Adjusts thermostats.

☐ N. Operates cleaning equipment and appliances.

☐ O. Uses coin-operated machines and equipment.

☐ P. Operates ticket machines found in bakeries, supermarkets, and stores.

☐ Q. Uses self-service elevators.

☐ R. Uses personal aids.

☐ S. Puts on and adjusts jewelry.

SUGGESTED ACTIVITIES

 ## Specific Objective A

The student plugs in and unplugs appliances.

Teacher Interventions

Primary and Secondary Levels. Assign jobs to the student within the learning area. As one of the student's jobs, make him or her responsible for unplugging the record player and tape recorder each afternoon just before dismissal. Expect the student to plug in the equipment the next morning so that it is ready for the day's use. Rotate jobs so that each student has a turn at each job.

Show the student an electric drip coffeepot with a detachable electrical cord. Point out the various parts: the glass pot, the cord and plug, the receptacle for the plug, and the plug that goes into the electrical outlet. Stress the difference between the plug that goes into the pot and the one that goes into the wall receptacle.

Family Interventions

Primary and Secondary Levels. Ask the parents to show their child the plugs on various household appliances and equipment. Tell them to point out two- and three-pronged plugs. (A three-pronged plug may be found on grounded plugs for equipment such as power tools and on most major appliances such as air conditioners.)

Ask the parents to show their child electrical wall outlets that are found throughout the home and point out the two or three slots in the outlet. Tell them to hold the appliance plug near the outlet and show the child how the prongs on the plug fit into the slots or openings in the electrical outlet. Tell the parents to warn their child that appliances must be turned off before the plug is inserted into the outlet. Also, caution him or her not to use cords or plugs that appear damaged, worn, or of an inappropriate size.

 ## Specific Objective B

The student uses light switches and switches that turn appliances and conveniences on and off.

Teacher Interventions

Primary and Secondary Levels. Show the student a variety of lamps with various types of on–off switches. Include a regular turning type of switch, one that is shaped like a key, a push button such as that on most fluorescent lamps, and a switch that is pushed in one direction to turn the light on and in the opposite direction to turn the light off. Demonstrate using each type of switch. Tell the student to imitate your actions and practice using the various types of switches.

Bring a few flashlights into the classroom or learning area. Show them to the student and point out the various parts of the flashlight: the body, the switch, and the lens. Demonstrate turning a flashlight on and off. Do this a number of times, telling the student what you are doing as you do it. Tell the student to imitate your actions and to practice turning the flashlight on and off.

Family Interventions

Primary and Secondary Levels. Tell the parents, when appropriate and if the carpet needs cleaning, to show their child a vacuum cleaner. Tell them to point out the on–off switch and demonstrate its use. (Note: Some vacuum cleaner on and off switches are built into the base of the cleaner, requiring your foot to push down as a way of activating the switch.) The parents should have the child vacuum the carpet.

During hot weather, tell the parents to demonstrate to their child turning an air conditioner or fan on and off. Tell them to allow their child to turn the air conditioner or fan on and off at appropriate times.

 ## Specific Objective C

The student locks and unlocks catches, locks, and chains on doors.

Teacher Interventions

Primary and Secondary Levels. Construct a locking board. Secure a variety of locks, chains, and catches on a heavy piece of wood. Tell the student to practice locking and unlocking the various locks, chains, and catches on the board. After this activity, find the same type of locks on doors and point them out.

Take the student to a door with a lock that locks and unlocks with a skeleton key. Show the student the skeleton key. Point out the section of the key that is inserted into the keyhole. Insert the key into the keyhole and turn it until the door locks. Encourage the student to imitate your actions and to practice locking and unlocking the door.

Family Interventions

Primary and Secondary Levels. Ask the parents to take their child to a door with a safety chain. Tell them to point out the chain and the slot into which the chain slides, and to grasp the end of the chain with a thumb and fore-finger. Next they should place the end of the chain into the wide end of the slot and slide the chain down or across to secure it. The child should imitate their actions and practice securing the safety chain. Have them emphasize the safety precautions that should be followed for using locks, catches, and chains on doors.

Tell the parents to take their child to an aluminum storm door or screen door. If one is not present in their home, they are available and on display in most building supply stores. Tell them to point out the small button or catch that locks and unlocks the storm door (this is usually located directly below the doorknob or handle). Tell them to lock and unlock the door and to ask the child to imitate their actions and lock and unlock the screen door.

 ## Specific Objective D

The student picks up and dials a regular and a push-button phone and engages in a telephone conversation.

Teacher Interventions

Primary and Secondary Levels. Demonstrate dialing both dial and push-button telephones. Tell the student to imitate your actions and to practice using these telephones.

Print both numbers on flashcards (e.g., the weather and time). Tell the student to practice dialing the printed phone numbers on both types of telephones.

Family Interventions

Primary and Secondary Levels. Ask the parents to show their child the telephones they have in their home. (Note: The parents may borrow practice phones and teletrainers from most local telephone companies if they are for educational purposes.) Tell the parents to point out the similarities and differences between the phones. The child should use the phones.

Tell the parents to give their child a personal list of important phone numbers. Tell them to assist their child in making calls to his or her family and friends.

Specific Objective E

The student raises, lowers, and adjusts venetian blinds and window shades.

Teacher Interventions

Primary and Secondary Levels. Point out window shades in the classroom or take the student to the cafeteria, a reception room or office, or a part of the school building where there are window shades. Point out the window shades and demonstrate how to raise and adjust each. Tell the student to adjust the shades all the way down, all the way up, and halfway open. When showing filmstrips, assign different students the job of raising, lowering, and adjusting the window shades.

Tell the student to imitate your actions and to raise and adjust venetian blinds. Use a variety of blinds, including vertical ones that require different actions in order to open, close, or adjust them.

Family Interventions

Primary and Secondary Levels. Ask the parents to demonstrate raising and lowering a window shade to their child. Tell them to describe what they are doing as they do it.

Ask the parents to demonstrate raising, lowering, and adjusting a variety of shapes of venetian blinds to their child. Tell them to describe what they are doing as they do it.

Specific Objective F

The student opens and closes cabinets, cupboards, drawers, and doors.

Teacher Interventions

Primary and Secondary Levels. Assign the student jobs involving opening cabinets and cupboards (e.g., art cupboards, kitchen cabinets, and storage cabinets). Tell the student to place art supplies in the cupboards; pots, pans, and canned goods in kitchen cabinets; and mops, brooms, and buckets in storage cabinets at appropriate times.

When appropriate and under supervision, send the student on errands outside the classroom. Require him or her to close the classroom door.

Demonstrate to the students closing a drawer that is crooked. First, center the drawer in the middle of its opening, allowing an equal amount of space on each side of the drawer (for example, if it is too far to the left, push the drawer to the right to even it out). Then close the drawer from the middle.

Family Interventions

Primary and Secondary Levels. Ask the parents to remind their child to close the door when he or she uses the bathroom. Tell them to stress privacy and to remind the child to close the door each time he or she uses the bathroom.

The parents should demonstrate opening and closing the refrigerator and freezer compartment drawers. They should do this several times and tell their child to imitate their actions, practicing opening and closing the refrigerator.

Tell the parents to demonstrate opening and closing a cabinet with a knob. Ask them to tell their child what they are doing as they do it.

 ## Specific Objective G

The student uses cooking utensils, including pots, pans, and kettles.

Teacher Interventions

Primary and Secondary Levels. Bring a selection of pots and pans with lids into the classroom. Show the student the various sizes of pots and pans and their corresponding lids. Practice matching them.

Do simple cooking activities that require placing lids on pots, pans, and casserole dishes and removing the lids.

Family Interventions

Primary and Secondary Levels. Ask the parents to demonstrate placing a lid on a pan and removing it and then have their child imitate these actions.

Tell the parents to demonstrate placing a lid on a casserole dish and removing it. Tell them to remind their child that casserole dishes are more fragile than pots and pans, so he or she should be gentle when placing the lids on casseroles and removing them.

Ask the parents to show their child a capped-spout teakettle. Tell them to explain that the spout must be opened to pour water in and out of the kettle. Tell them to show the two most common types of spout control: the kettle with a button on the handle that opens and closes the spout and the kettle with a curved hook under the handle that opens and closes the spout.

 ## Specific Objective H

The student operates small and large electrical appliances.

Teacher Interventions

Primary and Secondary Levels.   Bring an electric can opener into the classroom or learning area. Demonstrate its use. Tell the student to imitate your actions and to practice lifting and lowering the lever of the can opener. Give the student clean empty cans and let him or her practice opening unopened cans. Emphasize the safety factors involved in doing this activity.

Following a cooking activity that has resulted in soiled towels or dishcloths, take the student to a laundry room or area where there is an automatic clothes washer. Demonstrate to the student how to lift the lid and use the washing machine, and then wash the towels or other soiled materials.

Family Interventions

Primary and Secondary Levels.   Ask the parents to demonstrate to their child the use of the small appliances found in their kitchen. Tell them to determine which appliances are safe for their child to presently use, and then have the child practice using the appliances.

Ask the parents to prepare a breakfast of juice and toast, frozen French toast, or waffles that are cooked in the toaster. Tell them to make their child responsible for putting the bread into the toaster, pushing the appropriate lever down, or removing the bread from the toaster.

Ask the parents to prepare a simple lunch (e.g., canned soup or canned spaghetti, canned vegetables, and canned fruit). Tell them to have their child open the cans.

 ## Specific Objective I

The student uses bathroom facilities and accessories.

(Note: For Teacher and Family Interventions, refer to Unit 1, "Self-Care Skills," Goal I.)

 ## Specific Objective J

The student uses grooming accessories and appliances.

Teacher Interventions

Primary and Secondary Levels. Tell the student to wash his or her hair as part of classroom grooming activities. Once the student's hair has been washed, tell the student to use the hair dryer to dry it.

As part of grooming, assign the student a partner. Ask the partners to take turns washing and drying each other's hair, using the hair dryer.

Family Interventions

Primary and Secondary Levels. When appropriate, ask the same-sex parent to show his or her child how to use an electric shaver, and to tell the child that one should shave regularly in order to maintain a neat appearance. Suggest that the teachers allow the child to try a variety of electric shavers until one is found that is best suited for him or her.

Ask the female parent or designee to show her child how to set her hair. Tell her to practice using a variety of curlers, hot rollers, or curling irons.

 ## Specific Objective K

The student winds and sets clocks.

Teacher Interventions

Primary and Secondary Levels. Bring a number of alarm clocks that require manual winding into the classroom or learning area. Show the student the winding key and demonstrate winding the clocks.

Set the alarm clocks for different times: lunch, physical education, bus, bathroom, and recess. Tell the student to set the alarms so that they will go off at the appropriate times, reminding the student to proceed to the next class or activity.

Family Interventions

Primary and Secondary Levels. Ask the parents to show their child a variety of clocks found within the home. Tell them to point out which ones need to be wound (nonelectrical) and which ones are run by electricity or battery.

Ask the parents to encourage their child to use an alarm clock to wake him- or herself up in the morning. Initially, someone else may take responsibility for setting the clock and the child may take responsibility for winding it.

 ## Specific Objective L

The student operates recreational appliances for entertainment and information, including video games, televisions, radios, stereos, CD players, and VCR recorders and tapes/disks.

Teacher Interventions

Primary and Secondary Levels. Bring a cassette tape recorder into the classroom. Demonstrate the use of the cassette recorder and tell the student what you are doing as you do it. Point out the various parts of the recorder: cassette ejection button, record button, stop button, play button, and so forth. You may want to color-code the buttons for the student's convenience (e.g., red on the stop button, green on the play button, yellow on the record button, blue on the cassette ejection button, black on the rewind button, and orange on the volume button).

Make a chart using the color codings of the tape recorder buttons, showing the student the order to follow in using the cassette tape recorder (see Figure 4.10).

Use tape cassettes with coordinated storybooks.

Family Interventions

Primary and Secondary Levels. Ask the parents to demonstrate using a television set or stereo that uses knobs or push buttons for turning it on and off. Repeat the activity with recreational appliances that use a remote control for these functions.

Repeat the above activity using recreational appliances with push–pull on–off switches, or a rocker-type on–off switch. Also, have the parents demonstrate the way to adjust volume or select stations.

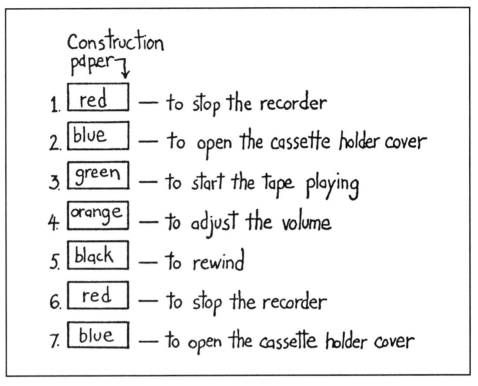

FIGURE 4.10. Color-coding chart for sequence of steps in playing a cassette tape recorder.

 Specific Objective M

The student adjusts thermostats.

(Note: This activity is best done at home because adjusting thermostats in school or in other facilities may pose problems with master heating and cooling plants.)

Family Interventions

Primary and Secondary Levels. Ask the parents to show their child a thermostat that is located in the home or living quarters. Tell them to point out the movable dial, the indicator, the arrow, and the numbers that represent the degrees of temperature.

Ask the parents to place a red dot above the number on the thermostat that indicates the desired temperature for the room in which the thermostat is located (e.g., 68 degrees in a bedroom). Tell them to show the child how to line up the arrow on the movable dial with the dot above the number.

The child should imitate the parents' actions and practice adjusting the thermostat by matching the arrow and the dot. (For the child's living quarters, the parents may want two different-colored dots: one for daytime temperature and one for evening or sleeping temperature. The appropriate temperature would, of course, depend upon the individual child.)

Specific Objective N

The student operates cleaning equipment and appliances.

Teacher Interventions

Primary and Secondary Levels.   If the school has a washing machine, ask the student to wash his or her dirty gym clothes in it. Point out the settings and the amount of detergent needed for the wash.

Develop classroom jobs that include using an electric broom or vacuum cleaner. Assign a cleaning job to the student that requires him or her to use the cleaning appliances.

Family Interventions

Primary and Secondary Levels.   Ask the parents to provide opportunities for their child to help in cleaning the house or his or her room. Tell them to demonstrate the use of the vacuum cleaner or electric broom, including how to empty its bag or cup when it is full. Tell them to monitor how appropriately their child uses the appliances.

The parents should suggest that the child offer to clean his or her room if he or she is a guest in a home for a period of time. The parents should tell the student to vacuum the rug or floor as part of this cleaning.

Specific Objective O

The student uses coin-operated machines and equipment.

Teacher Interventions

Primary and Secondary Levels. Take the student to a cafeteria or lunchroom with vending machines. Demonstrate operating the various types of vending machines, such as those with push buttons versus pull-out knobs. Insert the appropriate coin(s) into the coin slot. Make your selection and operate the machine. Tell the student to watch what you are doing and to imitate your actions.

Ask a female teacher to take the female student to a bathroom that has a sanitary napkin vending machine. Insert the appropriate coin(s) into the coin slot and follow the directions for releasing a sanitary napkin. Tell the student to watch what you are doing, and tell her what you are doing as you do it. Tell the student to imitate your actions.

Family Interventions

Primary and Secondary Levels. Ask the parents to take their child to a subway, light-rail, or any system that has a turnstile that is operated by inserting a token or coin. The parents should buy a token or give the child a coin and ask him or her to insert it into the turnstile.

The parents should buy bus tokens and take the child on a public transportation bus, telling the child to insert the tokens into the token box as he or she steps onto the bus.

Have the parents take the child to a laundromat or laundry room in an apartment building with coin-operated machines, telling the child to identify which coin(s) the machines require and to choose the appropriate coins. The parents should ask their child to insert the correct number of coins into the machines, helping him or her in identifying words on machines that illustrate operating instructions.

 ## Specific Objective P

The student operates ticket machines found in bakeries, supermarkets, and stores.

(Note: The following activities can be used as both Teacher and Family Interventions.)

Primary and Secondary Levels. Take the student to a bakery or supermarket that has a ticket machine. Demonstrate operating the ticket machine. Tell the student what you are doing as you do it. Tell the student to imitate your actions and to operate the numbered ticket machine.

Repeat the above activity when you take the student for ice cream at places like Baskin Robbins that have ticket machines.

Plan a small party. Take the student to the supermarket to buy luncheon food. (There often is a ticket machine at delicatessen and bakery counters.) The student must take a ticket at the delicatessen, wait his or her turn, and order his or her portion of cold cuts. The student must then go to the bakery, take a ticket, wait his or her turn, and order rolls, bread, or pastries for the party.

 Specific Objective Q

The student uses self-service elevators.

Teacher Interventions

Primary and Secondary Levels. Show the student flashcards of floor numbers and "B" and "L" for basement and lobby. Drill the student until he or she recognizes the numbers and letters.

Construct an elevator push-button panel out of corrugated cardboard. Paste or draw on buttons. Tell the student to find buttons with specific numbers and/or letters.

Family Interventions

Primary and Secondary Levels. Ask the parents to take their child to apartment buildings of friends or relatives that have self-service elevators. Ask them to observe how their child uses the elevator.

Ask them to repeat the above activity with places in the community that require the use of self-service elevators.

 Specific Objective R

The student uses personal aids.

Teacher Interventions

Primary and Secondary Levels. Bring sunglasses into the classroom (the student who wears glasses may use his or her own glasses). Point out the various parts of the glasses: the lenses, the frame, the bridge, and the ear-piece.

When appropriate, demonstrate the use of a hearing aid to the student. Check the hearing aid to be sure it is off (hearing aids should always be off before the earpiece is inserted into the ear). Read the directions on how to use the hearing aid and allow the student to demonstrate its use. Tell the student to watch what you are doing and explain what you are doing as you do it. Tell the student to imitate your actions and to practice operating the hearing aid.

Family Interventions

Primary and Secondary Levels. Ask the parents to demonstrate putting glasses on and removing them. Tell them to have their child watch what they are doing and to explain each action as they do it. Tell the parents to remind their child not to put his or her fingers on the lenses and to handle glasses with care.

Tell the parents to encourage their child who uses a hearing aid to wear it whenever appropriate. If the child does not wear a hearing aid, the parents should tell him or her to be understanding and supportive of a person who does.

 ## Specific Objective S

The student puts on and adjusts jewelry.

Teacher Interventions

Primary and Secondary Levels. Bring watches with buckle-type watchbands into the classroom or learning area. Demonstrate opening and closing the buckle on the watchband. Tell the student to watch what you are doing and explain what you are doing as you do it. Tell the student to imitate your actions and to practice opening and closing the buckle on the watchband.

Bring a variety of necklaces and neck chains into the classroom or learning area. Demonstrate opening and closing the clasp of the necklace or chain. Tell the student what you are doing as you do it. Tell the student to imitate your actions and to practice opening and closing the clasps of necklaces and chains.

Family Interventions

Primary and Secondary Levels. Ask the parents to assist their child in selecting and putting on jewelry. Tell them to point out that there are times when a lot of jewelry is not appropriate (e.g., funerals) and when it may be dangerous (e.g., when working with machines in which jewelry may be caught).

Ask the parents to take their child to plays, movies, or theaters. In preparation, have them dress for the occasion by wearing articles of jewelry as accessories, if they wish.

Sample Lesson Plan 1

Topic Area: Household Management and Living Skills

Designed by: William Livingstar

Time Recommended: 30 Minutes

Student Involved: Helen (Secondary Special Class)

Background Information:

The student has oral receptive language. She comprehends spoken words and will positively respond to requests. She does not read beyond a basic sight word vocabulary. She dresses appropriately for her age and has learned to select her own clothing each morning for school.

General Goal *(Household Management and Living Skills II):*

The student will be functionally independent in purchasing and maintaining her clothes in a manner that allows her to perform optimally.

Specific Objective *(Household Management and Living Skills II-F):*

The student packs clothes for trips and outings.

Lesson Objective:

The student will select clothing appropriate for an overnight stay at a friend's house.

Materials and Equipment:

- Suitcase
- Variety of pictures of clothing

- Variety of clothing items
- Selection of toiletries
- Sleepwear
- Pictures of medications, if appropriate for the student

Motivating Activity:

Plan a class slumber party for a Friday night as a culminating activity for the year. Discuss what types of clothing would be necessary for the student and what other items should be considered if the student sleeps over.

Instructional Procedures:

Initiation—Tell the student to identify the types of clothing and other toiletries that are used in preparing for bed at home. Guide the child through a discussion of each step of preparation for bed and dressing in the morning.

Guided Practice—Then say, "Let's start by selecting pictures and putting them into a pile to include on a list." As the student tells you what is needed, have the student select the picture, name the item, and put the item in order on the table. Review the necessary toiletries and other items that are specific to the student.

Independent Practice—Ask the student to select clothing from a pile and place it in a suitcase. Have the student assist a classmate in selecting the items for the overnight trip.

Closure—Ask the student to help you prepare a list for you to pack for the overnight trip for the class. Have the student select the appropriate pictures for your list and then compare the categories of items.

Assessment Strategy:

Observe the student to determine whether she correctly and quickly responded to the direction to select clothing for an overnight trip.

Follow-Up Activity or Objective:

If the student achieves the lesson objective, proceed to a lesson involving folding the clothing and packing the suitcase.

Sample Lesson Plan 2

Topic Area: Household Management and Living Skills

Designed by: Thames Roslyn

Time Recommended: 30 Minutes

Student Involved: Kathryn (Primary Special Class)

Background Information:

The student has developing oral receptive language. She utilizes single words, particularly related to food items with which she is familiar. She also appears to comprehend some gestural language, for example, (a) she looks at a person who is waving his or her hand for attention; (b) when an object is pointed to, she will look at that object; and (c) she responds appropriately when asked to hand the teacher a picture of an item with which she is familiar. She has yet to demonstrate an understanding for sight words but can discriminate colors and representational pictures.

General Goal *(Household Management and Living Skills I):*

The student will be functionally independent in planning meals and in purchasing, storing, and preparing food in a manner that allows her to perform optimally.

Specific Objective *(Household Management and Living Skills I-A):*

The student plans nutritious meals and snacks.

Lesson Objective:

When the student is asked to assist you in planning the snacks for the week, she is able to select nutritious snacks for the class.

Materials and Equipment:

- Pictures of nutritious foods with Velcro strips on the back
- A weekly chart

- Velcro strips on the chart

- Pictures of candy and high-calorie items on red poster board

Review the student's files to determine whether the items selected are safe for the entire class and to make sure no one has an allergy to any of the selected items.

Motivating Activity:

Make a simple snack with the cooperation of the student and one of the student's classmates (for example, peanut butter and jelly sandwiches). As you are preparing the snack, point out how nutritious the selections are and have the students assist you in serving the snack to the class.

Instructional Procedures:

Initiation—Tell the student that you would like to have her help in selecting the snacks for the next week. Discuss the nutritious value of each food and provide a picture of each, discussing why it is healthy for the student and the need for a variety of nutritious foods in a balanced diet. At this point show the pictures and explain that when she sees something she likes that is nutritious, you would like her to pick it up. Demonstrate with a picture of an apple and attach it to Monday on the snack chart.

Guided Practice—Then say, "Let's start by sorting the nutritious foods from those that would not be eaten for a healthy snack." Name each snack and discuss the food value of the selected item. If the food is inappropriate, point out the red backing on the food as a secondary clue.

Independent Practice—Ask the student to help a classmate to select a nutritious snack and to give her classmate the pictures of the nutritious snacks.

Closure—Ask the student to help you to plan a snack for one of the special class snack times.

Assessment Strategy:

Observe the student to determine whether she correctly and quickly responds to the direction to select a nutritious snack menu for the week.

Follow-Up Activity or Objective:

If the student achieves the lesson objective, proceed to a lesson involving preparing a nutritious snack for the class.

References

Amary, I. B. (1979). *Effective meal planning and food preparation for the mentally retarded and developmentally disabled: Comprehensive and innovative teaching methods.* Springfield, IL: Thomas.

Bender, M. (1994). Learning disabilities: Beyond the school years. In A. Capute, P. Accardo, & B. Shapiro (Eds.), *Learning disabilities spectrum, ADD, ADHD, and LD* (pp. 241–253). Baltimore: York Press.

Bender, M., & Valletutti, P. J. (1982). *Teaching functional academics: A curriculum guide for adolescents and adults with learning problems.* Austin, TX: PRO-ED.

Brolin, D. E. (Ed.). (1991). *Life-Centered Career Education: A competency based approach.* Reston, VA: Council for Exceptional Children.

Cuvo, A. J., Jacobi, L., & Sipko, R. (1981). Teaching laundry skills to mentally retarded adolescents. *Education and Training of the Mentally Retarded, 16,* 54–64.

Johnson, B., & Cuvo, A. J. (1981). Teaching cooking skills to mentally retarded adults. *Behavior Modification, 5,* 187–202.

Patton, J. R., Cronin, M. E., Polloway, E. A., Hutchinson, D., & Robinson, B. A. (1989). Curricular considerations: A life skills orientation. In G. A. Robinson, J. R. Patton, E. A. Polloway, & L. R. Sargent (Eds.), *Best practices in mild mental disabilities* (pp. 23–37). Reston, VA: Council for Exceptional Children.

Schloss, P. J., Smith, M. A., & Schloss, C. N. (1990). *Instructional methods for adolescents with learning and behavior problems.* Boston: Allyn & Bacon.

Stacy-Sherrer, C. J. (1981). *Skills necessary for contributive family and home living: Applicable to the moderately to severely retarded child and adult. A task analysis manual for teachers, parents and houseparents.* Springfield, IL: Thomas.

VanBuren, J. B. (1989). Documentation of basic skills in consumer and homemaking education curriculum. *Journal of Vocational Home Economics Education, 7,* 37–45.

Suggested Readings

Barnard, J. D., Christophersen, E. R., & Wolf, M. M. (1977). Teaching children appropriate shopping behavior through parent training in the supermarket setting. *Journal of Applied Behavior Analysis, 10,* 49–59.

Belina, V. S. (1975). *Planning your own apartment: Text workbook and teacher's guide; Reading level, 3.0; Interest level, Grades 7–12/ABE.* Belmont, CA: Fearon-Pitman.

Bellamy, T., & Buttars, K. (1975). Teaching trainable level retarded students to count money: Toward personal independence through academic instruction. *Education and Training of the Mentally Retarded, 10,* 18–26.

Bender, M., Valletutti, P. J., & Bender, R. (1976). *Teaching the moderately and severely handicapped* (Vols. 1, 2, and 3). Austin, TX: PRO-ED.

Brown, V. (1976). On reviewing cookbooks: From kitchen to classroom. *Journal of Learning Disabilities, 9,* 63–68.

Coon, M. E., Vogelsberg, R. T., & Williams, W. (1981). Effects of classroom public transportation instruction on generalization to the natural environment. *The Journal of the Association for the Severely Handicapped, 6,* 46–53.

Crnic, K. A., & Pym, H. A. (1979). Training mentally retarded adults in independent living skills. *Mental Retardation, 17,* 13–16.

Cronin, K. A., & Cuvo, A. (1979). Teaching mending skills to mentally retarded adolescents. *Journal of Applied Behavior Analysis, 12,* 401–406.

Cronin, M. E., Lord, D. C., & Wendlings, K. (1991). Learning for life: The life skills curriculum. *Intervention in School and Clinic, 26,* 306–311.

Doyle, E. (1980). *Skills for daily living series.* Baltimore: Media Materials.

General Services Administration. (1972). *Floor polish and floor care.* (Consumer Information Series No. 9). Washington, DC: Author.

George, R. (1978). *The new consumer survival kit* (Adapted from the series produced by the Maryland Center for Public Broadcasting). Boston: Little, Brown.

Hupp, S. C., & Mervis, C. B. (1981). Development of generalized concepts for severely handicapped students. *The Journal of the Association for the Severely Handicapped, 6,* 14–21.

Knox, C. (1980). *Using the telephone directory.* Baltimore: Media Materials.

Laus, M. D. (1977). *Travel instruction for the handicapped.* Springfield, IL: Thomas.

Leff, R. B. (1975). *How to use the telephone: The dial-a-phone kit.* Peoli, PA: Instructor/McGraw-Hill.

Levy, L., Feldman, R., & Simpson, S. (1976). *The consumer in the marketplace: Interest level, Grades 7–12.* Belmont, CA: Fearon-Pitman.

MacWilliam, L. J. (1977). You can get there from here. Travel and community experience for multiply handicapped students. *Teaching Exceptional Children, 9,* 49–51.

Mannix, D. (1992). *Life skills activities for special children.* West Nyack, NY: Center for Applied Research in Education.

Mastropieri, M. A., & Scruggs, T. (1987). Teaching for transition: Life skills, career, and vocational education. In M. Mastropieri & T. Scruggs, *Effective instruction for special education* (pp. 337–356). Austin, TX: PRO-ED.

Matson, J. L. (1979). A field tested system of training meal preparation skills to the retarded. *British Journal of Mental Subnormality, 25,* 14–18.

Matson, J. L. (1980). A controlled group study of pedestrian skill training for the mentally retarded. *Behavior Research and Therapy, 18,* 99–106.

Matson, J. L. (1981). Use of independence training to teach shopping skills to mildly mentally retarded adults. *American Journal of Mental Deficiency, 86,* 178–183.

McClure, L., Cook, S., & Thompson, V. (1997). *Experience-based learning: How to make the community your classroom.* Portland, OR: Northwest Regional Educational Laboratory.

Neef, N., Iwata, R., & Page, T. J. (1978). Public transportation training: In vivo versus classroom instruction. *Journal of Applied Behavior Analysis, 11,* 331–344.

Nettlebeck, T., & Kirby, N. H. (1976). Training the mentally handicapped to sew. *Education and Training of the Mentally Retarded, 11,* 31–36.

Nietupski, J., & Williams, W. (1976). Teaching selected telephone related social skills to severely handicapped students. *Child Study Journal, 6,* 139–153.

Page, T. J., Iwata, B. A., & Neft, W. A. (1976). Teaching pedestrian skills to retarded persons: Generalization from the classroom to the natural environment. *Journal of Applied Behavior Analysis, 9,* 433–444.

Polloway, E. A., Patton, J. R., Smith, J. D., & Rodrique, T. W. (1991). Issues in program design for elementary students with mild retardation: Emphasis on curriculum development. *Education and Training in Mental Retardation, 26,* 142–150.

Retish, P., Hitchings, W., Horvath, M., & Schmalle, B. (1991). *Students with mild disabilities in the secondary school.* New York: Longman.

Robinson-Wilson, M. (1977). Picture recipe cards as an approach to teaching severely and profoundly retarded adults to cook. *Education and Training of the Mentally Retarded, 12,* 69–73.

Roderman, W. H. (1979). *Getting around cities and towns: A Janus survival guide.* Hayward, CA: Janus Book Publishers.

Sarber, R. E., Halasz, M. M., Messmer, M. C., Bickett, A. D., & Lutzker, J. R. (1983). Teaching menu planning and grocery shopping skills to a mentally retarded mother. *Mental Retardation, 21,* 101–106.

Schloss, P. J., Alexander, N., Hornig, E., Parker, K., & Wright, B. (1993, Spring). Teaching meal preparation vocabulary and procedures to individuals with mental retardation. *Teaching Exceptional Children, 25,* 7–12.

Shultheis, P., Paine, R., Morgan-Brown, A., Smith, S., & Hanson, R. (1980). *Household mathematics.* Baltimore: Media Materials.

Shultheis, P., Paine, R., Morgan-Brown, A., Smith, S., & Hanson, R. (1980). *Shopping mathematics.* Baltimore: Media Materials.

Shultheis, P., Paine, R., Morgan-Brown, A., Smith, S., & Hanson, R. (1980). *Traveler's mathematics.* Baltimore: Media Materials.

Smith, M., & Meyers, A. (1979). Telephone-skills training for retarded adults: Group and individual demonstrations with and without verbal instruction. *American Journal of Mental Deficiency, 83,* 581–587.

Sowers, J. A., Rusch, F. R., & Hudson, C. (1979). Training a severely retarded young adult to ride the city bus to and from work. *AAESPH Review, 3,* 15–24.

Special Service Supply. (1977). *Arithmetic skill text for daily living.* Huntington, NY: Author.

Thompson, T. J., Braam, S. J., & Fuqua, R. W. (1982). Training and generalization of laundry skills: A multiple problem evaluation with handicapped persons. *Journal of Applied Behavior Analysis, 15,* 177–182.

Tiller, C., & Wyllie, C. (1978). *An activities of daily living curriculum for handicapped adults.* Twin Falls, ID: Magic Valley Rehabilitation Services, Inc.

Triebel, J., & Manning, M. (1976). *I think I can learn to cook or I can cook to think and learn.* San Rafael, CA: Academic Therapy Publications.

VanDenPol, R. A., Iwata, B. A., Ivancic, M. T., Page, T. J., Neef, N. A., & Whitley, F. P. (1981). Teaching the handicapped to act in public places: Acquisition, generalization and maintenance of restaurant skills. *Journal of Applied Behavior Analysis, 14,* 61–69.

Vogelsberg, R. T. (1980). Access to the natural environment: The first step to community independence. In R. Dubose & K. Stonecipher (Eds.), *Illinois' best practices for teaching severely handicapped students.* Springfield: Illinois State Board of Education.

Walls, R. T., Crist, K., Sienicki, D. A., & Grant, L. (1981). Prompting sequences in teaching independent living skills. *Mental Retardation, 19,* 243–246.

Wiederholt, J. L., & Wolffe, L. E. (1990). Preparing problem learners for independent living. In D. D. Hammill & N. R. Bartell, *Teaching students with learning and behavior problems* (pp. 451–503). Austin, TX: PRO-ED.

Williams, R. D., & Ewing, S. (1979). Consumer roulette: The shopping patterns of mentally retarded persons. *Mental Retardation, 19,* 145–149.

Yawkey, T. D., Dank, H. L., & Glosenger, F. L. (1986). *Playing inside and out: How to promote social growth and learning in young children including the developmentally delayed child.* Lancaster, PA: Technomic Publishing.

KITS/CURRICULAR MATERIALS

- *BCP—Behavioral Characteristics Progression: 2400 Developmentally Sequenced Skills with Curriculum*
  VORT Corp.
  PO Box 60880
  Palo Alto, California 94306
  (415) 322-8282

- *Brigance Inventory of Essential Skills*
  Curriculum Associates,® Inc.
  5 Esquire Road
  North Billerica, Massachusetts 01862-0901
  (800) 225-0248

- *Out in the World: A Community Living Skills Manual*
  Imaginart Communication Products
  307 Arizona Street
  Bisbee, Arizona 85603
  (800) 828-1376

- *Steps to Independent Living*
  Exceptional Teaching Aids
  20102 Woodbine Avenue
  Castro Valley, California 94546
  (800) 549-6999

VIDEOS

- *Appropriate Curriculum: The Role of the Teacher* (1 video)
  Kaplan School Supply Corp.
  1310 Lewisville-Clemmons Road
  PO Box 609
  Lewisville, North Carolina 27023-0609
  (800) 334-2014

- *Families Helping Families* Videotape Set (2 videotapes)
  DDM, Inc.
  PO Box 6919
  Denver, Colorado 80206-0919
  (303) 355-4729

- *A Place for Me*
  Educational Productions Inc.
  7412 SW Beaverton Hillsdale Highway
  Suite 210
  Portland, Oregon 97225
  (800) 950-4949

ASSISTIVE DEVICES

- *Battery Operated Quick Mixer*
  Fred Sammons, Inc.
  PO Box 32
  Brookfield, IL 60513
  (800) 323-5547

- *Caption Video Viewer*
  Hear You Are, Inc.
  4 Musconetcong Avenue
  Stanhope, New Jersey 07874
  (201) 347-7662

- *Large Button Speaker Phone*
  HARC Mercantile, Ltd.
  PO Box 3055
  Kalamazoo, Michigan 49003
  (800) 445-9968

- *Push-Button Peppermill*
  LJM Projects, Inc.
  PO Box 372
  Rochelle Park, New Jersey 97662
  (216) 382-9700

- *Talking Alarm Clock*
  Access with Ease, Inc.
  PO Box 1150
  Chino Valley, Arizona 86323
  (602) 636-9469

Notes

Notes

Notes

Notes

Notes

Notes

Notes

Notes